IRISH
HISTORY
MATTERS

Also by Brian M. Walker

Parliamentary Election Results in Ireland, 1801–1922 (edited)
Sentry Hill: An Ulster Farm and Family
Ulster Politics: The Formative Years, 1868–86
Province, City and People: Belfast and its Region (co-edited with
 R.H. Buchanan)
Ulster: An Illustrated History (co-edited with Ciaran Brady and Mary
 O'Dowd)
Parliamentary Election Results in Ireland, 1918–92 (edited)
Degrees of Excellence: The Story of Queen's Belfast, 1845–1995
 (co-authored with Alf McCreary)
Dancing to History's Tune: History, Myth and Politics in Ireland
Past and Present: History, Identity and Politics in Ireland
The Oxford History of the Irish Book (co-general editor with Robert
 Welch)
A Political History of the Two Irelands: From Partition to Peace
*A History of St George's Church Belfast: Two Centuries of Faith, Worship
 and Music*

IRISH
HISTORY
MATTERS

POLITICS, IDENTITIES
AND COMMEMORATION

BRIAN M. WALKER

The
History
Press
Ireland

For Don Akenson

First published 2019

The History Press
The Mill, Brimscombe Port
Stroud, Gloucestershire, GL5 2QG
www.thehistorypress.co.uk

© Brian M. Walker, 2019

The right of Brian M. Walker to be identified as the Author
of this work has been asserted in accordance with the
Copyright, Designs and Patents Act 1988.

British Library Cataloguing in Publication Data.
A catalogue record for this book is available from the British Library.

ISBN 978 0 7509 9129 2

Typesetting and origination by The History Press
Printed and bound by TJ International Ltd

CONTENTS

ACKNOWLEDGEMENTS

During the research and writing of these essays I have been helped by many people and institutions. I am much indebted to the staffs of the library of Queen's University Belfast, the Linen Hall Library, Belfast, the newspaper section of Belfast Central Library, the RCB Library, Dublin, the National Library of Ireland, Dublin, and the library of Trinity College Dublin. I must record special thanks to George Boyce and Marianne Elliott, who read parts of my manuscript and gave me good advice. Of course, they are not responsible for the final draft!

I have greatly valued the many conversations on historical matters that I have enjoyed with Bill Vaughan. I am very grateful to Eugenio Biagini for his support and advice. Many thanks are due to John Fairleigh, who gave me great encouragement in the writing of this book. Others who provided valuable help include Robin Bury, Vincent Comerford, Gordon Gillespie, Will Hazleton, Jacqueline Hill, Susan Hood, Brian Hughes, Jack Johnston, Greta Jones, Brian Kennaway, Liam Kennedy, Raymond Refaussé, Patrick Roche, Don Wood and Christopher Woods.

For their support and collegiality I am very grateful to former members of the Institute of Irish Studies at Queen's, in particular Ronnie Buchanan, Sophia Hillan, Dominic Bryan, Angelique Day, Catherine

Boone, Jane Leonard, Peter Francis and Margaret McNulty. The encouragement of former colleagues in the Queen's politics school, including Yvonne Galligan, Graham Walker, Margaret O'Callaghan and Cathal McCall, has been much appreciated. Many of the ideas in this book were first expounded at conferences or to my students over the years and I am very grateful for helpful comments received.

Chapter 1 on the past and present in Ireland appeared in my book, *A Political History of the Two Irelands: From Partition to Peace*, published in 2012, while chapter 2 on St Patrick's Day appeared in a collection of essays, *Representing Irish Religious Histories: History, Ideology and Practice*, edited by Jacqueline Hill and Mary Ann Lyons, and published in 2013. I acknowledge permission from the publisher, Palgrave Macmillan, to reuse this material. Chapter 6 on the Irish diaspora featured in the *Irish Studies Review*, vol. 15, no. 3 (April 2007), while chapter 8 on the 1885–86 elections appeared in my *Dancing to History's Tune: History, Myth and Politics in Ireland* (1996), published by the Institute of Irish Studies.

I must acknowledge especially Don Akenson, not only for his research on the Irish diaspora that inspired my own work, but also for his support for my varied research interests over a long period. I have dedicated the book to him. Many thanks are due to Alex Waite and Chrissy McMorris and the staff of The History Press Ireland for all their assistance towards publication. Finally, I must thank my wife, Evelyn, and our children, Katherine and David, for their constant support, and also their patient understanding of my state of distraction and absent-mindedness during the final stages of writing this book!

ABBREVIATIONS

DUP	Democratic Unionist Party
GAA	Gaelic Athletic Association
IRA	Irish Republican Army
MP	Member of Parliament
RIC	Royal Irish Constabulary
RUC	Royal Ulster Constabulary
SDLP	Social Democratic and Labour Party
TD	Teachta Dála (Dáil deputy)
UUP	Ulster Unionist Party
UVF	Ulster Volunteer Force

INTRODUCTION

In October 1996, the South African church leader Michael Cassidy remarked about Ireland: 'One notices how people are gripped by the past, remembering the past, feeding on the past.'[1] As revealed by the title, *Irish History Matters*, a major concern in this volume is how and why history *matters* in Ireland, north and south. An opening chapter looks at the way history, or, more correctly, 'views of the past', 'historical perceptions' or 'historical myths', have influenced the present in Ireland. History in Ireland has been heavily contested between communities. These views served in part to cause and to sustain the 'Troubles', which ran for three decades from the late 1960s until the late 1990s. Eventually, many of these historical perceptions were challenged, which helped to allow important reconciliation and to promote the peace process. Such historical views and the ways they altered are examined here. As indicated by the subtitle, other chapters look at politics, identities and commemoration. This book investigates how these issues have been influenced by historical developments – how and why Irish history matters. Public history and its impact on society and politics are studied. New approaches are taken to these issues in their historical context which allows better understanding of our contemporary world.

These essays are based on my research over the last three decades, and include already published material as well as new work. They reflect how my interests have grown over the years. Originally I studied modern history and political science at Magee College Derry/Londonderry and Trinity College Dublin. In the 1970s in Dublin, under the supervision of northerner Theo Moody, a leading figure in efforts to promote objective scholarship in the writing of Irish history, I researched Ulster parliamentary politics, 1868–86, and Irish elections, 1801–1922. I became a member of the politics school at Queen's University Belfast in 1979 and my teaching and research focus moved to the study of modern politics in Ireland, north and south, with special emphasis on the contemporary Northern Ireland 'problem'. My work at this time also concerned politics in other parts of Europe, which gave me a valuable comparative perspective on developments in Ireland.

I became assistant director in 1988, and then director in 1993, of the interdisciplinary Institute of Irish Studies at Queen's. Two areas of particular interest at the institute in the 1990s were the Irish diaspora and commemorations, and my research work now extended into these topics. In 1995, when President Mary Robinson delivered her groundbreaking speech at a joint sitting of the Irish parliament in Dublin on the subject of the Irish diaspora, I was invited to attend as a guest of the president. Her speech and the writings of historian Don Akenson, a former senior research fellow at the institute, radically changed our understanding and appreciation of the diaspora. They have informed my treatment of the subject in this book. In 2002 I returned to the politics school, where my main teaching and research concerns centred on political identities in twentieth- and early twenty-first-century Ireland. My career and interests are reflected in the following essays.

The first chapter looks at history, identity and the peace process. Over the years I have tracked and analysed how ideas of history have impacted on current politics in both Northern Ireland and the Republic of Ireland. The next part looks at a number of commemorative events in Ireland. These tell us much about public awareness and celebration of our history. I examine how a century ago St Patrick's Day and Armistice Day/Remembrance Sunday were marked widely, became restrictive, but are now again shared events. Attention then focuses on the ways in which the

Siege of Derry, 1688–89, and Theobald Wolfe Tone – two diametrically opposed, single-identity subjects – have been recalled annually by their respective political communities. Ian McBride has remarked: 'What is so striking about the Irish case is not simply the tendency for present conflicts to express themselves through the personalities of the past, but the way in which commemorative rituals have become historical forces of their own.'[2]

The next part is concerned with Irish identity in Ireland and among the diaspora. In the early 1900s most people in Ireland, including Ulster unionists, regarded themselves as Irish, but this is no longer the case. Today relatively few unionists in Northern Ireland consider themselves Irish. We examine the historical developments that caused this change, and consider current trends in relation to Irish identity. A chapter on the Irish abroad studies the great diversity among the diaspora. The next chapter looks at the Irish in America, drawing special insights from the example of former President Barack Obama's Irish ancestry. New information and the work of historians about the many millions abroad with an Irish background have implications for identity in Ireland. It is clear that over the years and in different places, in Ireland and abroad, Irish identity has been understood and expressed in many different ways, hence the title of this part is 'Identities' rather than 'Identity'.

In the final part, on the period 1885–1923, a chapter examines the 1885–86 general elections. As John Coakley has pointed out, the 1885 general election marks 'the birth of modern Irish party politics', while the 1886 general election confirmed and reinforced this outcome.[3] These elections were critical for the political confrontation in early twentieth-century Ireland that led to partition in 1921 and subsequent party politics and divisions in both parts of Ireland. The last chapter looks at the fate of southern Protestants, 1919–23 – a subject ignored until recently and now a matter of some controversy.

These essays reflect my interests as a historian and political scientist. To a certain extent they also reflect my personal background and interests. Questions of identity have long intrigued me. My father was Belfast born, a graduate of Trinity College Dublin and an army chaplain, D-Day veteran. He considered himself to be both a loyal British citizen and a proud Irishman. My mother's people were farmers from Tartaraghan, Co. Armagh, near Drumcree, the site of recent Orange/

Green confrontation. But she was born and educated in Glasgow, where her father, a second son, went to work in the early 1900s. After he retired, the family moved back to Bangor, Co. Down, where she met and married my father. I was born in Belfast.

In our Church of Ireland family home, St Patrick's Day was always more important than the 12th of July Boyne celebrations, probably because after the Second World War our father was rector of Saul parish outside Downpatrick, where St Patrick had his first church. We moved to Ballynahinch in mid County Down, the site of the Battle of Ballynahinch during the 1798 rebellion. Growing up, however, I knew nothing about the battle. I suspect that if I had lived in the neighbouring Presbyterian manse, rather than the rectory, I would have been aware of it.

My father then became rector of Knockbreda parish in south Belfast. His church, opened in 1737, was the work of the eminent German architect, Richard Castle, who was also responsible for the design of Leinster House, Dublin, home of the Irish parliament today. I attended Campbell College in east Belfast, which stands in the shadow of the Northern Ireland parliament buildings at Stormont. Little Irish history was available in northern state schools until the 1960s, when a course on Henry Grattan and his times, including the 1798 rebellion, was introduced. The subject was taught with great enthusiasm and knowledge by the Presbyterian chaplain Dr Liam Barbour, and this gave me a strong interest in Irish history.

In 1998 the bicentenary of the 1798 rebellion involved widespread efforts to deal with this historic episode in a new inclusive way. In September I was asked by Rev. Brian Kennaway of the education committee of the Orange Order to speak at an event in the Northern Ireland parliament buildings at Stormont, as part of an effort to 'build bridges'. The occasion was to mark the 1798 bicentenary, on the eve of the anniversary of the Battle of Ballynahinch. Ending my speech with reference to this battle, I recalled the brave Catholic soldiers of the Monaghan Militia who fought and died to save Ireland for the Crown and the gallant Presbyterian United Irishmen who fought and died for a new Ireland. That same year I was invited by my former Queen's University colleague, Mary McAleese, then President of Ireland, to speak at the first of her annual July Battle of the Boyne commemorative events at the Áras an Uachtaráin, the residence of the president, in Dublin. Aimed at offering commemoration of this 'history-changing episode' to 'both Williamite and Jacobite traditions', these receptions were part of her stated aim, also called 'building bridges'.

In 2015 I attended another special commemorative occasion in Dublin, at Trinity College. This involved the unveiling of a memorial stone in honour of the 471 'forgotten' students, staff and alumni of the college who died during the First World War. On Remembrance Sunday, 11 November 2018, I was present at ceremonies in Enniskillen to mark the hundredth anniversary of the Armistice. On the original Armistice Day in 1918 Enniskillen was the first town in either Ireland or Britain to celebrate the end of the war by the ringing of church bells (silent since 1914), thanks to a vigilant wireless operator in the army barracks who at 6.45 a.m. on 11 November 1918 picked up Marshal Foch's Morse code signal to the Allied commanders announcing the armistice. On Remembrance Sunday 1987 Enniskillen was the scene of an IRA bomb that caused twelve deaths. In 2018 Arlene Foster, former first minister of Northern Ireland, and Heather Humphreys, Irish government minister, were among those who laid wreaths at the cenotaph. In the parade from the cenotaph to the service in the cathedral there were not only members of the Royal British Legion but also a large contingent of veterans of the Irish army, wearing their blue United Nations berets.

No doubt my background and experiences, academic and personal, have served to inform my approach to the historical subjects in this book.

PART 1

PAST AND PRESENT

1

THE PAST AND THE PRESENT: HISTORY, IDENTITY AND THE PEACE PROCESS

A sense of history is often important for the identity of individuals, communities and, particularly, national communities. Ideas of history are communicated in various ways such as commemorations, academic histories, popular accounts, myths and songs. These are learned in the home, in the school or in the public arena. They serve to provide a historical narrative at the core of the identity of both individuals and national groups. This historical story helps to provide people with an understanding not only of their past but of where they are today. It can give members of society a collective memory that serves to give unity and sense of purpose for the contemporary world. All this is true as regards the role of history throughout modern Europe. Ireland, north and south, is no exception. Nor is it unusual in a European context that in Ireland there are often strongly different and conflicting views of history, arising from important national and religious divisions. What is unusual, in the case of Ireland, is the widespread belief held strongly by many until recently that matters in Ireland are greatly influenced by history and that events of the past determine the present to an exceptional degree.

The importance of the past for the present in Ireland has often been noted by people from outside as well as inside the country.

In October 1996 the South African church leader Michael Cassidy remarked about Ireland: 'One notices how people are gripped by the past, remembering the past, feeding on the past; people are constantly remembering this betrayal or that battle; … this martyr or this murderer.' He concluded that 'these realities of the past feed into the present in Ireland more than anywhere I have been'.[1] Indeed, in 1992, the novelist Dermot Bolger felt compelled to protest that in Ireland 'we must go back three centuries to explain any fight outside a chip shop'.[2] In speeches in the 1990s, the American President, Bill Clinton, made frequent mention of the role of 'ancient enmities' in Northern Ireland.[3]

In the comments of Ian Paisley we find many references to unionists' 'traditional enemies'.[4] In 1971 he declared: 'God has been our help in 1641, 1688, 1690, 1798, 1912, 1920, and He will not fail us in the future.'[5] In 1996 Ruari Ó Brádaigh of Republican Sinn Féin was reported to have stated: 'In Ireland we have no need of your Che Guevaras and your Ho Chi Minhs. We have Robert Emmet, O'Donovan Rossa, Cathal Brugha, Dan Breen.'[6] Later commentators have often seen the success of the peace process as evidence of triumph over such historical forces. During a visit to Northern Ireland in 2009 the American Secretary of State, Hillary Clinton, remarked on how 'ancient hatreds have yielded to new hopes'.[7]

Can we say that the history of Ireland has special importance for the present and that Ireland has a unique past? The answer to this is that history is as significant for the contemporary world in Ireland as for anywhere else, but no more significant than in other countries. The shape of politics and society in Ireland is influenced by historical developments, but that history is neither unique nor responsible for predetermining political conflict among the inhabitants of Ireland. In seventeenth-century Germany and the Netherlands, as in Ireland, there was also bitter religious and political conflict, but such a history does not *determine* events today in these countries, even though it has had influence on the modern world. What is very important in all these countries is the more modern history of the late nineteenth and twentieth centuries, which has affected the shape of their societies and influenced the present.

In the case of Ireland, it is not correct to say that historical events here were more dreadful or more deterministic for the future than elsewhere in Europe. In 1942 Nicholas Mansergh wrote that the history of Ireland 'is no more unhappy than that of other small nations in Europe, the Belgians, the Serbs, the Poles, or the Greeks'.[8] These comments by Mansergh are fair in relation to the early history of Ireland and these other countries. They are not fair, however, in relation to the more recent past, when these countries experienced dreadful events that Ireland avoided. The Greeks suffered very substantial population expulsions and deaths in the early 1920s, and all these countries were invaded by the German army, 1939–42, which led to heavy loss of life.

For Ireland, north and south, what has been critically important for the contemporary world has been matters relating to present-day problems, in particular over nationalism but also over religion. These problems have affected many other parts of Europe. Such challenges to both politicians and citizens do not relate to a special history that predetermines the present. At the same time, it is clear that many people have believed this to be the case. There has been a strong belief that these historical roots are especially important and lie at the heart of conflict in Ireland. Such a view is challenged here.

Nonetheless, it is clear that 'views of the past', 'historical perceptions' or 'historical myths' have been very important. Often, such ideas are part of a sense of history, which individuals or communities have created for themselves in response to contemporary challenges or needs. It is argued here that, even though the situation in Ireland is not influenced by special historical circumstances, such strongly and widely held perceptions are of considerable significance and must be taken seriously. These views have served to inform and shape the main political identities in Ireland and have helped in part to cause the conflict and violence that persisted for three decades from the late 1960s. Efforts to challenge these historical perceptions have played an important role in the emergence of reconfigured identities, which have allowed significant reconciliation.

Reasons for and Consequences of these Historical Perceptions

Anthony D. Smith has observed in his book, *National Identity*, that historical memories have been very important for the creation of national identity in our modern world.[9] It is a common feature of nineteenth- and twentieth-century nationalist movements in Europe that they developed or 'constructed' historical traditions as part of their ideology, and this has been true of both unionism and nationalism in Ireland.[10] It has also been noted that history remains more significant in modern societies divided over national and religious matters than in those where these problems have been resolved or do not matter.[11] This has certainly been the case in Ireland. History can provide the explanation and means of personal and public discourse by which people understand and artic- ulate the debate over the main national/religious problems.

Often these accounts of the past are selective or based partly on myths, and are closer to what Walker Connor has called 'sentient or felt his- tory' rather than 'chronological or factual history'.[12] Nonetheless, such views have remained important for many. This historical dimension has often seemed plausible, because in our dominant Anglo-American world people until recently have been unable to understand the importance of ethnic/national/religious conflict, so this historical explanation has appeared a sensible one.[13] For many, both in Ireland and outside, to blame the situation on history has seemed reasonable. In the early twenty-first century, of course, there is a better under- standing of such conflict.

Historical narratives, created from actual historical experiences and from myths and selective views that surround them, have served to give the past an important role in the identity of individuals and national communities in Ireland, north and south. A. T. Q. Stewart has remarked: 'To the Irish all history is applied history and the past is simply a conven- ient quarry which provides ammunition to use against enemies in the present.' He continued: 'when we say that the Irish are too much influ- enced by the past, we really mean that they are too much influenced by Irish history, which is a different matter.'[14]

We often find references to historical events in speeches by politicians from Northern Ireland, as, for example, in the debate at Westminster in 1985 on the Anglo-Irish Agreement.[15] John Hume talked of events of 1912, stating that the 'divisions in Ireland go back well beyond par- tition', and referred to the United Irishmen and C.S. Parnell. In the same debate, Ian Paisley declared: 'Anyone who has read history should understand that this did not start in 1920, but goes far back to the days of the plantation settlement and back into the dim and distant past.' In his presidential address to the Fianna Fáil Ard Fheis, on 26 February 1983, Charles J. Haughey declared that 'the right to territorial integrity is derived from history. From time immemorial the island of Ireland has belonged to the Irish people'.[16]

Members of paramilitaries have often been influenced by a strong historical sense. In his study of their many periodicals and journals over the period 1966–92, Richard Davis has described 'the attitude of republicans and loyalists to a history which both acknowledge as fundamental to their respective positions'.[17] A former IRA volunteer, Shane Paul O'Doherty, has described his reasons for joining the organisation: 'My attraction to the IRA was not initially based on the sight or experience of any particular social injustice, though, when I did join the IRA, injustices were foremost in my motivation. It was the discovery of the tragedies of Irish history which first caused my desire to give myself to the IRA …'[18] Others joined because of events after 1969, but then they would have become very aware of this historical dimension, with its emphasis on matters such as the 1916 Rising and the 1918 general election. A belief in the physical force of historical tradition was integral to the role of the IRA in the late twentieth century. When the first of the loyalist paramilitary groups was founded in 1965, it very consciously called itself the Ulster Volunteer Force, after the 1912 unionist organisation of that name. Loyalist paramilitaries, as psychologist Geoffrey Beatty has pointed out, have used the Battle of the Somme to 'sanction their own actions in a very different sort of combat'.[19]

Such historical narratives, however, have been not only an important part of people's identity in Ireland: they have also served to impede efforts to achieve political accommodation. They have helped to give selective, incomplete and often inaccurate pictures to communities of their own history, and little or no understanding of the experiences of other communities. In the past in Northern Ireland the formal school system had little direct part in the sense of history held by the public, because there was little Irish history on the curriculum. In a press interview in February 1998, the Northern Ireland Protestant playwright, 34-year-old Gary Mitchell, said: 'We never learned Irish history at school, which was really strange. It was all English history geared towards the exams. We didn't do 1798, even though, woops, Wolfe Tone and Henry McCracken were Protestants.'[20] People picked up knowledge of their history from songs, popular historical accounts or annual commemorations of important events or individuals from the past.

For many in the Protestant and unionist community, their sense of history focused on events such as the Siege of Derry and the Battle of the Boyne in the seventeenth century and the Battle of the Somme in the twentieth century, which served to explain themselves as a people who have faced siege and sacrifice from these earlier times to the present. This historical narrative does relate to historical experiences of that community, but is selective and contains myths. It ignores periods when Protestants were not greatly concerned about such events, when they were divided, and when they co-operated with Catholics, as in the United Irishmen of the 1790s.

Among nationalists, there was a historical narrative of an heroic Irish people who had suffered invasion and conquest but who always survived. In 1994 Bernadette McAliskey recalled how she learned her history from her father, 'everything from the tales of the Tuatha De Dannan, and Celtic mythology, to Larkin and Connolly'.[21] In a newspaper article in 1994, John Hume wrote of the 'traditional nationalist philosophy with which we all grew up – a philosophy that the essence of patriotism – à la 1916 – was the nobility of dying for Ireland and struggling against the British occupation of Ireland'. He referred not only to northern but also to southern 'traditional nationalist thinking'. He stated: 'All the major parties in the dáil were born out of that philosophy and their founders were the progenitors of it.'[22]

In the south, nationalist opinion retained a strong historical dimension, supported in this case by the education system and the state. In 1996 a Fianna Fáil deputy, Conor Lenihan, recalled his schooling in the 1960s: 'History was a heady and potent thing then. In our school in Athlone there were posters of the seven signatories of the 1916 proclamation hung up all over the place.'[23] This historical narrative of the nationalist and Catholic community does reflect its historical experiences, but is also selective and includes myths. This account leaves out periods when Irish Catholics did not pursue separatist goals, when they were divided among themselves and when they were aligned with Protestants, as in the British army in the First World War.

These historical views that inform and influence people's identities have helped to cause distrust between individuals and communities. The Mitchell Commission of 1996, which looked into the decommissioning of paramilitary arms in Northern Ireland, emphasised the importance of trust between parties. It noted how, because of the historical arguments about why the other side cannot be trusted, 'even well-intentioned acts are often viewed with suspicion and hostility'.[24] Another major problem about these historical views linking the current situation to the remote past is that they help to create what Arthur Aughey has called a 'historic culture of fatalism', which makes it difficult to achieve compromise and peaceful co-existence, both for people and for parties.[25] George Mitchell, formerly a member of the United States senate, who became the president's special envoy to Northern Ireland in 1995, has recorded how, when he arrived in Northern Ireland in 1995 to take up a mediating role, people welcomed him, but then said: 'You are wasting your time. This conflict cannot be ended. We have been killing each other for centuries and we are doomed to go on killing each other for ever.'[26] Strongly felt ideas of historical struggle or siege can make acceptance of change difficult.

Fascination with a supposedly unique history has led to a failure to learn from elsewhere. Other European countries have faced these vexed matters over nationality and religion and have dealt with them better than has been the case in Ireland. In their modern nineteenth- and twentieth-century histories, countries such as the Netherlands and Switzerland experienced serious religious divisions, while others including Norway and Italy had to deal with deep divisions over nationalism, but they have managed to cope successfully with these problems. Finally, these historical views have helped to legitimise the use of violence. In his 1993 study, *The Irish Troubles: A Generation of Violence, 1967–92*, J. Bowyer Bell observed that in other countries people were emboldened to act 'by Lenin's or Mao's example, by Allah's word or the people's need'. In Ireland, however, the enemy was killed to 'history's tune and the blare of those unseen trumpets, audible always to the faithful'. Bell continued: 'In Ireland legitimacy was won from history, a legacy and clearly defined responsibility.'[27] This historical dimension to contemporary identities helps to account for the actions and atrocities of loyalist and republican paramilitaries that cannot be accounted for only by political and social factors.

Changes in Public Discourse on History, from the Early 1990s to the Agreement

The period of the 1990s witnessed important changes in the ways that many people viewed and expressed their history in Ireland. The Opsahl Commission, which in 1992 and 1993 considered the future of Northern Ireland, received submissions from hundreds of individuals and groups. It found evidence of a widespread desire to question many current assumptions about community identity, including the historical dimension, and urged greater emphasis on a common Irish history and culture in the schools.[28] In schools in Northern Ireland, teaching of Irish history had increased since the 1960s. This was given impetus with the introduction in 1989 of a new common history curriculum, with textbooks looking at Irish history from a range of perspectives.[29] Other educational initiatives included an annual series of Irish history lectures, known as the Rockwell lectures, organised for schoolchildren between 1990 and 2000 at Queen's University Belfast, and a local history schools' competition, run by an interdenominational church group. At the Ulster Museum, two major exhibitions, curated by W.A. Maguire, addressed two of the most contentious events in Irish history in a manner that gained cross-community as well as academic respect. The first was 'Kings in conflict', marking the tercentenary of the Battle of the Boyne (1990); the second was 'Up in arms!', which marked the bicentenary of the 1798 rebellion (1998).

Organisations such as Protestant and Catholic Encounter and church groups ran lectures and seminars to explore popular historical myths. Different historical traditions were explored through the programmes and projects of the Cultural Traditions Group, established in 1989 under the Community Relations Council. The 1990s witnessed the appearance of new popular histories, such as Jonathan Bardon's *A History of*

Ulster.[30] In her study of identities in Northern Ireland, Máiread Nic Craith observed how historians 'have heightened public consciousness regarding the collective history of the region [Northern Ireland] and contributed to a non-partisan awareness of this past'.[31] During the period from the late 1980s until the early 2000s, more than 200 books on local history were produced by local publishers in Northern Ireland, such as Blackstaff Press, Friar's Bush Press and the Institute of Irish Studies. The Federation for Ulster Local Studies witnessed a large growth in the number and activities of local community historical societies.

In the south, new Irish historical writing helped to undermine simplistic views of past heroes and events, which were widely held. Books and journal articles explored various historical myths and also sought to provide a scholarly and non-partisan treatment of Irish history. One such major project, which began in the late 1960s, was the multi-volumed, *A New History of Ireland*, published under the auspices of the Royal Irish Academy, containing material from leading scholars in Ireland and aimed at a wide public. In the 1970s, authors such as Ruth Dudley Edwards and Conor Cruise O'Brien sought to challenge influential historical myths.[32] This revision of Irish history, however, had little immediate effect on public opinion.

It was not until the late 1980s and early 1990s that these new historical ideas started to percolate significantly from academic to both popular and government levels, perhaps because of the publicity caused by some opposition that emerged to revisionism in the late 1980s.[33] At the same time, there was a growing awareness of the harm of some historical myths. A number of best-selling books, including Roy Foster's *Modern Ireland* (1988), Marianne Elliott's *Wolfe Tone* (1989), Tim Pat Coogan's *De Valera* (1993) and Conor Cruise O'Brien's *Ancestral Voices* (1994), challenged widely held historical views.[34] Journalists such as Kevin Myers, Eoghan Harris and Ruth Dudley Edwards interrogated historical matters, as did broadcasters like John Bowman and Myles Dungan.

The change in attitudes to history was reflected in the way in which commemorations were now used by many to recall important events in their history. In her study of war commemorations, Jane Leonard remarked how 'in Ireland politicians and local communities have endeavoured to replace the partisan character of existing war commemorations with more inclusive, generous forms of acknowledging the Irish past'.[35] From the early 1990s, both unionist and nationalist politicians were involved together in Remembrance Day services in many places in Northern Ireland; previously this particular commemoration had largely been dominated by unionists and ignored by nationalists.

In the Irish Republic the 1990s saw a new effort to acknowledge the role of Irish servicemen in the two world wars. In 1995 a ceremony in Dublin, led by President Mary Robinson, to mark the end of the Second World War was attended by representatives of nearly all Irish parties, including Sinn Féin. In memory of the Irish who died in the First World War, a peace park was built by groups from the north and south of Ireland at Messines in Belgium and opened by Queen Elizabeth and President Mary McAleese in 1998. In her speech on this occasion, President McAleese declared: 'Those whom we commemorate here were doubly tragic. They fell victim to a war against oppression in Europe. Their memory, too, fell victim to a war for independence at home in Ireland.' She continued: 'Respect for the memory of one set of heroes was often at the expense of respect for the memory of the other.'[36]

In the course of commemorations for the Great Irish Famine, the prime minister, Tony Blair, apologised on behalf of the British government for not having done more to help during this catastrophe. The bicentenary of the 1798 rebellion in Ireland was commemorated widely, north and south, as a shared historical event. George Boyce has written how in the bicentenary celebrations of the event in 1998 'memory was directed towards the significance of pluralist thinking in the Irish past, and academics mediated between the state and the citizen, playing a public role'.[37] In the second half of the 1990s the Irish government actively supported a number of these commemorations, whereas in previous decades it had shown considerable reserve about historical matters.[38] The education committee of the Orange Order held a 1798 commemorative dinner on the eve of the bicentenary of the Battle of Ballynahinch, Co. Down, at the parliament buildings at Stormont, attended not only by members of the order, but also by the lord mayors of Belfast and Dublin, the heads of most of the universities of Ireland and leading journalists. The speaker on this occasion recalled all those who died at Ballynahinch in 1798, including 'the brave Catholic soldiers of the Monaghan Militia who fought and died to save Ireland for the crown and those gallant Presbyterian United Irishmen who fought and died for a new Ireland'.[39]

From the early 1990s we can see evidence of the beginning of a different attitude to the importance of the past in political speech and approach. These changes can be seen at popular, party and government level. They are apparent not only in the north and the south but also in Britain. Sometimes this new attitude has meant an outright rejection of any role for history or an effort to draw a line under the past. After a particularly gruesome murder by the IRA in South Armagh in 1992, Dundalk priest Father John Duffy declared: 'if that is how you write Irish history then it is not worth giving to anyone'.[40] In 1995 the author Eugene McCabe warned about the impact of myths in Ireland: 'Throughout the country, family mythology, local mythology, historical mythology, should all be tagged with a health warning: myth can induce a form of madness and zealotry that leads to death.'[41] More commonly, it has involved an effort to deal with the past or to draw either a different or more inclusive lesson from history. At the same time, however, it must be stressed that many people, including some who have at times taken this new approach, have continued to see events within the customary, historical framework discussed earlier.

Changes in Political Speech Regarding History, from the Early 1990s to the Agreement

This new approach was reflected among politicians and others in the development of the peace process from the early 1990s. In an important speech on government policy in Coleraine on 16 December 1992, the Northern Ireland Secretary of State, Sir Patrick Mayhew, declared that there was much 'in the long and often tragic history of Ireland for deep regret' and the British government 'for its part shares in that regret to the full'.[42] After a meeting of a unionist delegation and members of the Irish government in November 1992, unionist MP Ken Maginnis remarked that 'the real disappointment was that the Fianna Fáil party was caught

up by a large 1922 warp'.[43] In mid–April 1993, however, in response to
questions about changes to articles two and three of the Irish constitution, Albert Reynolds, the Fianna Fáil Taoiseach, declared: 'We are not
tied up in our past. We want to move forward, to look at the changes
required to ensure that both communities can live together.'[44] In an
address to the annual conference of his Fianna Fáil party in November
1993, Reynolds acknowledged that there was 'a more complex situation than existed during the war of independence struggle from 1916 to
1921'. He stated that 'We must not be prisoners of history' and that 'new
patterns must transcend the antagonisms of a century between the two
political cultures'.[45]

On a number of occasions in 1993, Dr John Dunlop, then modera-
tor of the Presbyterian Church, pointed to the danger of a historically
based siege mentality for the unionist community.[46] On 7 March 1993
he wrote:

> Protestants talk of siege and survival. For most unionists, the siege of
> Derry and the Battle of the Boyne only continue as powerful sym-
> bols from the past because they speak of the periodic and constantly
> renewed threats of being overwhelmed by the Irish majority, whether
> in 1641, 1690, 1798, the home rule crisis of the early 1920s or in the
> violence of the present.

Dunlop warned that: 'The trouble with the siege mentality is that it leads
to defensive thinking, which often does not have the flexibility or generosity of spirit to discern where its own self-interest lies, never mind the
legitimate interests of other people.' In late 1993, nonetheless, Ian Paisley
attacked talks between John Hume and Gerry Adams, accusing Hume of
trying to sell the people of the province 'like cattle on the hoof to their
traditional enemies'.[47]

In March 1993, Seamus Mallon, the SDLP MP, criticised the republican movement for being 'weighed down by history', while, the following
month, a South African journalist, Rian Malan, described republicans
being 'so steeped in ancestral memories of martyrdom that they can't see
straight any more'.[48] In April 1993 an IRA statement declared that 'the
root cause of this conflict is the historic and ongoing violent denial of

Irish national rights'.[49] On the BBC programme *Spotlight* on 21 October 1993, John Hume, the SDLP leader, spoke of the 'distrust of others based on the past', and argued that this was the time to leave the past behind. In an article in the *Irish Times* in April 1994, Hume acknowledged the importance in the recent past of the 'traditional nationalist philosophy' with its strong historical dimension, emphasised the importance of agreement and diversity in modern Ireland and urged the IRA to renounce its campaign of violence, which had been based on 'traditional Irish Republican reasons'.[50]

A number of key governmental papers now carried significant references to dealing with the past, in contrast to earlier documents, such as the Anglo-Irish Agreement and the Sunningdale Agreement, which contained no mention of history. The Downing Street Joint Declaration of 15 December 1993, signed by Prime Minister John Major and Taoiseach Albert Reynolds, stated that the most important issue facing the people of Ireland, north and south, and the British and Irish governments together, was to 'remove the causes of conflict, to overcome the legacy of history and to heal the divisions which have resulted'. In paragraph 5, Reynolds, on behalf of the Irish government, stated that 'the lessons of Irish history, and especially of Northern Ireland,' show that 'stability and well-being' will not be achieved by a political system which 'is refused allegiance or rejected on grounds of identity' by a significant minority. The statement advocated the principles of consent and self-determination.[51]

The Frameworks for the Future document of 22 February 1995, between the British and Irish governments, contained a foreword by John Major that declared that 'age-old mistrusts need to be consigned to history'. The paper stated that both governments recognised that there was 'deep regret on all sides in the long and often tragic history of Anglo-Irish relations, and of all relations in Ireland. They believe it is now time to lay aside, with dignity and forbearance, the mistakes of the past.'[52]

In October 1993, Gerry Adams, leader of Sinn Féin, declared that his party had now adopted 'a different approach which is more in keeping with the reality of Ireland in 1993 than perhaps harking back to Ireland in 1918'.[53] Again reflecting a change in attitude to the significance of history, Sinn Féin National Chairman and councillor Tom Hartley in January 1994 wrote of how 'modern republican ideology, while rooted in the past, is above all the result of a 25 year learning process …'[54] For a time, however, republicans expressed reservations about the Downing Street Declaration, one reason being, in Adams' words, that 'we are dealing with centuries of history'.[55] Eventually, at the end of August 1994, the IRA declared a ceasefire in a statement that did not dwell on the past, but referred briefly to all those who had died 'for Irish freedom'. The *Irish News* editorial, 1 September 1994, appearing the day after the ceasefire, saw this announcement in the 'tradition of Patrick Pearse's noble decision to lay down arms after the Easter Rising of 1916'. The ceasefire declaration of October 1994 from the loyalist groups carried no reference to the past beyond the recent 'Troubles'. Nonetheless, we may note that their statement was read out in North Belfast at Fernhill House – a building with historic links to the original UVF of 1912. The IRA ceasefire collapsed in early 1996 but was renewed in July 1997.

Over the next four years from 1994 we see continued reference to history in various ways. At government level there was often mention of the past and of the need to deal with or leave it behind. On St Patrick's Day 1996, in reference to his recent visit to Northern Ireland, President Bill Clinton spoke of how he had seen optimism 'in the faces of the two communities, divided by history' and how 'we must not permit the process of reconciliation in Northern Ireland to be destroyed by those who are blinded by the hatreds of the past'.[56] The Northern Ireland Secretary of State, Sir Patrick Mayhew, spoke in September 1995 of the government's desire for a 'political settlement to the ancient difficulties of Ireland' and in July 1996 of the difficulties of a process which is intended 'to overcome divisions which go back centuries'.[57]

At the opening of substantive all-party negotiations at Castle Buildings, Belfast, on 12 June 1996, Prime Minister John Major declared: 'For too long the history of Northern Ireland has poisoned the present and threatened the future. It is time to end all that, however difficult it may be. History has involved too many victims.'[58] In September 1996, Taoiseach John Bruton attacked the use of history to justify the renewal of IRA violence and went on to say: 'We cannot relive our great grandparents' lives … we are not obliged to take offence on their behalf, any more than we are obliged to atone for their sins.'[59] In June 1996 at Queen's University Belfast, George Mitchell remarked: 'You can't disregard history – that would be a fatal error – but try to break out of the bonds which history sometimes creates and imposes on a society.'[60] When Tony Blair first met Bertie Ahern officially in 1997, he told him that he 'came to the issues with no ideological or historical baggage' while Ahern then said that he 'too came to Northern Ireland with no historical baggage'.[61]

Attitudes among the parties in Northern Ireland over this period to the question of the past have reflected some of these changes. David Ervine, leader of the Progressive Unionist Party, in March 1995 urged unionists to 'break the myths and lay the ghosts', while in June 1995 Gary McMichael of the Ulster Democratic Party warned: 'I think in this society we have developed a very dangerous fashion of looking into history and using history as a weapon and a means of justifying actions that were taken.'[62] In August 1996 Cecil Walker, UUP MP, exhorted his political colleagues to 'scatter the historical cobwebs'.[63] Among members of the SDLP, in particular John Hume, there were various references to leaving the past behind. In December 1995, at the launch of a book on Daniel O'Connell, he stated that: 'If there is a lesson from Daniel O'Connell it is – the aislings [vision poetry] of our ancestors should inspire us, not control us.'[64] On 4 February 1998 he urged: 'In learning the lessons of the past we must not become prisoners of the past – the major obstacle to success is the unwillingness of certain parties to leave the past behind them and their continued use of the language of the past.'[65]

Surviving Difficulties over Historical Views

At the same time, ideas of the importance of the past continued to influence people and to hamper efforts to ameliorate the conflict. George Mitchell accompanied President Clinton during his stay in Ireland in 1995, and he later recalled separate meetings the president had with Ian Paisley and Gerry Adams. He described how Paisley launched into a thirty-minute account of the history of Northern Ireland from a unionist point of view, while later Adams gave a similar story, but from a national-ist point of view.[66] The report (published in 1996) of the international body on arms decommissioning, chaired by Mitchell, highlighted the problem of the 'absence of trust' between the various parties. It noted how 'common to many of our meetings were arguments, steeped in history, as to why the other side cannot be trusted', as a consequence of which 'even well-intentioned acts are often viewed with suspicion and hostility'. The report declared that: 'a resolution of the decommissioning issue – or any other issue – will not be found if the parties resort to their vast inventories of historical recrimination. Or, as was put to us several times, what is really needed is the decommissioning of mindsets in Northern Ireland.'[67]

The 1997 report of the independent review of parades and marches, chaired by Peter North, observed that 'remembering in Northern Ireland is complicated by opposing perspectives, by the long, lingering pain of remembered past suffering and conflict'. The report described how 'We met representatives of the Loyal Orders who have recently suf-fered at the hands of the Provisional IRA and who recall the deliverance of the Protestant people in a battle which took place more than 300 years ago'. It continued: 'Their Catholic neighbours meantime remem-ber the same battle as a defeat, along with their more recent experience of discrimination at the hands of the unionist administration.'[68]

Of great concern to many unionists in these years was the ban-ning of an annual Orange parade at Drumcree, Portadown, which they believed had been held every year since 1807. In fact, this parade had been cancelled on a number of occasions over the years (such as during the Second World War), but historical myths about unin-terrupted traditions were allowed to colour contemporary concerns about parading.[69] Eventually, a South African lawyer, Brian Currin, was brought in to mediate in the conflict over the Drumcree Orange parade. After initial discussions, he spoke in July 2000 of the problems involved and of the need to unpack 'hundreds of years of historical baggage' to come to a better understanding of each other's position.[70] His efforts were not successful.

Such concerns and problems served to hinder progress in the peace process. They made many people reluctant to accept change and caused the parties to be very cautious in their negotiations. As regards republicans over this period, historical perspectives continued to influence their attitude towards the peace process, in particular to the decommissioning of arms. It was noticeable, however, that at Sinn Féin annual conferences during these years the speeches of Gerry Adams made less mention of history than in the past, apart from general statements such as that 'Anglo-Irish history and the international experience, teaches us that the road to peace is often tortuous'.[71] On the unionist side, the speeches of Ian Paisley attacking the peace process often contained references to unionists' 'traditional enemies'.[72] On account of David Trimble's part in the dispute over Orangemen parading to Drumcree, the front page of the *Economist*, 13 July 1996, carried a picture of him with the headline 'Wedded to the past'. Later in the same year, Trimble was prepared to justify negotiations with representatives of the Irish government by referring to James Craig's discussions with southern government representatives in the early 1920s.[73]

An Agreement Emerges

Eventually, in spite of these difficulties, on 10 April 1998, after extensive and difficult talks between most of the parties and the two governments, the Belfast Agreement/Good Friday Agreement was concluded. A month later the document was endorsed by a large majority throughout Ireland, with a vote in Northern Ireland supporting the agreement and a vote in the Republic of Ireland accepting changes to the Irish constitution in support of the agreement.[74] The agreement carried virtually no historical references. It acknowledged that 'the tragedies of the past have left a deep and profoundly regrettable legacy of suffering' and remembered those who had died or been injured, and their families. The opening sentence in the document expressed the general belief that the agreement offered 'a truly historic opportunity for a new beginning'.

The document expressed commitment to 'partnership, equality and mutual respect' as the basis of relationships 'within Northern Ireland, between north and south, and between these islands'. Such relationships were expressed solely in contemporary terms. The agreement laid down important principles and institutions for the future of Northern Ireland, which represented a compromise on the part of the main sections.[75] Its aim was to reconcile opposing unionist/nationalist views on national sovereignty and the method of government and type of society for the conflicting groups. It established the acceptance of the consent of the people of Northern Ireland as to their future relations with the UK and Ireland, drew up a structure for a power-sharing government, affirmed various human rights and liberties, and declared an absolute commitment to peaceful means. The agreement created north–south and east–west dimensions and bodies.

While the agreement made only brief mention of the past, some participants and observers saw it as an important part of a historical process. On the eve of its signing, the British Prime Minister, Tony Blair, spoke of how he felt the 'hand of history upon our shoulders'.[76] Press coverage showed some confusion on its exact historical impact. An *Irish Times* editorial, 11 April 1998, referred to peacemakers who 'buried the quarrel of 400 years', while a *Belfast Telegraph* editorial, 21 May 1998, talked of a new partnership that will 'replace 800 years of enmity with trust and friendship'. In September 1998, President Bill Clinton praised the progress of Northern Ireland's peace process as helping the whole world to awaken from 'history's nightmares' by showing that 'ancient enmities' could be overcome. He then went on to claim that if the peace process was successfully concluded, then this example could be shown to 'conflict areas in the Middle East, the Aegean, the Indian sub-continent and to the tribal strife of Africa'.[77]

Changes in Public Discourse on History after the Agreement

Since the agreement was passed the impact of this historical dimension can be felt in a number of ways. For some there is now a clear understanding that history does not determine the present, that people are not slaves to history. This view was enunciated in a new approach by President Bill Clinton on his last visit as president to Ireland in late 2000, when he talked of the dangers of 'historical ghosts' and declared that what had happened in Northern Ireland provided proof 'that peace can prevail, that the past is history, not destiny'.[78] With others it has involved a belief that the 'positive' or 'shared' aspects of history should be emphasised. Prime Minister Tony Blair, in an address to the joint houses of the Irish parliament, on 22 November 1998, declared: 'No one should ignore the injustices of the past, or the lessons of history. But too often between us one person's history has been another person's myth. We need not be prisoners of our history. My generation in Britain sees Ireland differently today and probably the same generation here feels differently about Britain.'[79]

On 14 May 2000 President Mary McAleese spoke at a conference at the Kennedy Center, Washington, on the subject of 'Ireland: politics, culture and identity'. She remarked how in Ireland 'we have so often raided the past for proof of our difference, for reasons to remain strangers, for memories that prove the iniquity of the other, each piece of evidence shoring up our preconceptions of both self and the other'. She urged: 'As we strive to create a new future together in respectful partnership, might we not look more carefully at our histories and find in shared memories, sources of unity rather than division, sources of enlightenment about one another rather than mutual incomprehension.'[80]

At the popular level in Northern Ireland we can also see evidence of these changing attitudes. An example of shared historical commemorations was cross-party support at Belfast City Hall for the erection of a memorial sculpture to James Magennis, the Catholic holder of a Second World War VC. In April 2003 a special service at St Anne's Cathedral in Belfast to remember people from Belfast who had died in the First World War involved not only British crown and army representatives but also republicans such as the Sinn Féin lord mayor, Alex Maskey. Most council areas now regularly experience cross-party attendance at Remembrance Sunday. Recent years have seen unionist backing for the erection of memorials to supporters of the late eighteenth-century United Irish movement. There have also been efforts to make more inclusive the celebrations on 17 March for the historical figure of St Patrick.

For many groups there is still a strong belief in the importance of their own history, but we can also see some effort to explain this history to others and to make their commemorations more inclusive. Since 1998, the Apprentice Boys of Derry have held a week-long festival, before their annual August parade, to 'explain their ethos and culture to Derry's wider nationalist community'.[81] On 5 June 2006, for the first time, representatives of the 'loyal orders' met, at their request, the Catholic archbishop of Armagh to discuss the parades issue. Afterwards Archbishop Brady remarked that the desire of the leadership of the 'loyal orders' to meet him 'represents their willingness to go beyond the barriers of history [and] … to explain the customs, principles and values of their organisations to leaders of the Catholic community. This is to be welcomed.'[82]

Leading northern politicians have continued to seek to challenge this historical dimension. In his speech accepting the Nobel Peace Prize in 1998, John Hume expressed his hope that, with the new institutions in place, 'we will erode the distrust and prejudices of our past'. On the same occasion David Trimble spoke of the 'dark sludge of historical sectarianism' and declared that both communities must leave it behind. In a new approach to unionist history he acknowledged that 'Ulster unionists, fearful of being isolated on the island, built a solid house, but it was a cold house for Catholics'.[83] At other times, Trimble used the example of former unionist leader James Craig to support his actions over controversial matters.[84] On 2 March 2002, Dr John Reid, Northern Ireland Secretary of State, urged people to 'challenge the historical assumptions which drive the conflict in Northern Ireland'.[85] In 2007, Alliance Party leader David Ford warned that 'hiding in the 17th century isn't an option any more'.[86]

In the south, there was also a widespread determination to adopt a more magnanimous and less restrictive view of the past. A leading role in this effort was played by President Mary McAleese. On 7 May 2003, speaking at a conference on 'Re-imagining Ireland', she declared: 'The old vanities of history are disappearing. Carefully hidden stories like those of the Irish who died in the First World War are coming out of the shoeboxes in the attic and into daylight. We are making new friends, we are influencing new people, we are learning new things about ourselves, we are being changed.'[87] This issue of the Irish in the First World War, which traditional nationalist versions of Irish history had ignored, is one historical theme in particular that President McAleese, other Irish politicians and many members of the public sought to restore to common concern.

An even more extraordinary gesture by President McAleese to a broader view of Irish history, as part of a 'bridge-building' policy, was her annual reception for southern Orangemen and other Protestants around the 12th of July at the Áras an Uachtaráin, the Dublin residence of the president, to mark the Battle of the Boyne. In 2007 she noted how 'For 10 years now Áras an Uachtaráin has been the only place on the island of Ireland to offer an official commemoration of that major history-changing episode, the Battle of the Boyne, and to offer it jointly to both Williamite and Jacobite traditions'.[88] At the same time, leading southern figures, such as President McAleese and the Taoiseach Bertie Ahern, now felt able to give new attention to commemorating the 1916 Rising, as was seen in the major state commemoration of the event in 2006. Later Ahern wrote that he had been determined 'to take 1916 back from both the IRA and the revisionists for all the people of Ireland'.[89]

Despite all these developments, in special political arrangements and in changes to many people's attitudes, there remained problems, which caused the collapse of the assembly and power-sharing executive for a time. The deaths, suffering and bitterness of the last forty years of conflict have left a legacy that still influences the present.[90] While the Belfast Agreement initially brought wide agreement, it did so partly by certain ambiguity on important matters such as power-sharing, decommissioning and policing.[91] There was a failure to deal with these problems satisfactorily, mainly because they went to the core of the underlying national political conflict and proved difficult practically to solve to everyone's satisfaction. At the same time, there were difficulties due to the survival of what Norman Porter has called 'antagonistic elements of the historical self-understandings of unionism and nationalism'.[92] There were some special efforts post-1998 to develop aspects of a common history, identity and symbols, but more could have been done in this area.[93] For many people, historical perceptions continued to exert a powerful influence, which made political accommodation more difficult.

The delay in decommissioning of IRA weapons and in Sinn Féin involvement in policing can be seen in part as a result of traditional historical attitudes among many republicans. Denis Bradley, a former go-between for the Irish government and the IRA, commented in 2001 on the problem of decommissioning that 'it takes republicans, like a lot of other organisations that see themselves with long roots into history, quite a considerable time to get round to doing things, a long gestation period'.[94] The same year, at the inter-party and inter-government talks at Weston Park, Shropshire, England, Gerry Adams sought to explain the delays in progress: 'We are dealing with 100 years of conflict, dealing with quite difficult issues.'[95] Among republicans there emerged several small groups of dissenters who were not willing to embrace the peace process, which some saw as 'a total and a complete departure from the traditions of the past' and were prepared to resort to violence again.[96]

Among many unionists, especially members of the DUP, there remained opposition to power-sharing and the new 1998 arrangements, which can be viewed as arising in part from their historical sense of siege. In November 2002, at the DUP annual conference, Ian Paisley began his speech with the words: 'In every generation, since the plantation settlement in Ulster in the seventeenth century, traditional unionists have been forced to defend to the death their heritage.'[97] Jonathan Powell, chief negotiator for Prime Minister Blair, has written: 'Even after the Good Friday Agreement, the unionists and republicans were still unreconciled people. With all the history that had gone before, they simply could not make the necessary leap of faith in the other side after such a short period of time.' He observed: 'It took nine years to build that trust, step by painful step; nine years of allowing the history to work itself out of the system on both sides so that the war could be formally ended and true power-sharing happen.'[98]

New Accommodation

Eventually, however, it was possible to reach an agreement over these difficult issues. In 2007 a new Northern Ireland executive was formed with the DUP's Ian Paisley as first minister, and Sinn Féin's Martin McGuinness as deputy first minister. Various pragmatic factors lay behind this settlement, but some of the main figures involved saw matters in a changed historical light that helped to sustain the new arrangements. Such change was most explicit in the cases of Paisley and Ahern, and particularly in the realm of north–south relations. After their first official meeting, in Dublin in April 2007, First Minister Paisley and Taoiseach Ahern declared their intention to have a joint visit to the site of the Battle of the Boyne. Paisley stated how 'we both look forward to visiting the battle site at the Boyne, but not to refight it' and expressed his hope that this visit would help to show 'how far we have come when we can celebrate and learn from the past ... and trust that old suspicions and discords may be buried under the prospect of mutual and respectful co-operation'.[99]

A month later at the Boyne, Paisley declared: 'I welcome that at last we can embrace this battle site as part of our shared history.'[100] In his speech Ahern remarked: 'In recent years, many of us from the nationalist tradition have come to a greater appreciation of the history, traditions and identity of those of you from the unionist tradition with whom we share this island.' In September 2007 Paisley had his first official meeting with President Mary McAleese. The setting was again symbolic in a historical sense. It was held at the Somme Heritage Centre in Newtownards, Co. Down, on the occasion of their joint opening of an exhibition about the soldiers of the mainly Catholic 16th Irish Division.[101]

The significance of these wartime commemorations for engendering respect and reconciliation was underlined again in Paisley's words of praise for Bertie Ahern after the announcement of the latter's resignation. He singled out Ahern's willingness to acknowledge the role of Irish soldiers in the two world wars as an important reason for his respect for him.[102] In his memoirs published in 2009, Ahern stated: 'respect for our shared history was one of the ways that we were trying to build a shared future north and south. It was something that, probably to the surprise of both of us, Ian Paisley and I agreed about. It would turn out to be an important factor in implementing the Good Friday Agreement.'[103] On 30 April 2008 he spoke in Washington at a joint session of the United States Congress and mentioned his forthcoming visit to the site of the Battle of the Boyne to meet Paisley: 'Today, both sides, proud of their history and confident of their identity, can come together in peace and part in harmony.'[104] On 15 May 2008 Ahern addressed both houses of the British parliament. He made a number of historical references about relations between Britain and Ireland and declared: 'Now we look back at history not to justify but to learn, and we look forward to the future in terms not of struggle and victories to be won, but of enduring peace and progress to be achieved together.'[105]

In May 2011 Queen Elizabeth II visited Ireland. This visit was seen as very significant historically, not just as the first trip of a British monarch to the Republic of Ireland since 1921, but also, in the words of the London *Times*, as marking 'the final reconciliation between two peoples after centuries of misunderstanding and resentment'.[106] In the course of this four-day visit, there was frequent reference to history, but in a way that included regret for past conflict, an acknowledgement of each other's traditions and history, an appreciation for shared history and a determination to move together to the future. In her speech at Dublin Castle on 18 May, the Queen spoke of how so much of the visit reminded people of 'the complexity of our history, its many layers and traditions, but also the importance of forbearance and conciliation; being able to bow to the past but not being bound by it'. She declared: 'With the benefit of hindsight we can all see things we wish had been done differently or not at all.' She also referred to how recent 'events have touched us all, many of us personally, and are a painful legacy. We can never forget those who have died or been injured, or their families.' In her speech, President Mary McAleese commented on 'the difficult centuries which have brought us to this point' and referred to 'the colonisers and the colonised'. She then stated: 'The harsh facts cannot be altered, nor loss nor grief erased, but with time and generosity, interpretations and perspectives can soften and open up space for new accommodation.' President McAleese declared: 'We cannot change the past, we have chosen to change the future.'[107]

A number of events illustrated the 'new accommodation'. On the previous day, the British Queen and the Irish President had visited the Garden of Remembrance, where the Queen laid a wreath in honour of all those who died for Irish freedom. The following day she went to the Irish National War Memorial at Islandbridge, where both heads of state laid wreaths in honour of the many thousands of Irishmen who gave their lives in the British forces during the Great War. She also visited Trinity College and Croke Park, the main stadium and headquarters of the GAA. This royal visit, with its frequent historical references, had a great impact on many and in different ways. The ceremony in the

Garden of Remembrance was described by Taoiseach Enda Kenny as 'symbolism beyond words'.[108]

Many commentators remarked on the great symbolism of her visit to Croke Park, where in 1921 British soldiers killed fourteen civilians. At this place, described as a 'hallowed' place for nationalists, the president of the GAA, Christy Cooney, declared that 'while acknowledging the significance of the past, and honouring all those that died in this place, the GAA has consistently supported and helped the peace process in Northern Ireland'.[109] He referred to the future and spoke of the determination of people and leaders 'to stand together against violence and hatred'. After the event at Islandbridge, former leader of the Progressive Unionist Party, Dawn Purvis, remarked: 'I remembered my own family's involvement in the Great War. I was moved when the Irish Tricolour was raised to full mast in memory of those who had fought as Irishmen and Irishwomen. This is another part of the shared history of our island.'[110]

Several weeks later at the Church of Ireland Cork diocesan synod, Bishop Paul Colton spoke of the impact these events had made on him.[111] He talked of how recent acknowledgements of the complexity of Ireland's historical fabric gave 'the lie to the heresy … that there was only one way in which you could meaningfully be said to be an Irish person – mythical Celtic, oppressed and Roman Catholic'. The dispelling of this myth 'which many of us grew up with', he remarked, made it 'moving … to see the ceremony at Islandbridge when wreaths were laid by Queen Elizabeth and our President, Mary McAleese'. He explained that recently he had gone to France to visit the grave of his grandmother's soldier first husband, a former labourer at Guinness in Dublin. He saw the ceremony at Islandbridge as 'a public acknowledgement and validation of my ancestors, and, more deep than that, how a family such as mine came to be in Ireland'. He said he believed that this event had been an 'equally potent symbol for many others in our country'.[112]

Final Observations

In 2000, on his last official visit to Ireland, the US President, Bill Clinton, acknowledged that 'the past is history, not destiny'. Of course, this has been true always, not just in 2000. The situation in Ireland cannot be seen as the outcome of some sort of historical regression that has created an inevitable and unavoidable conflict. The problems involved were neither irrevocably rooted in the past nor the outcome of a special history of many hundreds of years of conflict. They are modern-day ones, in this case to do with serious divisions over nationalism, and to a lesser extent over religion, although, of course, they have historical roots. At the same time, consciousness in the form of ideas of 'ancient enmities' as part of people's identities has been influential. In other countries as well as Ireland, societies have faced serious national, ethnic and religious divisions, and perceptions of history have come also to play an important part in these places. In the case of the former Yugoslavia, for example, it has been pointed out that the main cause of the conflict there lay in twentieth-century problems and conditions, rather than 'ancient enmities'.[113] At the same time, historical narratives considerably increased tensions. Pal Kolsto has remarked: 'There is strong evidence that mythicized versions of the past have indeed influenced the thinking of many former Yugoslav citizens and induced them to accept their leaders' call to war.'[114]

Although the core of the difficulty in Ireland lies in this national/religious conflict, it is wrong to underestimate cultural factors in the form of strongly held historical ideas that have influenced identities. While these views reflect present realities rather than any immutable link with the past, they are still important in their own right and affect the values and actions of the people involved. A sense of history, including actual historical experiences as well as myths, has been a valuable source for the political identity of both individuals and communities. It has helped people to understand and articulate their identity and what it means to be a nationalist or a unionist or British or Irish. At the same time, however, historical narratives have served to sharpen differences between people: also they have strengthened ideas of fatalism and mistrust, as well as justified violence. Such historical views, integral to the contemporary identity of many, have contributed to conflict.

In recent years in Ireland there have been strong efforts to interrogate some of the selective and exclusive views of the past. These developments played an important role in changing the landscape of society and politics in the 1990s, which led to new political arrangements, first under the Belfast Agreement and subsequently in the effective accommodation of a decade later. George Mitchell, who chaired the inter-party talks leading to the Belfast Agreement, has described how people came to realise how 'knowledge of their history is a good thing, but being chained to the past is not'.[115] In his memoirs, Bertie Ahern recorded how 'the ability to reflect on our history in an open and tolerant way was a central priority of my period as taoiseach'. He continued: 'The 32 counties of Ireland had been a divided society in so many different ways, but we had a shared past. If that history could be commemorated respectfully, I believe that would make an impact on our shared future.'[116] Erosion of the idea of continual conflict back to early history helped to remove some of the distrust and hostility that existed. These developments have encouraged movement within society to allow the emergence of new structures and political arrangements.

The reasons for these changes in historical perceptions require comment. In part, no doubt, political events, such as the ceasefires of the mid-1990s or the Belfast/Good Friday Agreement, helped these developments by allowing many to feel more relaxed about new historical views. At the same time, however, changes in understanding and in public discourse about the importance of history have been an important part of the total picture and helped to bring about the new conditions that made political progress easier. This happened at both government and popular level, and is part of a process, which began well before the ceasefires or the 1998 Agreement. Various factors contributed to these changes, such as revisionism in Irish history, the exploration of different historical traditions by various groups, and a new approach to commemorations. Such alterations in historical perspectives can be seen as partly elite driven, by politicians and leading public figures, and by government agencies and intellectuals. At the same time, these changes enjoyed support from a wide section of people, from teachers, history enthusiasts and members of the general public, who also saw the need to challenge existing historical narratives. Changes in historical perceptions affected political identities and allowed space for change.

While difficulties remain in the peace process, efforts to achieve political accommodation have won a level of success that would have been unthinkable forty years ago. Changes in recent years in historical views at the centre of contemporary identities are an influential element of this evolving scene. This historical dimension had helped to deepen conflict and efforts to deal with it have been an essential part of efforts to resolve the situation. The new approach to these historical narratives has won wide although not full public support. An important lesson from the peace process in Ireland is that it is necessary not only to create institutions and systems of government that can win the allegiance of different groups, but also to challenge ideas of 'ancient enmities' that can strongly influence the identities of individuals and communities and so affect the working of such new structures. People have come to gain a better appreciation of their own history and the history of others, which has allowed them to deal with myths. This new understanding has allowed them to escape ideas of inevitability and continual conflict.

A final lesson from these events relates to the importance for contemporary identities of developing a shared sense of history. This has been most evident in the case of the new awareness of all those from Ireland who died in the First World War. A cross-border initiative, organised by former Co. Donegal Fine Gael TD Paddy Harte and former Derry loyalist leader Glenn Barr led to the building of the Island of Ireland Peace Park at Messines in Belgium to remember all the fallen Irish. The 'remarkable ceremony' to dedicate the park in 1998 was recalled later in a speech in Dáil Éireann by one of those who attended, the grandson of a Co. Donegal Orangeman, the British prime minister, Tony Blair. He described how 'Representatives of nationalists and unionists travelled together to Flanders to remember shared suffering. Our army bands played together. Our heads of state stood together.' He continued: 'With our other European neighbours, such a ceremony would be commonplace. For us it was a first. It shows how far we have come. But it also shows we still have far to go.'[117]

In Derry city in 2005, at a very different local level, the Battle of Messines was recalled with a parade, involving people from Waterford as well as Derry, to commemorate members of their families who had died at this battle, including a 14-year-old Waterford soldier, believed to be the youngest British army casualty in the entire war. For the first time ever, the Irish tricolour was flown alongside the union flag in the city centre at the cenotaph.[118] In 2007 at Galway Catholic cathedral, a service was held to remember Co. Galway servicemen killed in the First World War. Afterwards, a photograph in the press showed two leading politicians, from north and south and from very different backgrounds, standing together on this occasion.[119] One was Sir John Gorman, MC, former British army officer and RUC inspector, and Ulster Unionist Party member of the Northern Ireland Assembly. He was also the son of RIC officer Jack Gorman, Co. Tipperary-born and last adjutant of the RIC depot in Phoenix Park, Dublin. After the depot was formally vacated by the police in May 1922, he drove north, for 'loyalty to the crown', and joined the RUC. The other was Éamon Ó Cuiv, a Fianna Fáil member of Dáil Éireann and Irish government minister. He was also the grandson of New York-born Éamon de Valera, who commanded 'in the name of the Irish Republic' the Irish Volunteer garrison at Boland's Mills during the 1916 Dublin Rising, and later became Irish taoiseach and president. Their presence together at this event served to illustrate well how, in the present day, after all this time, there has indeed been a significant move, in politics and identities, from partition to peace.

PART 2

COMMEMORATION

2

ST PATRICK'S DAY: COMMEMORATION, CONFLICT AND CONCILIATION, 1903–2013

Presently in Ireland we are marking a whole series of commemorations of important events, which happened a century ago. At the same time, we continue to mark annually a number of other commemorations or anniversaries of significant historical events or individuals, such as the Battle of the Boyne on 12 July, the Dublin Rising at Easter and, of course, St Patrick's Day. On one level, these events are simply to do with important matters from our past that we choose to recall. On another level, however, such occasions are very much to do with the present and reflect contemporary attitudes. By looking at how St Patrick's Day has been celebrated, north and south, from the beginning of the twentieth century until the present, one can see how attitudes have changed in a wide range of areas. We can learn about people's sense of identity, their ideas of history and their religious and cultural views. In the case of Ireland, of course, we are talking about highly divided attitudes, north and south. A study of how St Patrick's Day has been marked can provide us with an insight into changing identities of the various communities in Ireland since the early 1900s.

In the recent past, such commemorations have often been occasions of discord and conflict. Referring to the 1960s, Sir Kenneth Bloomfield has written: 'Anniversaries are the curse of Ireland. Like saint's days, the dates of historically resonant events punctuate the Northern Ireland calendar, calling for an orgy of reminiscence, celebration and demonstration from some section or other of the population.' He continued: 'it does not seem to matter that some of these demonstrations annoy or infuriate other people: this is, indeed, for some at least of the participants, a principal attraction.'[1] It has been argued that the passion and confrontation aroused by the large number of commemorations in the 1960s, especially in 1966, was one of the factors that helped to destabilise political society and lead to the outbreak of the 'Troubles'.[2] In recent decades, however, new ways of viewing and celebrating these commemorations have emerged. Such changes indicate radically altered understanding of matters of identity in Ireland, north and south. To some extent, such developments reflect the recent peace process. At the same time, the new approach to these commemorations has helped to create the conditions that have led to conciliation between the different communities in Ireland.

St Patrick's Day Celebrations in the Early 1900s

In the early twentieth century St Patrick's Day was celebrated in many parts of the island. All the main denominations regarded St Patrick as the patron saint of Ireland. Many church and cathedral buildings of both the Catholic Church and the Church of Ireland were named in his honour. In 1903 a bill was introduced at Westminster to make St Patrick's Day a bank holiday and it quickly passed into law with the support of all the MPs from Ireland – an outcome that, as the *Belfast News Letter* commented, was 'rare good fortune' for an Irish bill.[3] That same year the paper also remarked: 'The anniversary helps to create a spirit of mutual tolerance and good will amongst Irishmen and this year perhaps the spirit is more evident than before.'[4] The rise in political controversy over the next decade did not dent this wide support for St Patrick's Day.

In Dublin there were usually two parades involving the lord mayor and the lord lieutenant. The *Church of Ireland Gazette* for 20 March 1913 reported that on St Patrick's Day holy communion was held in

St Patrick's Cathedral, Dublin, where Rev. J.E.H. Murphy, professor of Irish at Trinity, officiated. The *Gazette* noted that all over Ireland, in many cathedrals, the festival was duly honoured. To some extent, there were probably more popular celebrations in nationalist rather than unionist circles; for example the Ancient Order of Hibernians (AOH) organised their parades on this day, and Catholic parish churches throughout Ireland, not just cathedrals, held services in honour of the saint. Nonetheless, this day was held as important in all the main communities and was regarded as a special day for Ireland and expressions of Irishness. On 18 March 1914, an editorial of the Belfast unionist paper, the *Northern Whig*, noted: 'Irishmen, whatever their creed or politics, have an affectionate regard for St Patrick's Day and yesterday the shamrock was worn in honour of the festival by fully nine tenths of the population of the country.'

Significant differences, however, would now emerge between north and south in how St Patrick's Day was celebrated. This reflected the impact of the Ulster crisis, 1912–14, the Easter Rising of 1916, the War of Independence and the Civil War. The two new states sought to develop their own identities.

St Patrick's Day Celebrations in the South from 1922

In the new Irish Free State, St Patrick's Day quickly took on special significance. In 1922 it was made a general holiday and from 1925, thanks to the Irish Free State Licensing Act, all public houses were closed on that day. From the early 1900s a strong movement had grown up to express concern that alcohol was too closely associated with the day and with Irishness, and the founders of the new state were happy to endorse this change. In Dublin, an annual army parade now replaced the processions organised previously by the lord lieutenant and lord mayor. Throughout the country there were also parades, often involving army marches to church for Mass. Dances, sporting activities, theatrical events and excursions were run on the day. The Irish language was specially promoted, frequently with events organised by the Gaelic League.

In 1926 the southern premier, W.T. Cosgrave, made the first official radio broadcast on St Patrick's Day. He called for mutual understanding and harmony, and declared: 'The destinies of the country, north and south, are now in the hands of Irishmen, and the responsibility for success or failure will rest with ourselves. If we are to succeed there must be a brotherly toleration of each other's ideas as to how our ambition may be realised, and a brotherly co-operation in every effort towards its realisation.'[5] In his St Patrick's Day's speech in 1930, Cosgrave stated: 'as we have been Irish and Roman, so it will remain', but he took care to preface his statement with the remark that he was speaking for the majority of people in the state.[6] In 1931 in a St Patrick's Day broadcast to the Irish in America, and reported in the Irish press, Cosgrave again sought to make a reconciliatory gesture: 'whatever be your creed in religion or politics, you are of the same blood – the healing process must go on.'[7]

With the accession to power of Éamon de Valera and Fianna Fáil in 1932, however, St Patrick's Day took on new importance. Links between Church and State were stressed publicly with the annual procession on St Patrick's Day of de Valera and his executive council, complete with a cavalry troop, to the Dublin pro-cathedral for Mass.[8] The Patrician year of 1932, which included the eucharistic congress, gave an opportunity for large demonstrations, with considerable official involvement, emphasising connections between Ireland and Rome.[9] The Church of Ireland organised its own events in 1932 in the south but without any official involvement. While Cosgrave had sought to take a broad and conciliatory approach to St Patrick's Day, de Valera took a different line. In his St Patrick's Day broadcast of 1935 he reminded people that Ireland had been a Christian and Catholic nation since St Patrick's time. He declared: 'She remains a Catholic nation.'[10]

De Valera now used the St Patrick's Day broadcasts, which were transmitted to the USA and Australia, to launch vigorous attacks on the British government and partition. These speeches reached a peak in 1939 when de Valera broadcast on St Patrick's Day from Rome, where he had attended the inauguration of Pope Pius XII. He declared how he had made a pledge beside the grave of Hugh O'Neill that he would never rest until 'that land which the Almighty so clearly designed as one shall belong undivided to the Irish people'. He urged his listeners to do likewise.[11] At the same time, however, the links between Catholicism and Irish identity as expressed on St Patrick's Day were not absolute. In 1939 too, the Church of Ireland president of Ireland, Douglas Hyde, attended a St Patrick's Day service in the Church of Ireland cathedral of St Patrick's in Dublin.[12]

During the Second World War celebrations on St Patrick's Day were restrained, although de Valera continued to make his annual broadcast. In 1943 he spoke of the restoration of the national territory and the national language as the greatest of the state's uncompleted tasks. After the war St Patrick's Day became a major national holiday once again. In 1950 the military parade in Dublin was replaced by a trade and industries parade. In their St Patrick's Day speeches in the 1950s, heads of government Éamon de Valera and J.A. Costello continued to use the event to make strong denunciations of partition. In his St Patrick's Day broadcast in 1950, Costello declared that 'our country is divided by foreign interference'.[13] By the 1950s government ministers and spokesmen, such as Séan MacEntee, were also making public speeches on the day at a range of venues in Britain and the USA, usually concentrating on attacking partition.[14] In 1955 a rare discordant note was struck by Bishop Cornelius Lucy of Cork when in his St Patrick's Day address he suggested that emigration was a greater evil than partition, but this had no impact.[15] Irish leaders in their speeches continued to emphasise links between Ireland and Rome. By the mid-1950s it was common for either the president or the taoiseach to be in Rome on St Patrick's Day. The 1961 Patrician celebrations marked a high point in this religious aspect of the festival. It began with the arrival on 13 March of a papal legate, Cardinal MacIntyre, who, as described in the *Capuchin Annual*, was 'welcomed with the protocol reception given only to a head of state'. This included a welcome at the airport from the taoiseach and a full military guard.[16]

St Patrick's Day Celebrations in the North from 1922

In Northern Ireland from 1922, St Patrick's Day was still observed, but in a more understated way than in the south. During the 1920s and 1930s the shamrock continued to be worn widely and the day remained a bank holiday when banks, government and municipal offices, and schools were closed, although many shops and factories seem to have been unaffected.[17] In Catholic churches St Patrick's Day was an important feast day that was well attended. The AOH continued to organise demonstrations on this date and nationalist politicians often used the occasion to make speeches. From 1925 the BBC in Northern Ireland commenced an annual series of special broadcasts on St Patrick's Day.[18] The Patrician year of 1932, which marked the anniversary of St Patrick's arrival in Ireland, was observed by all the churches. At Saul, the site of St Patrick's first church, the Church of Ireland built a new church while the Catholic Church erected a statue of St Patrick on a nearby hill top. The Presbyterian Church also held events to mark St Patrick's arrival. Each of the main denominations took advantage of the occasion to reaffirm its belief that St Patrick belonged exclusively to its own tradition.[19]

Sporting activities took place on St Patrick's Day, including the Ulster schools rugby and Gaelic football cup finals; and special theatrical events, dances and dinners were well attended in the 1920s and 1930s. On 18 March 1939 the *Belfast News Letter* reported that 'in Belfast and all over the province Ulster folk said goodbye to St Patrick's Day with dances and other entertainments'. Special ceremonies of the trooping of the colour and presentation of the shamrock to Irish regiments remained a tradition (begun by Queen Victoria at the end of her reign). There was, however, no official involvement in or recognition of St Patrick's Day, apart from a number of dinners or dances on the day, organised by the Duke of Abercorn as governor of Northern Ireland.[20] On the unionist and government side there was no attempt to hold parades or make speeches on 17 March. The speeches of southern politicians on the day denouncing partition or declaring Ireland's attachment to Rome were reported regularly in the northern press and sometimes criticised in editorials but there was no attempt by the government in this period to respond.

After the Second World War, banks and government offices continued to close on St Patrick's Day, while the wearing of the shamrock remained popular and the tradition of presenting it to Irish regiments abroad continued. Catholic churches still observed it as a special feast day and the AOH organised parades and demonstrations as before. In the late 1940s and early 1950s the Northern Ireland premier, Lord Brookeborough, used the occasion of St Patrick's Day to issue public addresses to Ulster people abroad, while members of his Cabinet spoke at dinners organised by Ulster associations in Great Britain.[21] By the mid-1950s, however, these attempts to match the political use made of St Patrick's Day by the southern government had mostly ceased. In the late 1950s a government information officer urged the Northern Ireland Cabinet that it might be wise to 'quietly forget' St Patrick's Day and abolish it as a bank holiday.[22] The suggestion was rejected, but it is clear from newspaper reports in the 1950s that for many people St Patrick's Day was 'business as usual'. Many schools dropped it as a holiday, and shops and businesses remained open.[23]

It continued to be an important day for Catholics and national-ists, when AOH parades were usually addressed by northern nationalist politicians, often denouncing the 'six county system'. On St Patrick's Day in 1960 a statement from northern nationalist MPs and senators that 'towards the ideal of a united Ireland we will strive unceas-ingly' was published on the front page of the *Irish News*, alongside St Patrick's Day messages from the taoiseach and president, also calling for reunification.[24] Correspondents in the unionist press denounced the political overtones of the day in both the north and the south. One letter on 17 March 1961 in the *Belfast News Letter* stated that 'the day is now chiefly memorable to the average Ulsterman as the day on which repeated threats against his stand for constitutional liberty are pronounced in the republic and on which Ulster's position is vilified throughout the English speaking world'.[25]

Nonetheless, it should be noted that there were some in union-ist and Protestant Church circles who believed that more attention should be given to the event. From the mid-1950s the editorial in the *Belfast Telegraph* often urged that the day should be a full public holiday. We may note that Ian Paisley chose to open his first Free Presbyterian church at Crossgar, Co. Down, on St Patrick's Day 1951. In the 1950s the Church of Ireland inaugurated an annual St Patrick's Day pil-grimage and special service at Downpatrick and Saul, which was well attended. Such events were still strongly limited by denominational barriers, although small elements of change were occurring. In 1956 the nationalist members of Downpatrick council refused an invitation to participate in a joint wreath-laying ceremony at what was believed to be St Patrick's grave, on the grounds that the Catholic Church 'had arranged adequate celebrations for the Feast and they could not add anything to them'. Eight years later, however, when the archbishop of Canterbury was the special guest at the St Patrick's Day service at the Church of Ireland cathedral in Downpatrick, nationalist councillors turned up to greet the archbishop at the entrance to the cathedral, although they felt unable to enter the building.[26]

Changes from the 1960s

During the 1960s, celebrations of St Patrick's Day continued to reflect highly polarised views on this event, but elements of change can be discerned. On St Patrick's Day 1960, Irish President Éamon de Valera issued a greeting to the friends of Ireland overseas. He expressed hope that the occasion would strengthen 'your determination to continue your support of the motherland's just claims to the unity of the national territory'. In the same year, however, in his message to Irish men and women abroad, Taoiseach Sean Lemass declared that 'politically the aim of national objectives was the unity of Ireland, which would be achieved ultimately', but for the first time he expressed also his support for better understanding with the north.[27] In 1962 de Valera visited the Pope in Rome and, in a Radio Éireann broadcast from there on St Patrick's Day, he stated that 'loyalty to the See of Peter has been an outstanding characteristic of the Irish people's faith, and it is well that in commemorating St Patrick we should give national expression of this great historic fact and pledge continuance'.[28]

Nonetheless, subsequently, St Patrick's Day messages from the taoiseach, Sean Lemass and then Jack Lynch, often contained expressions of hope of co-operation and better understanding between north and south, although these were usually qualified by the stated belief that goodwill arising from this 'would surely hasten the day of reunification'.[29] Other leading politicians, such as Neil Blaney and George Colley, used the occasion in the mid-1960s to call for cross-border co-operation in matters such as tourism.[30] St Patrick's Day was observed widely in the south. It was a public holiday and there were various parades and church services. The ban on the sale of alcohol on St Patrick's Day was lifted in 1961. In Dublin throughout this period the main event was a trades and industries parade.

In Northern Ireland, celebration of St Patrick's Day in the 1960s was generally restrained, compared to the south. It remained a bank holiday, when government and public offices were closed, but the press reported usually that it was a 'working day for most people and shops and other businesses remained open'.[31] Shamrock was distributed specially to British army regiments from Northern Ireland, both at home and abroad, and to the Irish Guards. In Belfast, there was no parade, but a small number of cultural and sporting events normally took place. St Patrick's Day retained greater significance among members of the Catholic community and there were services in many Catholic churches to commemorate St Patrick's Day. The AOH continued to organise a number of well-attended demonstrations on the day. There were a few small-scale parades, as in Downpatrick and Armagh, connected with Catholic church services.

During this decade, however, we can see some effort to make the event more important and more widely appreciated. The government did not organise official events or issue statements, but the Northern Ireland premier, Capt. Terence O'Neill, took advantage of the day on a number of occasions to make special visits to Canada and America.[32] The pilgrimage and church services at Downpatrick, organised by the Church of Ireland, became more popular, and in 1961 both the diocesan synod of Down and Dromore and the annual conference of the Young Unionists, the young people's organisation of the Ulster Unionist Party, urged more support for the day.[33] In the north, Bishop Julian Mitchell of Down and Dromore seems to have been the leading Church of Ireland figure in promoting interest in St Patrick, as was also Archbishop Gerald Simms in Dublin. Some correspondents in the press argued that St Patrick's Day should be ignored in the north because of the way it had become politicised, but influential editorials in the *Belfast Telegraph* continued to back calls to give more importance to the day.[34]

From the early 1970s celebration of St Patrick's Day changed, especially in the south. The most conspicuous change was in the character of the Dublin parade after its organisation was taken over in 1970 by Dublin Tourism. There were now bands and majorettes as well as many visitors from the USA and Canada in the parade, which took on a new tourist and commercial aspect. Significant changes also occurred in other areas. An editorial in the *Irish Independent*, 16 March 1974, pointed out that 'since the Troubles began in the north' speakers at St Patrick's Day parades have become 'hyper-sensitive about words, concepts, tributes and ideologies which hitherto had been taken for granted' and talked of a new growing acceptance of different traditions and a slow redefinition of Irish patriotism. Speeches by leading politicians no longer contained strong condemnation of partition, and, both in America and at home, Irish government ministers often denounced violence and support for the IRA.[35] On a religious level also, efforts were made to overcome the denominational divisions associated with the saint's day. On St Patrick's Day 1972 a Jesuit priest, Father Michael Hurley, became the first Catholic priest since the Jacobite period to preach in St Patrick's Church of Ireland cathedral in Dublin. Interdenominational services were now held on the day and an ecumenical blessing of the shamrock became a regular feature of the Dublin parade.[36]

A new organisation was set up in 1995 to run the Dublin parade, which has become part of an all-day cultural and tourist festival. In 1996 the chairman, Michael Colgan, declared: 'The day is long gone when you could have an electrical company with washing machines on a float and a girl in a sash.'[37] Another new feature of St Patrick's Day has been efforts by the Irish government to promote Ireland abroad and to connect with members of the Irish diaspora. Previously some government ministers had attended celebrations of St Patrick's Day in Britain and the USA. By the early 2000s, however, more than a dozen government ministers and large numbers of councillors visited such events among the Irish diaspora, all over the globe. From the mid-1990s, it became an annual feature for the taoiseach to present shamrock to the American president at the White House. On 17 March 2004, an editorial in the *Irish Times* declared:

Ireland looks inwards and outwards on St Patrick's Day, celebrating Irish identity and communicating it to other peoples. The holiday … has a remarkable outreach to the Irish abroad, to their host societies and to the wider world. In recent years these dimensions have been projected even more strongly by a growing internationalisation of Ireland's economic, cultural and political life.

It observed: 'St Patrick remains an appropriate figure to express these changing realities. He has been reimagined to fit them, as is often the case with such national symbols.' Such changes reflected a gradual weakening of the main denominations' influence in society, as well as the impact of globalisation and a new interest in the Irish diaspora.

In Northern Ireland changes in the marking of St Patrick's Day were slower to come. During the 1970s and 1980s the occasion continued to be celebrated in an unremarkable way. It remained a bank holiday but there was little special about it apart from some sporting events, several AOH parades and a number of religious services. There were celebrations in Newry, Armagh and some other towns, and occasionally parades on the Falls Road in Belfast and in Derry. There were new instances of interdenominational co-operation on the day. The first joint Protestant/Catholic service in Down Church of Ireland cathedral was held on 17 March 1985, while on 17 March 1990 in Armagh Catholic cathedral an ecumenical service commemorated the laying of the cathedral foundation.[38] Nonetheless, such events did not arouse widespread support. On 17 March 1992 an editorial in the *Belfast Telegraph* commented: 'A casual visitor to Ulster would need to be very perceptive to realise that this is St Patrick's Day. Our celebrations are so muted as to be invisible. Yet across the border, March 17 is an occasion for national rejoicing by people and government.'

From the early 1990s, however, the event began to assume greater importance. Parades in nationalist towns such as Newry and Downpatrick were revitalised. At the same time there was an effort to give these events a cross-community focus, especially in Downpatrick, due in large part to the work of Edward McGrady, MP, of the Social Democratic and Labour Party. From 1994, at unionist instigation, the flag of St Patrick was flown at Belfast City Hall. By the late 1990s members of the Apprentice Boys of Derry in the city of Derry and a number of Ulster Scots groups had become involved in celebrations on the day. Efforts to organise a major parade in Belfast were dogged by controversy over flags and emblems. The first such parades in the late 1990s and early 2000s proved controversial, but subsequently they achieved wider, if not universal, support. By 2006 the event in Belfast had become a major festival, organised by Belfast City Council.

From 1994 unionist politicians began to visit Washington on 17 March to attend events at the White House, where SDLP and Sinn Féin leaders had already been guests on St Patrick's Day. After 1998 the first and deputy first ministers were received at the White House by the president on the day. These visits by Northern Ireland politicians on St Patrick's Day to Washington provided the occasion for a number of important initiatives in relation to the Northern Ireland peace process.[39] In 1999 the speaker of the Northern Ireland Assembly, John Alderdice, organised the first official reception on St Patrick's Day at the assembly buildings at Stormont, and this has continued annually (although cancelled in 2010, so that the speaker could attend the St Patrick's Day celebrations in the White House). Politicians, including Ian Paisley, have urged that St Patrick's Day be made a public holiday in Northern Ireland.[40] This has not happened, but St Patrick's Day now enjoys markedly wider support than before. On St Patrick's Day 2003 a *Belfast News Letter* editorial declared that:

> March 17 is increasingly seen as a day when the peoples of the two main traditions in our province can share the Christian legacy and inheritance of St Patrick. Marking St Patrick's day in an appropriate way should not be seen as a threat to the culture and aspirations of the pro-union population and the events should be celebrated in a manner that offends no one.

Final Observations

Some final observations are appropriate. Celebration of St Patrick's Day has changed greatly in its form over the last hundred years. In the early days, it was marked by most of the main communities and traditions in Ireland. Then it became dominated by one major group and the other major group walked away. This separation, however, was never complete. There continued to be some in the northern unionist and Protestant tradition who retained a strong interest and involvement in the day. Southern Protestants also continued to honour the feast day. Nonetheless, in the context of the political changes that occurred between 1912 and 1923, this event came largely to be monopolised by the nationalist and Catholic community, north and south. Such involvement was seen by many as an important part of Irish identity, which moved from a more conciliatory spirit to one linked to a strong sense of (Catholic) nationalism and anti-partitionism. This latter approach can be seen clearly in speeches by Éamon de Valera on St Patrick's Day in Rome, in 1938 and again in 1962.

Northern Protestants, by and large, withdrew from celebration of this event, partly because of the way these religious and political dimensions became linked. At the same time they wanted to emphasise their ideas of British and Ulster identity, with no place for any Irish identity, which St Patrick's Day celebrations seemed to embody. At the beginning of the twentieth century most northern unionists had been happy to acknowledge their Irish nationality alongside their British citizenship.[41] By the late 1960s, the number of Protestants/unionists in Northern Ireland who still identified themselves as Irish as well as British had fallen to about 20 per cent; by the late 1970s this had collapsed to 8 per cent.[42] These developments in the celebration of St Patrick's Day reflected the broader political and religious divisions in Ireland. At the same time they served to heighten such divisions.

In recent decades, however, efforts to respect different traditions and also to seek common ground have changed how we approach St Patrick's Day. St Patrick's Day is once again experienced as a shared event that unionists and nationalists, Catholics and Protestants, can enjoy. This reflects a new ecumenical spirit whereby St Patrick is viewed not in restrictive denominational terms but as a common saint for all the churches. Such developments reflect also new approaches to Irish identity. From the 1970s onwards, there was a strong effort in the south to replace the Catholic and anti-partitionist characteristics of St Patrick's Day with a more pluralist and conciliatory spirit.

These changes were part of important developments that would eventually lead to the amendment of the Irish constitution, after the Belfast/Good Friday Agreement, with the removal of the territorial claim on the north and the acceptance of the principle of consent. At the same time, the new second article of the Irish constitution acknowledged the importance of the Irish diaspora. A central feature of today's celebrations of St Patrick's Day is worldwide outreach to the Irish diaspora. On 4 June 2011, at the Irish Pontifical College in Rome, President Mary McAleese gave a different view of religion and Irish identity from that espoused earlier by Éamon de Valera in Rome on St Patrick's Day. She declared that despite 'past political and religious conflicts', modern Ireland has emerged as 'a country, a family, which is at once Catholic, Protestant, agnostic, atheist, Islamic, Jewish', and that all are to be 'cherished equally'.[43]

In Northern Ireland there have also been important changes in how St Patrick's Day is celebrated. In the last two decades there have been strong efforts to make St Patrick's Day an important and inclusive event for all religious and political communities. The celebration of the day has encouraged conciliation and has promoted a non-political and non-threatening sense of Irishness. While opinion polls still show that a low number of northern unionists claim an Irish identity, from the late 1980s there has been a rise in those who see themselves as 'Northern Irish'. The Belfast/Good Friday Agreement recognises the right of the people of Northern Ireland to 'identify themselves and be accepted as Irish or British or both', which has allowed many unionists to be more relaxed about accepting a sense of Irishness alongside their Britishness.

In 2004 at an Ulster Unionist Party conference, David Trimble declared: 'We are pluralist in our culture … For us, unionism is not the same thing as protestantism. We wish to add to the glory of being British the distinction of being Irish.'[44] In April 2007, at his first public meeting in Dublin with Taoiseach Bertie Ahern, Ian Paisley stated: 'I am proud to be an Ulsterman, but I am also proud of my Irish roots.'[45] Given the importance of St Patrick to the arrival of Christianity in Ireland, it is appropriate that celebration of his day is no longer a source of conflict but one of a sense of a common heritage and conciliation. Surely St Patrick would have approved!

COMMEMORATING THE SIEGE OF DERRY AND THEOBALD WOLFE TONE AT BODENSTOWN: PARADES, PILGRIMAGES AND POLITICS

History continues to be important for modern-day identity in Ireland, north and south. Annual commemorations remind us of our history, especially those parts that are seen to have contemporary relevance. Today, some, such as St Patrick's Day and Remembrance Sunday, reflect multiple or shared identities, although this has not always been the case. Others, however, reflect single-identity concerns and are meaningful to particular communities. Two such commemorative events are examined here. The first recalls the siege of Derry/Londonderry, 1688–89, when the Protestant citizens held out for nine months against the forces of the Catholic King James. For most of the first century after the siege, there was only limited public commemoration of the event. Subsequently it was commemorated annually, first by Derry citizens and later by others, with parades, religious services and other celebrations. For many in the unionist community this event has come to symbolise both siege and victory, and is one they see as an integral part of their history.[1] The second concerns Theobald Wolfe Tone, the leader of the 1798 rebellion, who was buried at Bodenstown graveyard in Co. Kildare. His burial place received little public attention until nearly 100 years later. In the twentieth century his grave became a popular site of pilgrimage and commemoration, which included parades, wreath-laying and graveside orations, for nationalists and republicans, both constitutional and non-constitutional. For many in the nationalist/republican community he is hailed as the first prophet of an independent Ireland and an important part of their history.[2]

Early Commemorations of the Siege

For most of the first hundred years following the siege, public commemoration of the events of 1688–89 in Derry was sporadic and without wide support. Reports in the local press in the 1770s indicate that there had been some earlier celebrations of the siege but these had lapsed and were only renewed towards the end of the century. In August 1772 the *Londonderry Journal* carried a resolution from a local guild that thanked the city's mayor because he had 'revived' the 'ancient custom of commemorating the equally glorious and memorable deliverance of this city'.[3] August commemoration of the lifting of the siege now became an annual event. From 1775 the anniversary of the shutting of the gates in December was also marked, while in December 1788 an effigy of the traitor of the siege, Colonel Robert Lundy, was burned for the first time. By this stage there is also evidence of the involvement of clubs or societies of local citizens, which can be seen as forerunners of the nineteenth-century Apprentice Boys of Derry clubs (so named after the apprentice boys who shut the city gates in face of the forces of James II).

In 1788 and 1789 there were special centenary anniversary commemorations.[4] In August 1789 a thanksgiving service for the relief of the city included a sizeable procession to St Columb's Church of Ireland cathedral that involved not only the members of the corporation but also the Catholic bishop and clergy, as well as the Presbyterian clergy and elders. In his sermon the preacher, Rev. George Vaughan Sampson, urged that the message from the example of their forefathers was not just 'Glory be to God in the highest' but also 'on earth, peace, goodwill towards men'.[5] In late eighteenth-century Ireland, with the rise of a tolerant Irish patriotism, the events of 1688–89 were seen as part of the Glorious Revolution with its constitutional benefits for all, and they embraced Presbyterians, Catholics and members of the Church of Ireland.[6]

The next century, 1789–1889, witnessed important changes in how the siege was commemorated in Derry. Reflecting the rise of Protestant/ Catholic tension in the early nineteenth century, the siege came increasingly to be seen primarily as a Protestant victory. The Apprentice Boys of Derry Club was the first nineteenth-century club, formed in 1814, to be followed by the No Surrender Club of Apprentice Boys in 1824. The Ordnance Survey memoirs of the early 1830s recorded the existence of three such clubs in the city, but noted that they were losing influence and would 'doubtless become gradually extinct'.[7] In 1828 a stone column with statue was erected on the city walls, in memory of Rev. George Walker, governor of the city during the siege. Celebrations of the 150th anniversary of the siege were markedly low key compared with the centenary.

The following fifty years, however, saw growth in the popularity of the siege commemorations and the fortunes of the Apprentice Boys. A number of new clubs were formed, a general committee was established to co-ordinate the clubs, and the position of governor as head of the committee and clubs was created in 1867. An impressive Apprentice Boys' Memorial Hall was opened in the city. Participation in ceremonies associated with these commemorations involved growing numbers. The Party Processions Act banned Orange parades in 1850–71, but not these commemorations, which were regarded as civic rather than political events, and this increased their popularity. New rail transport brought visitors to the events as well as 'honorary' members for some of the clubs. The emergence of unionist/nationalist confrontation in the 1870s and 1880s gave a new relevance to the story of the siege, especially for Derry Protestants. Nonetheless, the Apprentice Boys clubs were restricted to inhabitants of Derry, which prevented wider involvement in these events. In 1888–89 the bicentenary of the siege was marked by extensive commemorations involving the Apprentice Boys and the corporation.[8] While most of the customs and practices associated with the siege commemorations, which are evident today, were in place by this stage, the extent of popular involvement was still limited mainly to the Protestant inhabitants of Derry and its neighbourhood.

Rise in Popular Support for Siege Commemorations, 1889–1960s

The period 1889–1939 witnessed a complete transformation in the amount of popular support for the commemorations in Derry and the Apprentice Boys clubs. An important key to this change was the decision taken in the late 1880s to allow the Derry-based clubs (now known as parent clubs) to establish branch clubs outside the city. All members continued to be initiated within Derry's walls. To begin with, the growth of these clubs was slow. By August 1900 there were just eight branch clubs (four from Belfast, two from Co. Antrim, one from Co. Armagh and one from Co. Down), plus seven parent clubs. By August 1912 there were seventeen branch clubs.[9] From 1911 the general committee of the Apprentice Boys clubs was allowed to nominate six members to the Ulster Unionist Council. A small number of clubs were established in England, Scotland and Canada. During the First World War the annual commemorations continued, but in a restricted form.

In 1923 a press report on the August parade recorded the presence of seventeen branch clubs, similar to the figure for 1912.[10] From this time on, however, expansion in the number of clubs and initiations occurred rapidly. In 1924, for the first time, a Presbyterian minister preached in the cathedral at the August anniversary. The next day, the *Northern Whig* devoted an editorial column to the celebrations, declaring that 'every loyalist in the province loves and claims a patriotic interest in the stones of Derry'.[11] This special interest by the paper may be explained by the fear expressed in its editorial that under the threatened redrawing of the border Derry would be lost to the Free State. Following the erection of a war memorial in the Diamond in 1927 the laying of wreaths became an important feature of the parades. By the 1920s the August commemorations no longer included meetings for political speeches, but centred largely on the parade, a march around the walls, and in the cathedral the annual thanksgiving service for the relief of the city in 1689. Each December there continued to be ceremonies to mark the shutting of the gates.

Branch club numbers on parade at the August commemorations increased to thirty-one in 1924, fifty-one in 1930, and eighty in 1936.

In 1924 several hundred new members were initiated, but by 1936 annual initiations totalled 800.[12] Among those initiated in 1933 were Sir Dawson Bates, minister of home affairs, and W.H. Price, attorney general of Toronto, Canada. In 1939 700 new members were initiated and the number of branch clubs totalled ninety-three, including six from Co. Donegal, six from Scotland and two from England. The previous year the Apprentice Boys' Memorial Hall had been extended to provide a large assembly room for 2,000 people, rooms for the meetings of clubs and Orange and Black lodges, and new social facilities.

Celebrations in Derry city in 1938–39 to mark the 250th anniversary of the siege were extensive. The *Londonderry Sentinel* reported that at the 12 August 1939 demonstrations for relief of the city 'all morning until noon, Apprentice Boys and their friends, who grow more numerous every year, poured into the city from every part of Northern Ireland and the border counties of Éire'.[13] A total of twenty-one ordinary and special trains, about a hundred buses and many cars brought upwards of 20,000 people to the city. At the service in the cathedral, the preacher was Dr James Little, Presbyterian minister and MP for Co. Down. His sermon was primarily a religious one but he referred to current threats from the southern government and militant republicans. He declared: 'To all who are seeking in one way or another to undermine our state we send today this message from the historic walls of Derry, that to neither politician nor terrorist will we ever consent to surrender any portion of the inheritance which God has entrusted us.'[14] Also on the day, there were demonstrations in Cos Tyrone and Fermanagh, run by the Black Institution, to mark the 250th anniversary of the siege.

During the Second World War the public celebrations of the siege in Derry were cancelled by the Apprentice Boys' general committee. In August 1946, at the first peacetime demonstration since the war, a record number of 2,500 to 'nearly 3,000' members were initiated at ceremonies that, according to the *Londonderry Sentinel*, 'continued from 9.00 a.m. till 5.00 p.m'.[15] In the same year it was reported that the procession contained 7,000 Apprentice Boys and ninety bands. In 1947 the preacher at the August cathedral service, Rev. J.G. MacManaway, MP for Derry City at the Northern Ireland parliament and Church of Ireland clergyman, declared: 'We in Ulster have our own Holy Place, our own religious shrine to which our history as Protestants forever joins us. The Protestant shrine of Protestant Ulster is forever Derry.' He continued: 'We do not meet together to provoke anybody or criticise any man's faith. But, just as our forefathers before us, we are resolved that we shall not be driven out of this country by political pressure or economic measures to deprive us of our freedom and our faith.'[16] During the late 1940s and 1950s the numbers of members initiated frequently reached or passed 1,000. This period saw the formation of a number of amalgamated committees for different areas. The parades continued to attract large numbers of Apprentice Boys, bands and onlookers.

By the 1960s the initiation of prominent unionist politicians was commonplace, although few of them seem to have played a regular part in commemorations. Two prime ministers of Northern Ireland, Lord Brookeborough and Captain Terence O'Neill, were initiated in 1960 and 1964 respectively. At the 275th anniversary of the siege in 1964, the number visiting the city on 12 August was put at 35,000. It was reported that the 2½-mile-long parade contained more than 100 clubs, 5,000 Apprentice Boys and 100 bands, and took one hour and ten minutes to pass Carlisle Square. It was estimated that on the same occasion nineteen Ulster Transport Authority trains, 160 Ulster Transport Authority buses and 3,000 cars were required to bring the visitors to the city. The Lough Swilly Company brought 500 visitors from Co. Donegal. The press reported that there were representatives from Canada, Scotland, Liverpool and Philadelphia.[17]

Siege Commemorations and Changed Times, 1970 to Present

Since 1970 the siege commemorations have continued but in new circumstances. Tension between Derry's Bogside residents and the marchers at the 12 August 1969 parade led to serious rioting. In 1970 and 1971 a ban was imposed on Apprentice Boys' parades in the city, although services continued in the cathedral. From 1972 to 1974 the August procession was restricted to the Waterside. In 1975 the parade was allowed into the walled city during the August commemoration, but it was confined to the upper part of the city and marches around the walls continued to be banned; only from 1995 have parent clubs been allowed to march around the city walls again. In 1973 the Walker Memorial was destroyed by an IRA explosion. Figures for those present at the commemorations in August ranged from 5,000 in 1972 to 20,000 in 1985: the security situation sometimes affected numbers.[18] As regards the number of clubs during these decades, there were 178 in existence in 1971 and more than 200 by 1988.[19]

The tercentenary of the siege in 1989 was the occasion of extensive celebrations in the city. There were civic events, involving the nationalist-run council, to mark the occasion. On the morning of 12 August, however, there was an IRA explosion in the city centre. In spite of this, it was reported that crowds reached 15,000 and there were 700 new Apprentice Boys. At the cathedral service the preacher, Rev. James Kane, spoke of the many deaths and destruction of the previous twenty years. He mentioned how the cathedral had suffered bomb damage on a number of occasions. He declared that in the face of IRA violence 'men had become filled with a determination to remain under the British flag and all it stood for'. He expressed hope that 'mutual trust and forbearance may lead to mutual co-operation'.[20] In the Apprentice Boys' tercentenary brochure, which referred to both the general political situation and the local reduction of the number of Protestants on the west bank of the city, the chairman of the tercentenary committee wrote: 'the siege of Derry is, in many senses, still going on.'[21]

Over the last three decades commemoration of the siege of Derry has retained its popularity. On 12 August 2014 there were reckoned to be around 35,000 visitors to the city.[22] This included up to 8,000 members of the clubs on parade. It was reported that there were 145 bands and 250 Apprentice Boys clubs. Two new clubs, from Kent in the south of England and Dundonald, were on parade. This popularity reflects a growing interest in loyal orders and parades in the unionist community in response to political changes and challenges to unionist and loyalist identity.[23] Many continue to see the siege as an important part of their historical and cultural heritage. On 12 August 2012, Jim Brownlee, governor of the Committee of Apprentice Boys of Derry, called on people to remember that 'the freedoms they enjoy today came as a consequence of the siege and of the relief of this city'.[24]

In recent years the Apprentice Boys clubs have reached a new accommodation with the nationalist residents of Derry over these events. In the late 1990s and early years of the new century the Apprentice Boys' parades experienced confrontation and violence between marchers and local nationalist residents, as happened with other parades, such as at Drumcree in Co. Armagh. In this case, however, mediation organised by some leading Derry citizens, between Apprentice Boys leaders and the Bogside Residents' Group, has led to a new understanding between parties and a reduction in tension, which has brought about relatively peaceful parades.[25] As well, an annual week-long 'Maiden city festival', before the August parade, run since 1998 by the Apprentice Boys' committee, 'to explain their ethos and culture to Derry's wider nationalist community', has helped to improve community relations.[26] At the cathedral in August 2002 Dean William Morton gave thanks for the relief of the city in 1689.[27] He spoke also of good relations with St Eugene's Catholic Cathedral. He praised the way people had achieved a new understanding and accommodation about the commemorations and said there were lessons from this for elsewhere in Northern Ireland. In 2016 an impressive museum extension to the Apprentice Boys' Memorial Hall was opened to tell the story of the siege and the Apprentice Boys of Derry.

Early Pilgrimages to Bodenstown, 1798–1914

During the first three decades after Theobald Wolfe Tone's death it appears that little public attention was paid to his grave at Bodenstown, Co. Kildare. In 1843 the Young Ireland leader, Thomas Davis, visited the grave, after which he wrote a poem on the subject that received wide circulation. In the following year a memorial stone was laid at the grave by a number of Young Irelanders.[28] An American who visited the grave in 1861 later described how since 1848 few visitors had come to Bodenstown. He recalled: 'the ground beneath the tombstone was dry, hard and bare; and, judging from the feathers scattered around it, had apparently become a favourite resort for domestic fowl.'[29] As Christopher Woods has shown, organised visits to the grave, sometimes called pilgrimages, began in 1873 but ceased in the 1880s, only to resume in 1891, from when well-attended annual commemorations were held on the Sunday nearest to 20 June (the date of Tone's birth).[30] By the mid-1890s these commemorations were attracting large numbers, partly thanks to cheap rail transport from Dublin and partly due to the split in Parnellite politics. Parades would proceed from Sallins railway station to Bodenstown graveyard, a distance of some 2.5km. Wreaths were laid at the grave and orations were delivered. A Wolfe Tone Memorial Committee was established in 1898 to fund and erect a statue of Tone in Dublin but its plans were not successful (at least not for another seventy years).

In the first decade of the twentieth century it seems that there was little support for the Bodenstown event. From 1911, however, the annual pilgrimages to Tone's grave were revived by members of the Irish Republican Brotherhood (IRB).[31] In June 1913 the main speaker at Bodenstown was Patrick Pearse. He described Tone as the 'greatest of Ireland's dead' and quoted his lines about breaking the connection with England and replacing the denominations of Protestant, Catholic and Dissenter with that of Irishman.[32] For Pearse and other advanced nationalists the example and writings of Tone were important, but before the First World War these ideas had only limited support. In 1914, Sean MacDermott, addressing members of the IRB in Co. Kerry, stated: 'Nationalism as known to Tone and Emmet is almost dead in the country and a spurious substitute, as taught by the Irish parliamentary party, exists.'[33]

Rising Support for Bodenstown Event, 1922–1960s

Thanks to the Easter Rising and consequent events, the public June pilgrimage to Tone's grave at Bodenstown did not occur again between 1916 and 1921. When this annual commemoration recommenced in 1922, however, the character of the occasion had changed markedly. Due to the political success of followers of Tone, it attracted many of the leading politicians of the day. Reflecting the divisions within republicanism after the Treaty, rival organisations marked the event separately. On

23 June 1924 the *Irish Independent* described how 'a national tribute to the memory of Wolfe Tone was paid yesterday at Bodenstown. President W.T. Cosgrave, the heads of the Irish army and judiciary and eight hundred Irish soldiers assembled to do honour to the great patriot.' Later, an anti-treaty party, consisting of contingents of Cumann na mBan and Sinn Féin clubs, held a parade to the grave.

In 1925 the official graveside oration was delivered by the minister of defence, General Richard Mulcahy, who acknowledged Tone as the founding father of the Irish army.[34] From this time on it was the role of the defence minister, in the presence of other Cabinet members, to take the lead part in the government commemoration. Also in 1925, Éamon de Valera, in the company of Pearse's mother and Countess Constance Markievicz, addressed anti-treaty supporters. By 1927 numbers at the unofficial republican parade included representatives of Fianna Fáil. The event attracted large numbers of the general public. On these occasions speakers selected from Tone's life and writings according to their own political agendas. In his 1924 oration, Cosgrave pointed to similarities between Tone and Michael Collins. He also lauded Tone's efforts to substitute the 'common name of Irishman for that of Protestant, Catholic or Dissenter'. He even mentioned Tone's education at Trinity College, 'an institution which gave Ireland many illustrious sons'.[35] Very rarely, however, in subsequent decades, did any speech at Bodenstown repeat Tone's call for unity of Protestant and Catholic, or refer favourably to Trinity. In 1926 republican TD J.A. Madden asserted that 'Tone had never deviated from the object of his life – complete separation from England and the establishment of an Irish Republic'.[36]

The 1930s began with increased emphasis on the Bodenstown event in June by both government and non-government sides. In 1930 the official commemoration included a flypast by the Irish air force. The next year the unofficial parade included not only a Fianna Fáil party but also a large contingent of IRA members. In response to this IRA turnout led by Sean MacBride, the government attempted but failed to prevent the use of military orders and marching by republicans. After the election of the Fianna Fáil government, the following year, 1932, saw neither government nor Fianna Fáil representation at the June Bodenstown commemorations. In 1933, however, the minister for defence held an official parade on the morning of 25 June, while in the afternoon there was a Fianna Fáil parade, led by de Valera, to the graveside. A week earlier there had been an unofficial parade attended by forty-five IRA units, accompanied for the first time by members of the newly formed Irish communist party. In 1934 there was a similar schedule with parades on different days. Among those in the republican parade were members of the breakaway socialist group, the Republican Congress, including men from Orange areas of Belfast, including the Shankill Road, who belonged to the congress. Fighting broke out, however, when they refused to lower their flags on republican orders and they were then forcibly prevented by republicans from getting to Tone's grave.

In speeches spokesmen from the various parties paid tribute to Tone in different ways. At the government commemorations, the main speaker continued to be the minister of defence, Cumann na nGaedheal or Fianna Fáil, who usually stressed the value of the example of Tone for the state's armed forces. Republicans frequently quoted Tone's objective of breaking the connection with England and often attacked the British and Irish governments. In 1932 the IRA leader, Sean Russell, declared: 'Tone's ideals have not yet been realised … we have two regiments of the British army – one dressed in khaki in the north and the other dressed in green in the south.'[37] Many speakers used Tone's name to call for unity, but this usually meant the unity of nationalists or republicans. Only rarely was there even oblique reference to uniting 'Protestant, Catholic and Dissenter'. In 1933 republican Maurice Twomey declared that republicans honoured the words of the proclamation of the republic that guaranteed religious freedom to all citizens, but did not mention Protestants and instead devoted the rest of his speech to denying accusations that the IRA was against the Catholic Church.[38]

By 1935 the Bodenstown parade had become a massive display of IRA strength with a large number of units from all over Ireland on parade, along with thousands of supporters. By the following year, however, the government had declared the IRA an illegal organisation and steps were now taken to prevent IRA participation at the Tone event in June. The *Irish Independent*, 22 June 1936, declared that 'Bodenstown yesterday was an armed camp'. It described how 'about 1,000 troops, with full army equipment, and supported by aeroplanes, were quartered in the vicinity of the cemetery ... and about 500 gardai were also on duty'. In the next two years both official and republican parades occurred but with relatively small numbers of supporters. In 1939, because of an upsurge in IRA activity, the government banned the June Bodenstown commemorations and stationed troops and gardai at the graveyard to ensure that they did not take place. During the Second World War there seems to have been no public commemoration of Tone at Bodenstown, but the event recommenced in 1946.

In 1948, on the 150th anniversary of the death of Wolfe Tone, numbers at Bodenstown were low, probably because of a major 1798 commemorative event at Enniscorthy, Co. Wexford. Nevertheless, in the morning there was a military parade after which the minister for defence, T.F. Higgins, laid a wreath on the grave on behalf of the officers and men of the army. In the afternoon, wreaths were laid on the grave on behalf of the National Commemoration Committee. Tomás MacCurtain delivered the oration. He declared that Tone had discovered that 'there was only one policy which the British Empire recognised as effective – that was the policy of force'.[39]

During the 1950s and the 1960s there continued to be official army, Fianna Fáil and republican attendance at commemorative events at Bodenstown, but numbers involved were relatively small. There was a large turnout in 1966, no doubt influenced by the 1916 anniversary celebrations, and thereafter the occasion remained popular because of the growing crisis in Northern Ireland. On 18 November 1967, after the government gave a £10,000 grant to the Wolfe Tone Memorial Committee, established in 1898, a statue of Wolfe Tone was erected finally on St Stephen's Green in Dublin at a ceremony attended by President Éamon de Valera.[40] On 1 November 1969, however, loyalist paramilitaries destroyed Tone's memorial at Bodenstown with a bomb and two years later they were responsible for blowing up the Tone statue on St Stephen's Green. On 25 April 1971 a new memorial was unveiled at Bodenstown by the National Graves Association at an event involving some 1,000 people and attended by Church of Ireland, Catholic and Presbyterian clergy. The memorial contained thirty-two paving stones, each dedicated to one county of Ireland. According to a press report, 'The only protest came from the Breton nationalist, Yann Goulet; he was upset by the playing of *Marseillaise* (Tone was a brigadier-general in the French army).'[41]

Controversy and Division at Bodenstown, 1970 to Present

From the early 1970s, reflecting the new divisions in republicanism, the two wings of Sinn Féin marked the event separately. Sinn Féin (Gardner Place) paraded on the same occasion as the army and Fianna Fáil while Sinn Féin (Kevin Street) paraded on the Sunday before the main commemoration. From 1974 the army stopped attending those June commemorations, 'illustrative of the backlash of northern violence', as an *Irish Times* editorial put it.[42] By 1980 Sinn Féin (Kevin Street), now called Provisional Sinn Féin, celebrated the ceremony on the Sunday closest to 20 June, along with Fianna Fáil, while Sinn Féin (Gardner Place), now called Official Sinn Féin or Sinn Féin the Workers' Party, held its parade on the previous Sunday. The Irish Republican Socialist Party also ran a commemorative event at Bodenstown. These events often attracted considerable numbers, with bands and colour parties. In 1981, on the morning of the Tone commemoration on 21 June, the Fianna Fáil party cancelled its appearance at Bodenstown, apparently as the result of concern about the Provisional Sinn Féin parade that year, which included a number of prisoners who had escaped from the Crumlin Road jail in Belfast. Fianna Fáil switched its annual commemoration to a Sunday in September and from this time on marked the Bodenstown event in October, while Provisional Sinn Féin continued to hold its commemoration on or near 20 June.

Speeches at Bodenstown reveal major differences in approach to Tone and his contemporary relevance. By 1969 violence had erupted in Northern Ireland and from that time on northern matters tended to influence speeches. At the Fianna Fáil wreath-laying ceremony in 1968, Ruari Brugha TD described Tone as the founder of the Irish independence movement and a believer in the 'ultimate unity of the nation as a natural right'.[43] In 1972, however, Senator Neville Keery declared: 'Respect for Tone, his achievements and virtues is one thing. Recognition of the realities of changing times is another. No one familiar with the detailed narratives of 1798 would have history repeat itself.'[44] The split of the republican movement into two wings led to each side attacking the other as well as the British and Irish governments in their speeches.

Bodenstown speeches were often used by republicans to set out their current policies. From 1972 speakers from Official Sinn Féin rejected armed struggle. In 1972, Sean Garland condemned terrorism as 'not being a weapon that anyone genuinely concerned for the revolutionary organisation of the working class will employ' and called for a left-wing alliance.[45] Provisional Sinn Féin orations continued to support violence, Geároid MacCarthaigh in 1976, saying that Tone too 'was a man of violence'.[46] A year later, in a speech written by Danny Morrison and Gerry Adams, Jimmy Drumm declared: 'we can see no future in participating in a restructured Stormont, even with power-sharing and a bill of rights. Nor will we ever accept the legitimacy of the Free State [Republic of Ireland] … No! To even contemplate acceptance of either of these partitionist states would be a betrayal of all that Tone preached and died for.'[47]

There were no longer speeches at Fianna Fáil commemorations between 1975 and 1981. They recommenced in September 1982 with an oration by Taoiseach Charles Haughey. He condemned violence: 'today legitimate political means are available for us, and these and these only must be availed of.'[48] From the late 1980s speeches on behalf of Provisional Sinn Féin continued to justify armed struggle but also backed political action and the possibility of negotiations. From 1969 the provisional republican movement had used an IRA colour party, with paramilitary trappings, to head their parade but in June 1987 the colour party was 'civilianised', to mark this ideological shift.[49] On 21 June 1992, at the Sinn Féin rally at Bodenstown, Jim Gibney stated that republican thinking was not stuck in the 1960s and had evolved greatly in the last ten years.[50] On 20 October 1991 at a Workers' Party event at Bodenstown to mark the bicentenary of the founding of the United Irishmen, Tomás MacGiolla TD urged peace and called for 'an end to sectarianism and an end to terrorism'.[51]

Speeches by the various party spokespersons at Bodenstown over the next six years reflected the difficulties of negotiations until the Belfast/Good Friday Agreement of April 1998 delivered a political settlement.

The new arrangements involved renunciation of violence and accept-ance that there could be no change in the status of Northern Ireland without the consent of a majority of the population. Although it had not brought a united Ireland, in his June 1998 Bodenstown speech Gerry Adams welcomed the agreement and referred to Tone.[52] He said that republicans would play a full part in the assembly, the executive and the all-Ireland ministerial council, to which they would bring their repub-lican analysis. He stated his belief that its all-Ireland element would help 'the transition to our goal of unity'. In his October 1998 Bodenstown speech Taoiseach Bertie Ahern praised the agreement, quoted from Tone and expressed his hope that a bright future lay in prospect for the whole island.[53] Quotations from Tone at this time often mentioned his wish to unite the people of Ireland and to substitute the name of Irishman for the different denominations.

Since 1998 the number of those attending these commemorative occasions at Bodenstown is less than in the 1980s and 1990s. Nonetheless, Fianna Fáil, Sinn Féin, the Workers' Party and other groups have contin-ued to mark the event. Difficulties in operating the 1998 Agreement were a key feature of the speeches in the early years of the twenty-first century, after which southern political rivalries have tended to dominate speeches. All see the occasion at Bodenstown as a valuable occasion to stress their republican credentials. In June 2013, Sinn Féin TD Pearse Doherty stated: 'In the Ireland of 2013, the message of Tone is more rele-vant than ever … Let's make Tone's republic a reality.'[54] In October 2015 Fianna Fáil leader Micháel Martin declared: 'True republicanism belongs to no party or sect, it belongs to the Irish people.'[55] Even after 200 years, commemoration of Theobald Wolfe Tone at Bodenstown remains an important part of the Irish political calendar.

Final Observations

These two annual commemorative occasions show how people con-tinue to look to individuals and events from their history to inspire or inform their political position today. Over a long period of time the significance and popularity of these commemorations have changed greatly. For many generations of Ulster Protestants, the siege of Derry has been seen as an important part of their history. Ian McBride has noted: 'While the narrative has retained its basic structure, each generation has found fresh meanings, emphasising or suppressing different components according to its own ideological needs.'[56] In the late eighteenth century the message of the siege was 'peace, goodwill towards men', but in the nineteenth century it was viewed primarily as a story of siege and victory for Protestants. At the same time, the numbers involved remained relatively small, until the political and religious conditions of post-1921 Northern Ireland caused more of the larger Protestant and unionist community to be actively involved. In recent decades the siege of Derry has remained a potent symbol for many unionists and loyalists in Northern Ireland. Celebration of this historical event is seen as an important part of their cultural and political identity. In the past there has been tension between nationalist residents of Derry and those who want to mark these commemorations. Recent years, however, have seen important accommodation and new understanding between the various parties.

Theobald Wolfe Tone, as Marianne Elliott has noted, is the 'recognised founder of Irish Republican nationalism'.[57] Every year republicans of all shades go on pilgrimage to his grave at Bodenstown. Writing in 1989, she observed: 'Today his name still arouses heated passions.' For the first hundred years after his death, his grave attracted little public attention. With the emergence of the new Irish state in 1922, however, his name and political ideas took on a special importance, which led to new public attention to his burial place. Straightaway, a wide range of political parties reflecting different strands of republicanism were involved in these commemorations. The Irish government was formally represented at Bodenstown until the early 1970s. Marianne Elliott has commented: 'Each takes from the Tone tradition only what it needs to sustain its own image.' This tradition has involved ideas of a republic, the use of armed force and uniting the people of Ireland. In the conditions of political strife and violence in the decades after 1969, starkly different interpretations about Tone were very apparent. In the new conditions of recent decades, however, some of these interpretations have undergone considerable revision. It can be said that his name no longer arouses 'heated passions'. Nonetheless, the various parties continue to attend these commemorative events at Bodenstown and to expound why the Tone story remains important to them. For unionists and republicans alike, commemoration of certain events or individuals in their history continue to provide the means to explain or justify their contemporary political and cultural concerns.

COMMEMORATING THE TWO WORLD WARS, 1919–2017: REMEMBERING, FORGETTING AND REMEMBERING AGAIN

Commemoration in Ireland of those who served or died in the two world wars has changed radically over time. During the last two decades I have attended a number of world war commemorative events but three in particular illustrate these changes very clearly. In September 2015 at Trinity College Dublin a ceremony took place in memory of the 471 students, staff and alumni who died during the First World War.[1] A memorial stone, the work of sculptor Stephen Burke, was placed in Front Square at the steps of the Hall of Honour, which had been erected in remembrance of all those who lost their lives and formally opened in a ceremony on 10 November 1928. On this earlier occasion, no government representative was present, and in his speech, Lord Glenavy, vice-chancellor of the university, referred to 'a growing conspiracy of silence' about the memory of the war dead in the Irish Free State. The building was completed by the addition of a new reading room for the library and opened in 1937 by Éamon de Valera, head of the Irish government. In the speeches at this event there was no mention of either the Hall of Honour or the war. In time even in the college the significance of the memorial faded. I was a student at Trinity in the late 1960s and early 1970s but remained unaware of its existence. On 26 September

2015 I attended this special ceremony to unveil the memorial stone. Tomás Irish, historian of Trinity during the war, wrote for the occasion: 'It is hoped that the inauguration of the Memorial Stone will help to re-integrate the Hall of Honour – and the story of Trinity's war experience – into the consciousness of the college community.'[2]

The two other events that I attended occurred in Belfast. In 1999 Belfast City Council finally honoured James Magennis, the Belfast Catholic submariner and the only Northern Ireland holder of a VC, awarded for 'extreme valour', in the Second World War. When he returned to the city in 1945, he was at first honoured by the local citizens, but the city corporation, on which there was a unionist majority, declined to give him the freedom of the city. When he visited his old school, the De La Salle brother who introduced him to the pupils said that he was a brave man but he had not been brave for Ireland.[3] On 8 October 1999 I was invited to a ceremony to unveil a memorial sculpture, by Elizabeth McLaughlin, in Magennis's honour, erected in the City Hall grounds. On 30 April 2003 I attended a special service at St Anne's Cathedral in Belfast to remember all those from the city, nationalist and unionist, who died in the First World War. The congregation included the lord lieutenant for Belfast, Lady Carswell, the General Officer in Command, Northern Ireland, General Philip Trousdell, the Sinn Féin lord mayor, Alex Maskey, and an ex-IRA member, Martin Meehan, whose grandfather died in April 1916, not in Dublin but in northern France, as a soldier in the Inniskilling Fusiliers.[4] A survey of war commemorations in Ireland over the past century will set these events in context.

Early Southern Commemorations

During the First World War an estimated 200,000 people from Ireland served in British armed forces. It is reckoned that some 40,000 died. The first Armistice Day, 11 November 1919, was described by the *Irish Times* as follows:

> The two minutes silence in recognition of the first anniversary of Armistice Day proved a markedly impressive event in Dublin yesterday.

When the eleventh hour of the eleventh day of the eleventh month was chimed, a calm and stillness pervaded the entire city that was manifestation of the feelings of the people in regard to the solemnity of the occasion ... pedestrians stood still on the footpath with hats doffed and heads reverently bowed, and in all other departments of work-a-day life the same regard for the solemnity of the occasion was observed.[5]

This dignified occasion was marred only by scuffles between students from Trinity College waving union flags and from the National University of Ireland waving tricolours. In Cork, there was a march of men of the Discharged and Demobilised Soldiers' and Sailors' Federation with their president, the lord mayor of Cork, William F. O'Connor. Subsequently, however, these events to remember the fallen became controversial. Jane Leonard has observed: 'Division rather than dignity surrounded the commemoration of the war in Ireland.'[6] Nationalists and unionists had served together in the war but with the War of Independence and partition there were new political dynamics and divisions in Ireland.

In the twenty-six counties that became the Irish Free State, the War of Independence and the Civil War curtailed war commemorations, although we can note a press report in November 1922, during the Civil War, that the poppy sellers in Grafton Street, Dublin, were 'virtually besieged ... stocks were cleared and replenished time and time again'.[7] From 1923 there was a period of well-attended commemorative events and dedication of memorials. Armistice Day was marked not just by a two-minute silence but also by parades and assemblies of ex-servicemen and their friends and families. The Sunday after Armistice Day became known as Remembrance Sunday when special services were held in churches to remember the fallen. On 11 November 1924 before a temporary cenotaph at College Green in Dublin some 20,000 veterans observed the silence along with a crowd estimated at 50,000.[8] That same day there was an assembly of a reported 500 ex-servicemen in Tipperary.[9] Such events were organised by a number of ex-servicemen's organisations until they were brought together under the British Legion in 1925.

Public war memorials were erected. In Castlebellingham, Co. Louth, a Celtic cross was dedicated to 'those of the parishes of Kilsaran, Dromisken and Togher who died for Ireland in the Great European War of 1914–18'.[10] The most common memorials are the headstones, reckoned to number some 2,000 in all of Ireland, erected by the Commonwealth War Graves Commission.[11] Memorials to those who served or died were put up in most Protestant churches. A brass plaque in Waterford cathedral records that Col E. Roberts lost five grandsons: four in France and one in Gallipoli. A stained-glass window in the First Presbyterian Church in Monaghan commemorates two sons of the Black family, aged 18 and 22, who were killed at Gallipoli. Some Catholic churches had memorial plaques or other memorials. In the parish church at Dromin, Co. Louth, there is a stained-glass window in memory of Fr Willie Doyle, SJ, a chaplain killed in France in 1917.[12] The poppy was sold widely.

Official attitudes were ambivalent but generally tolerant in the 1920s. Aware of the many Irish people who had died during the war, including members of their own families, the Free State government sent representatives to the wreath-laying ceremonies in Dublin and London. The message on the wreath laid by Colonel Maurice Moore, the Irish government representative, at the temporary cenotaph cross in College Green in Dublin on 11 November 1924 read: 'This wreath is placed here by the Free State government to commemorate all the brave men who fell on the field of battle.'[13] In 1923 southern premier W.T. Cosgrave and some Cabinet colleagues attended an Armistice Day Mass in Cork.[14] Conscious of nationalist and republican susceptibilities, members of the Free State government looked askance at proposals to build a large Irish national war memorial in central Dublin, and insisted that it be erected in the outskirts at Islandbridge.[15] At the same time, the government provided the site at Islandbridge for the memorial and financially contributed towards its construction.

Early Armistice Day commemorations in Dublin met with a certain amount of opposition, expressed in actions such as the snatching of poppies. From the mid-1920s, however, the intensity of this opposition grew, with various republican groups organising anti-Armistice Day rallies to protest against the 'flagrant display of British imperialism disguised as Armistice celebrations' and with physical attacks being made on some of the parades.[16] In 1926 this led to the main ceremony being moved from the centre of Dublin to the Phoenix Park. Éamon de Valera spoke at one of the anti-Armistice Day rallies in 1930 and the formation of a Fianna Fáil government in 1932 led to a further downgrading of the commemorations. Official representatives were withdrawn from the main wreath-laying ceremony in Dublin from November 1932, although the Irish government continued to be represented at the Cenotaph in London until 1936. Permits for the sale of poppies, previously allowed for several days in the week before 11 November, were now reduced to one day only.[17] Work on the national war memorial park at Islandbridge was completed and handed over to the government in early 1937, but the official opening was put off a number of times by de Valera, until the outbreak of the Second World War led to its indefinite postponement.[18]

Armistice ceremonies were held at the Phoenix Park in 1939 and at Islandbridge in 1940, but without parades.[19] Thereafter, public demonstrations in Dublin relating to this event were banned during the war. Indeed, the government maintained its ban in November 1945, even after the end of the war, because it did not want to see any public demonstration of Irish involvement in the Allied war effort. In fact, it is estimated that at least 60,000 men and women went from the twenty-six counties to join the armed forces of the Allies.[20] These include nearly 5,000 members of the Irish army who deserted to fight for the Allies against fascism; after the war the government drew up a blacklist of these men to deny them any publicly funded employment. The number of war dead has been calculated at 2,302.[21]

After the war, in Ireland, as in Britain, Remembrance Sunday became the main day of commemoration. Names of those who died were added to existing war memorials (although not to public war memorials). The event continued to be marked annually by parades of ex-servicemen, including both First World War veterans and those who had served in the Second World War. In Dublin, separate denominational parades on the morning of Remembrance Sunday to St Patrick's Cathedral and to St Mary's Pro-Cathedral, were followed in the afternoon by a joint parade from Smithfield Market along North Quays to the Irish National War Memorial at Islandbridge. There were discreet wreath-laying ceremonies elsewhere in the country. These parades and other commemorative events continued during the 1950s, but for many of those involved, as declining numbers attending Remembrance Day and veterans' memories showed, there was a clear sense that they had become marginalised and excluded from the new Irish identity and sense of history that had now become dominant. Jane Leonard has described the growing personal isolation of many of the veterans: 'They matured into middle age and retirement, aware that they were excluded from the national cultural identity forged after independence in 1922. This identity declared that: "T'was better to die neath an Irish sky, Than at Suvla or Sedd el Bahr".'[22]

Early Northern Commemorations

Northern commemorations were both similar and different to those elsewhere in Ireland. The *Irish News* reported how, on the first Armistice Day, 11 November 1919, 'the two-minute pause was generally observed in Belfast yesterday … on the lines suggested by the King, all work in the shops and factories and all traffic in the streets being stopped at 11 o'clock for the space of two minute.'[23] From the early 1920s the event was commemorated not only with a two-minute silence and church services, but also with parades to new war memorials, erected in many towns. The first major memorial, however, was not in Northern Ireland but in France at Thiepval on the Somme. Sir James Craig was the leading figure on a committee established in November 1919 to raise funds and plan a memorial to the 36th (Ulster) Division. It was decided to erect a replica of 'Helen's Tower', a tower in the grounds of Clandeboy estate, Co. Down, where many Ulster volunteers had trained in 1914 and 1915. This Ulster Memorial Tower was dedicated on 18 November 1921 in memory of the officers and men 'of the 36th (Ulster) Division, and of the sons of Ulster in other forces who laid down their lives in the Great War'.[24]

There is evidence that in the early days there were efforts to keep these events open to all sections of the community. At the unveiling of the Enniskillen war memorial in 1922, Protestant and Catholic war orphans laid wreaths.[25] In Ballymena at a ceremony on 11 November 1924, Major General Sir Oliver Nugent, who had commanded the 36th (Ulster) Division at the Somme, declared that 'the service given by the Ulstermen in the war was not confined to one creed or one denomination; it was given by Ulstermen of all denominations and all classes'.[26]

The ceremony for the unveiling of the Portadown war memorial in 1925 involved the Catholic parish priest along with the other clergy, and wreaths were laid by representatives of the Orange Order and the Ancient Order of Hibernians.[27] On this occasion speeches were made by Major D.G. Shillington, a unionist MP, and R.M. Cullen, a Catholic ex-NCO of the Connaught Rangers. Cullen remarked that their joint participation was 'emblematic of the brotherhood that was born in the gullies of Gallipoli and cemented on the firing steps of Flanders'.[28] On 12 November 1924 the *Irish News* reported commemorations in both Northern Ireland and the Irish Free State with the headline, 'Brotherhood of bereavement – north and south pause to salute the dead'.

In spite of these comments and inclusive incidents, however, the Armistice Day commemorations in Northern Ireland became largely linked with unionism. To some extent this arose because of a reluctance in certain Catholic and nationalist quarters to acknowledge the Catholic role in the war. Cardinal Patrick O'Donnell, Catholic archbishop of Armagh, declined to attend the unveiling of the County Armagh war memorial in 1926.[29] More importantly, many unionists came to see Armistice Day as an occasion for the affirmation of their own sense of Ulster and British identity. As Keith Jeffery has commented: 'For them the blood sacrifice of the Somme was equal and opposite to that of Easter 1916.'[30] At the unveiling of Coleraine war memorial in 1922, Sir James Craig declared that 'those who passed away have left behind a great message to all of them to stand firm, and to give away none of Ulster's soil'.[31] Only Protestant clergy attended the unveiling of the cenotaph at the Belfast City Hall in 1929 and there were no official representatives from the 16th (Irish) Division, in which Belfast Catholics had tended to serve.[32]

The government played no direct role in organising events on Armistice Day and speeches were rarely made on the occasion. Nonetheless, the large parades and well-attended services on the day, often with army involved, were seen by many not only as an expression of grief but also as a mark of the British link among the unionist community. It would be wrong, however, to write off entirely Catholic and nationalist involvement in the Armistice Day commemorations. Catholic ex-servicemen continued to mark the occasion in some places. In Newry in the 1930s, on Armistice Day ex-servicemen held a parade before making their way to their respective Catholic and Protestant churches for memorial services.[33] During the 1930s Armistice Day wreaths were laid in Belfast for the men of the 16th (Irish) Division, in Derry for the 'Irish Catholic officers and men who fell in the great war', and in Portadown for the Connaught Rangers, in which many local Catholics had served.[34]

During the Second World War, some 60,000 volunteers from Northern Ireland served in the British armed forces. It has been estimated that 2,241 died.[35] After the war, names of those who had served or died in the war were added to existing church and public memorials. Parades and services continued on Remembrance Sunday as they had done on Armistice Day, and they remained largely the concern of the Protestant and unionist community. While the government had no formal involvement in these events, it was quite common for the prime minister or a Cabinet minister to take the salute of ex-servicemen on these occasions. The sense of alienation felt by Catholics was described in 1995 by Gerry Fitt, a merchant seaman during the war and later a member of the House of Lords, who recalled being noticed by some people from unionist York Street while he was on his way to VJ celebrations at the Belfast City Hall in 1945:

> They weren't too friendly and shouted insults about me being a Catholic and Irish neutrality. I remember looking at Union Jacks that were being waved about. I had served under it during the war and had been glad to do so but I realized that here it was a Protestant unionist flag and it looked different then.[36]

At the same time we should note that in some places, such as Dungannon, Newry and Sion Mills, parades of Catholic and Protestant ex-servicemen continued to take place as they had done in the 1930s.[37]

Commemorations and Controversy in the 1970s and 1980s

By the 1960s commemoration of Remembrance Sunday in the Republic of Ireland in honour of those from Ireland who had died during the two world wars was no longer prominent or widespread, compared with Armistice Day commemorations in the 1920s and 1930s. The main commemorative events on that day were held in Dublin. On that morning there were usually two parades of members of the British Legion and the Old Comrades Association, to the Church of Ireland national cathedral, St Patrick's, and to the Catholic pro-cathedral, St Mary's, where services were held. In the afternoon or evening there was a joint parade from the Dublin Quays to the Irish National War Memorial at Islandbridge.[38] This latter event was attended by members of the diplomatic corps from many countries, who laid wreaths, but no Irish government representatives. In 1966, on the anniversary of the 1916 Rising, Taoiseach Sean Lemass made a positive statement about the Irishmen who fought in the First World War: 'In later years it was common – and I was also guilty in this respect – to question the motives of those who joined the new British armies at the outbreak of the war, but it must, in their honour and in fairness to their memory, be said that they were motivated by the highest purpose.'[39] Nonetheless, the government continued to ignore these commemorative events. Some Remembrance Sunday ceremonies continued elsewhere. In 1967, for example, there was such an event at the war memorial in Sligo town, presided over by John Fallon, who was secretary of the Sligo branch of the British Legion, and chairman of Sligo County Council.[40]

In Northern Ireland by the 1960s Remembrance Sunday continued to be marked widely, but this was an event viewed differently by unionist and nationalist communities. In the early 1960s, the Belfast unionist paper, the *Belfast News Letter*, carried detailed reports of commemorative services and ceremonies in many centres throughout Northern Ireland.[41] Such services were held most often in Protestant churches, but occasionally in Catholic churches, as in Newry and Strabane; attendance, of course, was strongly denominationally based. At parades and other ceremonies there were normally no speeches, although often unionist politicians were reported as present. In sharp contrast, the Belfast nationalist paper, the *Irish News*, carried virtually no mention of these commemorative events. Such polarisation continued during the 1960s but there were occasional instances of change. In 1965 two Catholic members of the Ballymoney council, both ex-servicemen, attended for the first time the Remembrance Sunday service in Ballymoney First Presbyterian Church. In 1967, for the first time, a Catholic priest, a D-Day veteran, participated in the ceremony at the cenotaph in Bangor.[42]

The 1970s and 1980s witnessed important developments in how Remembrance Sunday commemorations were held. In 1971 the British Legion in both Northern Ireland and in the Republic of Ireland cancelled all public parades and ceremonies on Remembrance Sunday because of the deteriorating situation in Northern Ireland. The following year such public events resumed in the north but not in the south. At many of the northern services and commemorative events tribute was paid not only to those who had died in the two world wars but also to members of the security forces killed in the conflict in Northern Ireland. As before, these events involved primarily but not exclusively members of the unionist and Protestant communities. In 1978 considerable controversy arose when Democratic Unionist Party members of Ballymena council objected to and prevented a Catholic priest taking part at the annual remembrance service at the town war memorial, even though Father Hugh Murphy was an ex-Royal Navy chaplain and holder of the Military Cross. Their actions were widely condemned and the British Legion withdrew from the event.[43] We can still find occasions when an effort was made to keep the occasion a broad one. For example, in Irvinestown, Co. Fermanagh, during the 1970s and 1980s, it was customary for the Remembrance Sunday parade to halt to lay wreaths at both the Sacred Heart Church and the war memorial, before proceeding to the memorial service in the Church of Ireland church.[44] From the early 1980s, Father Hugh Murphy, now Canon, represented the Catholic diocese of Down and Connor in a Remembrance Sunday service in Belfast at St Anne's Church of Ireland Cathedral.[45]

In Dublin in 1972 the parade to the Irish National War Memorial at Islandbridge was cancelled by the British Legion on police advice, owing to the northern 'Troubles'. Subsequently, in face of republican hostility, neither this event nor other public occasions of commemoration of the Irish dead from the two world wars were restored in the south. Annual collections for ex-servicemen's charities ceased largely and many British

Legion branches closed.[46] In 1973, however, an ecumenical service of remembrance was held in Dublin on Remembrance Sunday afternoon in St Patrick's Church of Ireland Cathedral.[47] Under the direction of Victor Griffin, dean of St Patrick's from 1969 until 1991, this became an important annual event, attended by members of the public and the diplomatic corps. In Church of Ireland, Presbyterian and Methodist churches Remembrance Sunday services continued to recall the fallen of both world wars.[48] At Islandbridge the state of the National War Memorial and gardens deteriorated until by 1979, as Kevin Myers later recalled, they were 'a vandalised tiphead, covered in weeds and grazing horses, the great stonework festooned with graffiti'.[49]

In 1980 considerable controversy arose when the Irish president, Patrick Hillery, turned down an invitation to attend the Remembrance Sunday service in St Patrick's Cathedral. He acted on the instructions of the taoiseach, Charles Haughey, that it would be inappropriate for the president to attend, what were described as, memorial services for the armed forces of other countries.[50] Embarrassed over this matter, the Fianna Fáil government sent a minister to the service in 1980 and in the following year, but declined to do so in 1982, owing to poor Irish–British government relations.[51] A new coalition government in 1983 agreed to attendance at St Patrick's Cathedral of government ministers and representatives of the Irish defence forces who participated in the service, in spite of protest from Fianna Fáil spokesmen and others. In 1987, after the return of a Fianna Fáil government in that year, no minister was present at the St Patrick's service. In the mid-1980s, partly in response to criticism over this matter, the Irish government instituted a National Day of Commemoration to be marked at the Garden of Remembrance in Dublin on 11 July, the anniversary of the Truce in 1921, to commemorate the deaths of all Irishmen and women in all wars and conflicts as well as United Nations service.

Changes in Commemoration, 1987–98

Over the following decade, however, the nature of these world war commemorations, north and south, changed markedly. An important factor was the reaction to the eleven deaths caused by an IRA bomb at the war memorial in Enniskillen, Co. Fermanagh, on Remembrance Sunday, 8 November 1987. There was immediate widespread condemnation in the south of this bombing. In addition, as Jane Leonard has pointed out, public revulsion over the matter 'fuelled a recent desire in the Republic of Ireland to remember the Irish who served in both world wars'.[52] As a result of this change of opinion, over the following years a number of war memorials were restored, and public parades and commemorative events were held once again on Remembrance Sunday, in some places such as Limerick and Drogheda.[53] The sale of poppies increased greatly. A key moment in this development was Remembrance Sunday 1993 when, for the first time, the Irish president, Mary Robinson, attended the Remembrance Sunday service in St Patrick's Cathedral, Dublin.[54] The president's husband, Nicholas Robinson, wore a poppy, although the president did not. The following day, an editorial in the *Irish Independent* remarked that President Robinson, as the first president to attend this event, had 'made her own contribution to the on-going process of healing old wounds'. It concluded: 'There will be real peace on this island when the government officially attends such ceremonies, and it does not make news. We will have turned our backs on old prejudices.'[55] During the rest of her term of office, President Robinson continued to attend the Remembrance Sunday service in St Patrick's Cathedral, as have her successors, President Mary McAleese and President Michael D. Higgins.

From 1988 the British Legion and the Irish government worked together to restore the Irish National War Memorial at Islandbridge. The memorial park was opened officially in 1994 by the Fianna Fáil minister for finance, Bertie Ahern. Afterwards, *Irish Times* journalist Kevin Myers described his presence as signifying 'a change in attitude towards Irishness, in definitions of what it is to be Irish and how many forms of Irishness there can be without betrayal of anybody or anything'.[56] In the following year, a ceremony was held there to mark the end of the Second World War and to honour those Irishmen and Irishwomen who had served in British or Allied forces. Present on this occasion were the taoiseach, John Bruton, and representatives from all southern parties, as well as the Northern Ireland Secretary of State, Sir Patrick Mayhew, and representatives from the north of the Ulster Unionist Party, the Social Democratic and Labour Party and the Alliance Party. For the first time at any such event, Sinn Féin was represented, the party's national chairman and Belfast city councillor, Tom Hartley, attending.[57] The following Monday morning an *Irish Times* editorial talked of the breaking of taboos created by history and described this event as being on 'enormous importance'.[58] The editorial declared:

> The Taoiseach, Mr Bruton, found the words to express what has never been said aloud by any of his predecessors when he told the gathering at Islandbridge that the Second World War had been brought to an end 'by the courage, the struggle, and the sacrifice of Europeans some of whom were Irish, whose bravery we remember today'.

In Northern Ireland, the decade that followed the Enniskillen bomb also witnessed important changes in how Remembrance Sunday was marked. The sense of outrage caused by this event, and admiration for the courage and forbearance of many of the survivors, as well as a growing concern to promote reconciliation led, eventually, to efforts to view Remembrance Sunday in a more inclusive way, once again. In the late 1980s and early 1990s, Dorita Field, a Second World War South African veteran and SDLP councillor, attended the ceremony in Belfast on behalf of her party. In 1994 all five SDLP councillors in Belfast attended the remembrance ceremony in what their leader on the council, Alex Atwood, termed as 'an act of reconciliation'.[59] On 8 November 1992, Paddy McGowan, the SDLP chairman of Omagh District Council, was the first nationalist councillor to lay a wreath at the town's cenotaph.[60] In the early 1990s in Derry, some SDLP councillors attended the ceremony at the cenotaph in an individual capacity. For the first time, on 12 November 1995, a Catholic mayor, John Kerr of the SDLP, laid a wreath at the cenotaph.[61] As a reflection of the considerable changes which took place in this decade, we can note that on Remembrance Sunday 1997 wreaths were laid at their local cenotaphs by SDLP mayors or chairmen of councils in Belfast, Derry, Omagh, Armagh and Dungannon, a SDLP councillor in Ballynahinch and an independent nationalist chairman in Enniskillen.[62]

Other developments reflected the new-found desire to view these commemorations and the events they recalled in a broader and more inclusive way. In some cases there was a strong concern to promote reconciliation. The Somme Association was founded in 1990 under the chairmanship of unionist councillor Dr Ian Adamson to 'ensure that the efforts of Irishmen to preserve world peace between 1914 and 1919 are remembered and understood'.[63] Another aim was 'to coordinate research into Ireland's part in the First World War and to provide a basis for the two communities in Northern Ireland to come together to learn of their common heritage'. The led to the establishment in 1994 at Newtownards, Co. Down, of the Somme Heritage Centre, which remembered all soldiers from Ireland, not only members of the 36th (Ulster) Division, who had died at the Battle of the Somme. Interest in the Somme had been a central focus of Ulster unionist war commemorations for decades, but, as Keith Jeffery observed, what was significant was the widening of the scope of the association beyond the Protestant and unionist community.[64]

An important cross-border initiative to build a peace park at Messines in Belgium, in memory of all the Irish who died in the First World War and to promote reconciliation in Ireland, involved Paddy Harte, a Fine Gael deputy for North-East Donegal, and Glenn Barr, a former Derry loyalist leader and community worker, as well as many young volunteers from north and south. On 11 November 1998, the eightieth anniversary of the 1918 armistice, a ceremony was held to inaugurate the Island of Ireland Peace Park with the recently constructed Messines Peace Tower, based on an Irish round tower. It was attended by Queen Elizabeth II, President Mary McAleese, King Albert and large numbers of people from all over Ireland. In a joint speech, Harte and Barr declared: 'As Protestants and Catholics, we apologise for the terrible deeds we have done to each other and we ask forgiveness.' They recalled the 'solidarity and trust that developed between Protestant and Catholic soldiers when they served together in these trenches'. Together they affirmed that a 'fitting tribute to the principles for which men and women from the island of Ireland died in both world wars would be permanent peace in Ireland'.[65] For Harte and Barr, the main aim of the project was to remember these forgotten soldiers and to promote reconciliation in Ireland. These words are part of a peace pledge now inscribed at the entrance to the park. Others saw it as part of a bigger picture. The day after the inauguration, a *Belfast News Letter* editorial commented: 'Yesterday's poignant events marked a further thawing in the unofficial cold war that has existed between the two countries for most of this century.'[66]

Changes to Commemoration in the Twenty-First Century

These changes have continued into the present century. In 2002 the *Irish News* reported an account by a County Donegal woman, Nellie O'Donnell, of what happened to her father James Duffy, VC, when he returned to the county after the First World War. She described how because he had received the award of the Victoria Cross from the British Crown, and he attended VC reunion events in England, he was treated as a 'traitor', and he and his family were shunned in their neighbourhood for many years.[67] That same year, 2002, however, reflecting the great change in attitude to this matter, a Fianna Fáil government minister, Noel Dempsey, chaired the launch of a *County Donegal Book of Honour*, a publication organised by Fine Gael Paddy Harte, to remember all Donegal men and women who were killed in the First World War. In 2006 the Irish government organised a formal event to commemorate the Battle of the Somme. Two years later, Brian Lenihan, the Irish minister for finance, commented: 'The impact the ceremony had was on Irish people in the street, Catholic people mainly, who felt that part of that history had been hidden and concealed from them and was now revived by the Irish state.'[68]

In February 2008, a delegation from Roscommon County Council, accompanied by four senior officers of the Irish defence forces, laid a wreath of poppies at the Round Tower in the Ireland Peace Park at Messines to honour those from Ireland who died in the First World War, including an estimated 330 from the county itself. A card attached read: 'Thank you for your efforts and sacrifice. You have helped to shape the Ireland, the Europe and the freedom that we enjoy today. From the people of Roscommon.'[69] On 24 September 2009, President Mary McAleese unveiled in Killarney a new memorial 'erected in memory of those from Killarney and surrounding areas who served and died in the 1914–1918 war'. She congratulated the memorial committee for 'healing' the memory of Killarney's dead 'and drawing them back into memory and drawing them back into the community'.[70] An unusual memorial to war dead was unveiled at Glasnevin cemetery in Dublin on April 2016, as part of ceremonies to commemorate the Easter Rising of 1916. It was in the form of a memorial wall that listed all those who died during the Rising, and included the forty-one Irishmen serving in the British army.[71] On 10 July 2016 at the Irish National War Memorial, Islandbridge, there was a major ceremony attended by political leaders from both sides of the border to remember more than 3,500 Irishmen, north and south, who died at the Battle of the Somme.[72]

On 1 July 2002, at the annual ceremony in Belfast to mark the Battle of the Somme, the Sinn Féin lord mayor, Alex Maskey, laid a laurel wreath at the cenotaph outside the City Hall, although he did not partic-ipate in the official commemoration ceremony.[73] After a brief Sinn Féin ban on party members attending 'British military commemorations', on 1 July 2008 another Sinn Féin lord mayor, Tom Hartley, again placed a laurel wreath on the Belfast cenotaph to remember those who fell at the Somme.[74] On 6 November 2005, a parade and ceremony, organised by Glenn Barr, was held at the Derry cenotaph to honour all those from Ireland who had died at Messines, including 14-year-old John Condon from Waterford (believed to be the youngest Allied soldier to die in the war), whose family attended the event. At their request, for the first time, the Irish tricolour was flown at the cenotaph, alongside the union flag. Afterwards Barr commented: 'It was an excellent service involving people from both sides and from all walks of life … The whole theme of our work is reconciliation through remembrance for all and that was reflected in the service.' He added: 'It's been a long time in coming to have the British and Irish flags flying together at the cenotaph here in this city, but I always knew this day would come.'[75] On 2 June 2016, at Thiepval in France, Martin McGuinness, Sinn Féin MLA for Derry, and deputy first minister, paid tribute to all those Irish soldiers who died at the Somme. He said: 'We have a shared and complex history on the island of Ireland.' McGuinness continued: 'We all have a responsibility to con-duct ourselves in a way that is respectful and encourages reconciliation among our people. I hope that my presence here today contributes to that reconciliation process in a positive and meaningful way.'[76]

In 2007 the first official meeting of the Irish president and the Northern Ireland first minister (Mary McAleese and Ian Paisley) took place at the Somme Heritage Centre at Newtownards, Co. Down, to open an exhibition on the 36th Ulster Division and the 16th Irish Division. Ian Paisley declared how the purpose of the Somme Centre was 'to remember all the heroes of this entire island who fought so that our freedoms could survive. Mary McAleese and myself have come here to pay tribute in unity to all those who fought and died for us. There may have been division then, but not now.'[77] The first official visit to the centre for members of Sinn Féin came when Belfast deputy lord mayor Danny Lavery and councillor Tom Hartley visited there on 26 January 2010. Margaret Ritchie, leader of the SDLP, in November 2010, became the first nationalist leader to wear a poppy on Remembrance Sunday in Northern Ireland. She said that it was a signal of a new 'progressive nationalism' and that 'it was about moving the community forward'. She stated that thousands of nationalists died in two world wars and 'it was no longer acceptable for Irish nationalism to airbrush them out of history'. She declared: 'If you want to share the future then you have to be able to understand our history and our past.'[78]

Commemorative events on Remembrance Sunday 2017 show very clearly the great changes compared to thirty years ago in how people in Ireland remember the dead of two world wars.[79] Not everyone agrees with these developments, as can be seen by the placing of a viable pipe bomb in Omagh by dissident republicans that led to postponement of the wreath-laying ceremony at the town's cenotaph. Elsewhere, however, in many parts of Ireland, the memory of those who died was marked in respectful ceremonies. In St Patrick's Cathedral, Dublin, President Michael D. Higgins laid a wreath at the war memorial. For the first time, a member of Sinn Féin, Mary Lou McDonald, attended the service. In Belfast, a two-minute silence was held at the cenotaph, led by SDLP lord mayor Nuala McAllister, and during the memorial service, wreaths were laid, including one by Heather Humphreys, the Irish minister of culture and arts. In Enniskillen, the DUP leader, Arlene Foster, welcomed to the remembrance ceremony Taoiseach Leo Varadker, continuing the tradition of Enda Kenny, who came first on the twenty-fifth anniversary of the Enniskillen bomb. He wore a shamrock poppy, as he had done several days before in the Dáil. In an interview afterwards he quoted from Captain Willie Redmond, MP, in one of his last letters home before his death at Flanders: 'It would be a fine memorial to the men who died if we could over their graves build up a bridge between north and south.'[80]

Explanations for Recent Changes in Commemoration

How do we explain these developments? In part they reflect changes in the understanding of our history, encouraged by writers, historians and journalists. Jennifer Johnston's novel *How Many Miles to Babylon* (1974) had a First World War setting. Frank McGuinness's play *Observe the Sons of Ulster Marching Towards the Somme*, staged first in Dublin in 1984 and then widely toured, gave a special view of the war for one community. McGuinness recalled: 'it was an eye-opener for a Catholic republican, as I am, to have to examine the complexity, diversity, disturbance and integrity of the other side, the Protestant people.'[81] In his poetry Michael Longley has written of the wartime experiences of his father.[82] Only some of the extensive historical literature that appeared at this time can be recorded here, but the work has been discussed by Keith Jeffery in a bibliographical essay in 2000 on recent writing about Ireland and the First World War.[83] *Ireland and the First World War* (Dublin), the first Trinity College History Workshop book, published in 1986, was edited by David Fitzpatrick, who was responsible for other writing on the war. Philip Orr's *The Road to the Somme: Men of the Ulster Division Tell their Story* (Belfast) appeared in 1987. *Ireland's Unknown Soldiers: The 16th (Irish) Division in the Great War 1914–1918* (Dublin) by Terence Denman was produced in 1992. In 1994 George Boyce wrote an article in *History Ireland* on 'Ireland and the First World War' for the southern school curriculum, which now covered the war. Work by Myles Dungan included *Irish Voices from the Great War* (Dublin), published in 1995.

In the 1990s, Jane Leonard, based at the Institute of Irish Studies, Queen's University of Belfast, and later the Ulster Museum, wrote a series of important articles on commemorations and the fate of veterans north and south, as referred to above. Research by Keith Jeffery, then at the University of Ulster, on war memorials throughout Ireland, led to articles and the publication in 2000 of his book, *Ireland and the Great War* (Cambridge). Among the literature on Irish participation in the Second World War was Richard Doherty's *Irish Men and Women in the Second World War* (Dublin), published in 1999. Since 2000 there have been many books recording Irish participation in both world wars, especially with the centenary of the First World War. In their newspaper columns, Kevin Myers in the *Irish Times* in the 1980s and 1990s, and Eoghan Harris in the *Sunday Times* in the 1990s, drew attention to commemorations and the Irish war dead and veterans. A special concern of Myers was the restoration of the Irish National War Memorial at Islandbridge.

In part also, these developments reflect concern for change among the public at large. At a personal level, people wanted to discover and to tell the story of their own families.[84] Others wanted to learn the history of these events that had been hidden from them in the past. Original war memorials in various localities were restored and new memorials erected. A number of key figures, such as Ian Adamson, Paddy Harte and Glenn Barr, headed initiatives to remember the war dead from Ireland, north and south. In 1992 the Royal Munster Fusiliers Association was formed with the aim of perpetuating 'the memory and traditions of the regiment'.[85] The foundation of the Royal Dublin Fusiliers Association in January 1997 led to an extensive series of public lectures and exhibitions, which received wide publicity.[86] Northern regimental museums continued to be an important focus for those in Northern Ireland interested in these war events and those involved. The publication in 2002 of the *Donegal Book of Honour*, listing all from the county who died in the First World War, was followed by many other similar books, often involving local history societies, recording the names of the war dead and covering counties and towns from all over Ireland. County and district councils, north and south, have financially supported publication of these volumes. Since 2014 there have been many events at local level to remember the fallen of the Great War. On 1 July 2016 at the Theatre in the Mill, Newtownabbey, a play, *Tom*, by Philip Johnston, recalled through his letters and diaries the short life of local man Tom McKinney, who died at the Somme.

As well, these developments arise from important political and cultural factors. In 1993 George Boyce pointed out that the conflict in Northern Ireland had consequences for how these events were remembered.[87] Reaction to the Enniskillen bomb caused many in the south to rethink the importance of remembering the Irish dead in two world wars. More broadly it highlighted the need for reconciliation. Commemoration of these events has provided a strong sense of shared history that has aided reconciliation. This need has continued to be important, especially as more recent history has remained very divisive. It can be seen as part of an effort in society, north and south, from the late 1980s to respect different traditions. It reflects also a new confidence in how people view their Irishness and Britishness, which have become more inclusive as a result. Since the early 1990s these changes have influenced not just individuals and communities, but also relations between communities, between north and south and between the UK and the Irish Republic. If members of the general public have seen value in the new enthusiasm for these commemorations, so also have their political leaders. Such commemorative events have become an important part of the peace process. It is now more than a hundred years from the end of the First World War and nearly seventy-five years from the end of the Second World War. In spite of the passage of time, commemoration of those from Ireland who served or who died in the world wars is today marked widely and inclusively once again.

PART 3

IDENTITIES

5

IRISH IDENTITY, PAST AND PRESENT

Over the past century, Irish identity has been subject to both change and contest. How Irishness and the Irish people are understood and whom they involve are matters that have been strongly affected by political, religious and cultural factors. The Irish nation has been variously interpreted in inclusive or exclusive terms. In the early years of the twentieth century, most people in Ireland, unionist and nationalist, shared a sense of Irishness. In the course of the century, however, this ceased very largely to be the case. In the two new states established in Ireland after 1920, identities became sharply polarised and exclusive, with important consequences for how Irish identity was viewed in both polities. Today, most people in the Republic of Ireland and most nationalists in Northern Ireland regard themselves as Irish. Most unionists in Northern Ireland, however, do not regard themselves as such and choose a British rather than an Irish identity. Recent decades, however, have seen the emergence of a new respect for diversity in both parts of Ireland and this has affected how people view their identity. Changes to Irish identity, influenced by contemporary political and cultural developments, have had an important influence on modern society and politics. This study will examine how Irish identity has evolved over the last century.

Identity in the Early 1900s

In the early 1900s most people in Ireland viewed themselves as Irish. This included unionists, of both north and south. They strongly supported the union between Great Britain and Ireland. They were Irish, loyal to the British Crown and citizens of the United Kingdom. Even in 1912, at the beginning of the crisis over the Third Home Rule Bill, we find still a sense of Irishness, associated with the British link, among Ulster unionists. At a meeting of women unionists in the Ulster Hall, Belfast, on 30 September 1912, the chairwoman's speech began with the words: 'We are here because we love our country. We love Ireland …'[1] Then she proceeded to state their firm commitment to the union between Great Britain and Ireland. Elements of an Ulster consciousness can be observed in these years, but this did not necessarily exclude an Irish dimension. In 1912 at Westminster T.P. O'Connor challenged Ronald McNeill, later Lord Cushendun, on this point: 'I observe the hon. gentleman called himself an Ulsterman. Does he mean by that he is an Ulsterman and not an Irishman?' McNeill replied: 'I used the expression "Ulsterman" as a more particular phrase. Of course I regard myself as being an Irishman.'[2] We can note a resolution passed by the governors of Campbell College, in east Belfast, in June 1915 in opposition to the headmaster's efforts to run the school on the lines of an English public school: 'Campbell College, founded by an Ulster merchant, is essentially an Irish institution and should primarily aim at satisfying Irish wants and ideals.'[3]

At the beginning of the twentieth century Irish nationalists wanted home rule for Ireland. In general, as Gearóid Ó Tuathaigh has pointed out, the leaders of the nationalist home rule movement were 'comfortable with an Irish identity which could find institutional expression in a parliamentary assembly in Dublin …' It was 'an identity which combined a strong sense of patriotism and pride in membership of an ancient historic nation with an easy acceptance of Ireland's place in the larger family of the British empire'.[4] Even Arthur Griffith, founder of Sinn Féin, did not originally advocate a republic but proposed a form of dual monarchy by which Ireland would have a separate government and share a monarch with Britain. In the late nineteenth and early twentieth centuries Ireland experienced the growth of a cultural movement of 'Irish Ireland', which involved language, sport and theatre, and which sought to develop a special Irish dimension in these areas. This led to the founding of organisations such as the Gaelic League and the Gaelic Athletic Organisation. Some unionists were influenced by this movement, but its main impact was to be found among the nationalist community. The emphasis on cultural matters 'radically altered the meaning of Irishness itself', and gave an added cultural element to Irish identity for many.[5] During these early years there were some, in particular members of the revolutionary Irish Republican Brotherhood, whose identity included a republican agenda, but they had no significant influence on broader society or politics in Ireland at this time.

Robert Lynd, a Belfast-born Presbyterian, was a fluent Irish speaker and a member of both the Gaelic League and Sinn Féin. In his book, *Home Life in Ireland*, published in 1909, he asked: 'What is an Irishman?' He replied:

> The truth is, there is a great deal of nonsense talked about 'the real Irishman and the typical Irishman' – to mention two phrases common among thoughtless people. The real Irishman is neither essentially a Celt nor essentially a Catholic. He is merely a man who has had the good or bad fortune to be born in Ireland or of Irish parents, and who is interested in Ireland more than any other country in the world. The Orange labourer of the north, whose ancestors may have come from Scotland, has all the attributes of an Irishman no less than the Catholic labourer of the west, whose ancestors may have come from Greece, or from Germany, or from Spain, or from whatever you care to speculate.[6]

D.P Moran, in his journal, the *Leader*, gave an alternative view. In 1901 he wrote:

> The only thinkable solution of the Irish national problem is that one side gets on top and absorbs the other until we have one nation, or that each develops independently. As we are for Ireland, we are in the existing circumstances on the side of Catholic development and we

see plainly that any genuine non-Catholic nationalist must become reconciled to Catholic development or throw in his lot with the other side.[7]

Organisations such as the Ancient Order of Hibernians emphasised links between Catholicism and Irish nationality. 'Faith and fatherland' was an important motto for many who believed that only Catholics could be truely Irish.[8]

Thanks to events in Ireland from 1912, in particular Ulster unionist resistance to home rule, 1912–14, and the Easter Rising in Dublin in 1916, differences grew over how people viewed their Irish identity. With the Ulster Covenant, northern unionists sought to maintain the existing constitutional position for the whole of Ireland, but this changed to a determination to retain just six of the nine counties of Ulster for the link with Great Britain. For many unionists Ulster became more important ideologically and institutionally than Ireland.[9] Events led to the Government of Ireland Act of 1920 and the establishment of Northern Ireland. During Easter week 1916 republicans staged a rising in Dublin. They proclaimed 'the Irish Republic as a sovereign independent state'.[10] The rising was viewed by the insurgents as an opportunity to affirm the Irish national spirit in this republican form. Following the suppression of the rising there was a significant shift in political identity among Irish nationalists from acceptance of home rule for Ireland to demands for a republican form of government, without links to Great Britain and the British Crown. Sinn Féin emerged as the dominant political party for nationalists in 1918. This was followed by the War of Independence between British Crown forces and the IRA, which ended in a truce in July 1921 and the Anglo-Irish Treaty of December 1921, leading to the establishment of the Irish Free State.

New States and New Dynamics

By the early 1920s a new political settlement had emerged in Ireland that was very different from the expectations of the pre-1914 period. Only six counties of Ulster, with a substantial Catholic minority, remained a part of the United Kingdom, now known as Northern Ireland, while just twenty-six counties, with a smaller Protestant minority, became the new Irish Free State, still with links to the United Kingdom. There is evidence of initial efforts to create inclusive societies and identities and to encourage north–south cooperation. In an address on 12 July 1923, Sir James Craig declared: 'It is our earnest desire to live in peace and amity with the Free State, and to encourage in every way a better understanding between all classes and creeds.'[11] Northern Ireland's first lord chief justice was the Catholic Sir Denis Henry. The Irish Free State constitution was a liberal, secular document. In 1922 more than twenty Protestants and former unionists were elected or appointed to the new senate. The Tripartite Agreement of 1925, between the British, Northern Ireland and Irish Free State governments, stated that they were 'united in amity … and resolved to aid one another in a spirit of neighbourly comradeship'.[12] In the end, however, such efforts proved unsuccessful, with the result that exclusive and confrontational identities emerged in both parts of Ireland, with consequences for how Irishness was defined.

Why did this happen? In part it was because of existing political, religious and cultural factors. More importantly, it was due to the dynamics associated with the establishment of new states. Rogers Brubaker has observed how the post-war settlement led to the founding of countries elsewhere in Europe, like Poland, Romania and Czechoslovakia, which also lacked homogeneity.[13] Conflict arose where the majority 'nationalising' state sought to develop the new country in its own image, while there was a minority whose national or religious interests were different. In the case of the two polities in Ireland what was important was not just the relationship between majorities and minorities within each state and between north and south, but also the ongoing relationship between the two states and Great Britain.

Such new states face other problems. As Basil Chubb observed, a heightened self-consciousness is often exhibited in their early years, especially when some national or security issue has not yet been resolved.[14] There is usually a desire to prove that they are different from before and also distinct from their neighbours. Brubaker has emphasised how the main groups often faced not only inter- but also intra-group contest. Post-1921 in the south the main nationalist movement, Sinn Féin, split over the national question, leading eventually to the formation of the two main modern Irish parties. In the north the unionist movement had to deal not only with nationalist opponents but also with independent unionist and labour divisions. Political leaders are often keen to find issues to distinguish them from their rivals. The necessity for a fledgling state to gain stability and legitimacy is paramount, as is the need to create a uniting sense of community.[15] These factors would impact heavily on the development of identities in both new states in Ireland. Any other possible settlement for Ireland, such as a thirty-two-county Irish state, or a smaller four-county Northern Ireland, would still have experienced these contemporary problems.

The Irish Free State and Éire

Thanks to the Anglo-Irish Treaty, the new Irish Free State enjoyed extensive self-government. At the same time the country remained part of the British Commonwealth. This fact caused not only bitter division and civil war that led to the emergence of new political parties, but also continued conflict over national identity and the connection with Britain. From the foundation of the Irish Free State, the tricolour was used as the official flag of the country, while in 1926 the 'Soldier's Song' was confirmed as the national anthem. Both had strong links to the 1916 Rising and were important to help define a national identity and also to respond to the government's opponents and to reinforce the state's legitimacy. As Ewan Morris has noted, the Cumann na nGaedheal government believed that these emblems would both 'make the state as distinct as possible from Britain' and also strengthen their own position against criticism that they had failed to achieve a republic.[16] At the same time, the government sent representatives to conferences of the British dominions and helped bring about the Statute of Westminster of 1931 that meant dominions no longer had to refer legislation back to Westminster. The rise to power of Éamon de Valera and Fianna Fáil in the early 1930s led to additional expressions of a separate identity. In 1931 de Valera declared: 'We are not a British dominion. We are a separate nation. Our rights are inherent.'[17] The oath of fidelity to the British

Crown was abolished. A new constitution in 1937 changed the name of the country to Ireland, or Éire, and carried no reference to the British Crown or the UK, but did not declare a republic.

For de Valera and the Irish government, neutrality in the Second World War related in considerable part to their Irish identity. Joseph Walshe, Secretary of the Department of Foreign Affairs, stated that neutrality 'is just as much a part of the national position as the desire to remain Irish and we can no more abandon it than we can renounce everything that constitutes our national distinctiveness'.[18] In 1949, Dáil Éireann passed the Republic of Ireland Bill, introduced by the Fine Gael-led inter-party government, in order to end, in Taoiseach J.A. Costello's words, 'this country's long and tragic association with the institution of the British crown'.[19] This declaration of a republic was backed by Fine Gael ministers partly due to internal pressure from other Cabinet members, particularly from Clann na Poblachta, led by Sean MacBride, a former IRA leader, and partly due to a desire to outmanoeuvre de Valera and Fianna Fáil.[20] At the time a British diplomat in Dublin observed: 'The fact is that the Fine Gael party had a sudden brainwave that they would steal the "Long Man's" [de Valera's] clothes.'[21]

Attitudes towards Northern Ireland changed considerably over these early decades. Initially, the new Irish government had been very hostile towards the northern state. In 1925, however, the Tripartite Agreement between the Irish Free State, the Northern Ireland and British governments confirmed the 1921 boundary and recognised the position of Northern Ireland.[22] In December 1925 William Cosgrave, the southern premier, declared that 'a new atmosphere of friendship and brotherhood had been created'.[23] The first Irish Free State government continued to express hope for an end to partition but stated its belief, in the words of Ernest Blythe in 1928, that 'the end of that can only come about by consent'.[24] De Valera took a more strident view on the north. Article 2 of the 1937 Irish constitution declared that 'the national territory consists of the whole island of Ireland, its islands and the territorial seas'. His ideas to bring about an end to partition ranged widely. He argued that increased prosperity in the south would attract the north to a united country. Another approach, which he spelt out at the 1939 Fianna Fáil Ard Fheis, was that 'the people who were opposed to unity and who did not want to be Irish, could be transferred out of Ireland if they preferred to be British rather than Irish'.[25] In 1946, David Gray, the US minister to Ireland, described de Valera's ideas for expelling unionists as 'about as practicable as expelling the New Englanders from Massachusetts'.[26] In 1948, Taoiseach J.A. Costello announced the intention to declare a republic and also stated that he considered himself prime minister of all Ireland, 'no matter what the Irish in the north say'.[27]

For the builders of the new state, these political dimensions were only part of the official Irish identity established in the early years. As Margaret O'Callaghan has noted: 'Language and religion were the most obvious indicators of separateness.'[28] The Irish language provided both 'a badge of identity' and an 'intact cultural ideal' for a society deeply divided by the Civil War.[29] The 1922 Irish Free State constitution declared that 'the national language of the Irish Free State … is the Irish language, but the English language shall be equally recognised as an official language'.[30] In the 1937 constitution Irish was recognised as the first official language, while English was recognised as a second official language. The Irish language was made a compulsory subject in all primary schools in 1922 and in all secondary schools two years later. Proficiency in the Irish language became an essential qualification in a wide range of state and local authority employments.

This leading role for the Irish language in the new Irish identity was initiated by the Cumann na nGaedheal government and continued by Fianna Fáil when in power. In 1934, the department of education directed that other subjects, in particular mathematics and English, should be allowed to decline to promote Irish. In February 1939, in response to a call to consider the impact of these policies on northern unionists, de Valera stated: 'I would not tomorrow, for the sake of a united Ireland, give up the policy of trying to make this a really Irish Ireland – not by any means – I believe that as long as the Irish language remains you have a distinguishing characteristic of nationality which will enable the nation to persist.'[31] In 1942, the government sought to make it a criminal offence for parents to send their children to schools where Irish was not taught, in the north or in England. A bill to this effect was passed by both houses of parliament but was referred by

President Hyde to the supreme court, which rejected it as unconstitutional on grounds that it interfered with the constitutional rights of parents in educational matters.

Religion also played an important part in this new identity. Support from the Catholic Church helped to provide legitimacy and stability to the new government. Although originally not especially deferential to the Catholic Church, the Cumann na nGaedheal government became increasingly so. Divorce was prohibited in 1923 and book censorship was introduced in 1929. De Valera and members of Fianna Fáil sought to rebuild relations with the Church that had been damaged during the Civil War, and to reassure Catholic clergy about the party's soundness on social and moral issues – all necessary for their political success. At the 1931 Fianna Fáil Ard Fheis, de Valera reminded people of his long-standing views: 'I declared that, if all came to all, I was a Catholic first.'[32] At a Dublin election meeting in February 1932 he stated: 'The majority of the people of Ireland are Catholic and we believe in Catholic principles. And as the majority are Catholics, it is right and natural that the principles to be applied by us will be principles consistent with Catholicity.'[33] The importation and sale of contraceptives was prohibited by the 1935 Criminal Law Amendment Act. In his 1935 St Patrick's Day speech, de Valera declared that Ireland had been a Christian and Catholic nation since St Patrick: 'She remains a Catholic nation.'[34] The 1937 constitution reflected the denominational nature of the new Irish identity. It declared the 'special position' of the Catholic Church (while recognising certain other faiths), prohibited the introduction of divorce and based some of its social principles on papal encyclicals.[35]

The early years of the southern state saw efforts to reconcile members of the Protestant and former unionist community to the new state. In Dáil Éireann in September 1922 Kevin O'Higgins declared: 'It comes well from us [the majority] to make a generous adjustment to show that these people were regarded, not as alien enemies, not as planters, but that we regard them as part and parcel of this nation, and that we wish them to take their share of its responsibilities.'[36] The first Irish Free State senate, formed in late 1922, included sixteen former southern unionists, nominated by W.T. Cosgrave, head of the government, and another seven Protestants who were elected.[37] Southern

Protestants continued to regard themselves as Irish. Nonetheless, they found that they were now often called 'Anglo-Irish'. Stephen Gwynn, a former Protestant nationalist MP for Galway, remarked in 1926: 'I was brought up to think myself Irish without question or qualification, but the new nationalism prefers to describe me and the like of me as Anglo-Irish.'[38] Lily Yeats, sister of W.B. Yeats, expressed her annoyance at this development: 'We are far more Irish than all the saints and martyrs – Parnell – Pearse – Maude Gonne – de Valera – and no one ever thinks of them as Anglo-Irish.'[39] In a lecture in 1933, Edmund Curtis, the Trinity College historian, rejected this term because it 'seemed to separate them in some way from the Irish nation', which implied that they were not wholly Irish.[40]

Some southern Protestants, such as Douglas Hyde, founder of the Gaelic League and later the first Irish president, were prepared to accept the new ethos. Cumann Gaelach na hEaglaise (the Guild of the Church), founded in 1914, continued to promote Irish in Church of Ireland services. Others, however, felt excluded. Speaking in 1939, Church of Ireland Archbishop John Gregg described how 'we are outside the close-knit spiritual entity which the majority constitutes'. Nonetheless, he insisted that 'our smaller community … is yet conscious of an identity of its own, an identity genuinely Irish'. He spoke of the danger of 'the wholesale adoption of the culture of the majority' and stated that it was 'not necessary to be Gaelic to be Irish'. He warned particularly of the danger of 'Gaelicisation', which 'added to other factors in our environment, would involve our absorption'.[41] For Gregg and other southern Protestants, concern about 'Gaelicisation' referred not just to compulsory Irish but also to much of the new culture that imposed a strong 'Gaelic' and nationalist narrative on Irish identity. An *Irish Times* editorial, 18 June 1934, expressed concern that those who declared pride in Irish involvement in British armed forces in the First World War were represented as 'West Britons' and 'anti-Irish', and complained: 'the heirs of their tradition are regarded as aliens in Ireland today.' The promise of an inclusive society as seen in the membership of the early senate did not survive. Protestant numbers in the senate fell to around ten in 1934 before its abolition in 1936. In the Dáil their numbers declined to twelve in 1932, seven in 1937 and three in 1948.[42] This reflected the marginalisation of the Protestant community in society and in relation to the dominant Irish identity.

Northern Ireland

What happened to matters of identity in Northern Ireland? While the southern state developed its sense of Irish identity in a largely exclusive way, so the northern state adopted a heightened sense of British identity embracing Ulster or Northern Ireland, which increasingly denied a sense of Irishness. From the beginning the unionist government had a majority in parliament, but it faced special challenges. There was concern that under the arrangements of 1920 Northern Ireland's constitutional position could be altered at any time by Westminster, as threatened in 1923 by the boundary commission and in 1940 by the offer of Irish unity in return for the south joining the Allied cause. The threat of disunity in unionist ranks over various social issues remained a worry.

Symbols were important. Ewan Morris has noted: 'In the face of an assertive, separatist Irish nationalism, it became more difficult to maintain that unionism and Irishness were compatible, so it is not surprising that the Northern Ireland government turned to Ulster and British rather than Irish national symbols for official emblems of the new state.' The government stressed 'those symbols which were honoured by all unionists; the Union Jack and the emblems of the monarchy'.[43] They served to both emphasise their Britishness and reinforce a sense of unity for unionists. On 12 July 1933 James Craig (ennobled as Craigavon in 1927) stated: 'British we are and British we remain.'[44] His speeches often stressed links with the British empire, especially Canada, Australia and New Zealand. In 1938 Craigavon declared: 'The British empire, and all it stands for, is the sun and air of our existence.'[45] With the outbreak of the Second World War he gave strong support to the Allied war effort with the words: 'We are king's men and will be with you always.'[46] As Tom Hennessey has observed, for unionists the role of Northern Ireland in the war 'reinforced their sense of Britishness'.[47] In 1948, thanks to the Northern Ireland war record and also in response to the declaration of an Irish Republic, the UK parliament passed the Ireland Act, which removed constitutional uncertainties from the 1920 settlement. The act declared that 'in no event will Northern Ireland or any part thereof cease to be part of the United Kingdom without the consent of the parliament of Northern Ireland'.[48]

At well as maintaining this British aspect of their identity, there developed what J.C. Beckett described in 1972 as a kind of 'Ulster patriotism'.[49] He described how it served to give 'the new state a kind of continuity with the past: it implied that it represented a recognised and well-established territorial division'. A sense of belonging to Ulster, rather than just the United Kingdom, grew as an important part of identity for many unionists. At the same time, the government took care to moderate this sentiment, in case it undermined the British connection.[50] The added emphasis on an Ulster identity helped to highlight differences with the south and to diminish an Irish identity among unionists. The Irish language continued as an optional subject in Catholic schools. In 1933, however, a campaign against the Irish language by some unionist and independent MPs led to the ending of grants for the teaching of Irish as an extra subject in secondary schools. In the early 1940s, Prime Minister J.M. Andrews pressed J.H. Robb, minister of education, to prohibit the Irish language in all schools. Robb refused, on grounds that he explained to Andrews: 'the choice is for them, and is part of that freedom of the individual for which we profess to be fighting this war.'[51] In 1934, after complaints from various quarters, including Lord Craigavon, the BBC stopped broadcasting Gaelic football results in Northern Ireland; it recommenced in 1946, but initially the results of matches played on Sunday were broadcast on Monday.

This British/Ulster identity was directed primarily at members of the Protestant and unionist majority. In the early years of the new state, however, there is evidence that Sir James Craig and his government made some effort to avoid being identified with only the Protestant section of the population, especially the Orange movement. In 1922 in the Northern Ireland parliament, Craig rejected a call to have 12 July made a general holiday.[52] Subsequently this was agreed but between 1923 and 1927 he did not attend twelfth demonstrations.[53] On 12 July 1927, an editorial in the *Irish News* noted: 'a greater toleration is spreading … a better understanding is helping to remove the ancient antagonisms and assuage the bitterness of years of conflict and controversy.' It continued: 'the great dividing lines are fading away, and Orangemen and nationalists are being brought to recognise their common bond as Irishmen.'

That same day, however, for the first time in five years, Craig attended a 12th of July Orange demonstration in Belfast. On this occasion his speech was not concerned with the south or northern nationalists, about whom he made friendly remarks, but with the threat to unionism from independents and splits within unionist ranks, and with the need for unionist unity.[54] At the 1925 general election the unionist party had lost seven seats to Labour and independents. In 1927 the main threat related to the temperance issue (a special problem for Craig given his family distillery background).[55] In his speech Craig justified the government's plan to abolish proportional representation in Northern Ireland parliamentary elections. This move was not designed as an attack on nationalists (who won an extra seat in 1929 after abolition of PR, although republicans lost their two seats), but, as he explained, to curtail unionist splinter groups, independents and Labour. Both unionists and nationalists were well aware that the unionists had to lose only another seven seats to forfeit their parliamentary majority. From this time onwards Craig and his Cabinet members developed strong public links with the Orange Order. At the 1929 general election the unionist party regained five seats.

By 1930 Lord Craigavon made a point of attending the 12th of July proceedings in a different county of Northern Ireland. This Orange connection served to help unite unionism in face of other internal divisions over social and economic issues, especially in the 1930s with rising unemployment, and also the new threat from de Valera's government. An editorial in the *Belfast Telegraph*, 12 July 1932, observed: 'Divided as they are into different churches, it is necessary that protestants should have … a bond of union which will enable them to face assaults from any and every quarter. Such a bond is provided by the Orange Institution.' Speeches by leading unionist politicians at these Orange demonstrations now became more strident than they had been in the 1920s. On 12 July 1932 at Drumbanagher, Co. Armagh, Craigavon declared:

'Ours is a Protestant government and I am an Orangeman.'[56] In parliament in April 1934, he stated that he was very proud to be 'grand master of the loyal county of Down ... I prize that more than I do being prime minister'.[57]

In the years after the 1925 Tripartite Agreement, the unionist government remained well disposed to the south. On 22 January 1928, at a meeting of the Ulster Unionist Council, Craigavon declared that he was glad to say that 'the friendly relations existing between the Free State and ourselves had been growing every day'.[58] With the election of de Valera and the Fianna Fáil government in 1932, however, this positive attitude changed. Events in the south were closely followed in the north and politicians were reactive to events there. In the Northern Ireland parliament in April 1934 Craigavon made his often-quoted statement about a 'Protestant parliament and a Protestant state'. His fuller comment read: 'In the south they boasted of a Catholic state. They still boast of Southern Ireland being a Catholic state. All I boast of is that we are a Protestant parliament and a Protestant state.'[59]

In 1937, following the acceptance of the new Irish constitution with its claim to all Ireland, Sir Anthony Babington, Northern Ireland attorney general, declared that this constitutional claim could only be meant as 'a warning and a menace to them'.[60] He also suggested that the name of the state should be changed to Ulster. Craigavon declined to criticise the constitution over its religious aspects, in particular the 'special position' of the Catholic Church: 'while the government of the south is carried on along lines which I presume are very suitable to the majority of Roman Catholics in that part. Surely ... the government of the north, with a majority of Protestants, should carry on the administration according to Protestant ideas and Protestant desires.'[61] At the 1949 general election, Costello's decision to declare a republic and a vocal southern anti-partition campaign caused a northern reaction that helped the unionist party to achieve a major electoral victory against Labour opponents. Sir Basil Brooke, the new prime minister, declared: 'We have now on our southern border a foreign nation. Today we fight to defend our very existence and the heritage of our children.'[62] Writing in 1948 about relations between north and south, Hugh Shearman observed:

'Reaction in Éire will produce and seem to justify a counterbalancing reaction in Northern Ireland.'[63]

Initially the northern nationalist leaders rejected the institutions of the northern state, although later there was a possibility for a time that they might reach an accommodation with the new arrangements.[64] Nationalists boycotted the early days of the Northern Ireland parliament but they started to take their seats from 1925. At a meeting of the Belfast Rotary Club in early January 1926, nationalist Joseph Devlin explained how he felt it his duty 'once this northern parliament had been established, and the reasons why they should remain outside it had disappeared, to recognise that parliament is a sacroscant [sic] institution of democracy'. J.M. Andrews, unionist minister of labour, responded to say that 'they were united in the desire that the better spirit which had been growing in Northern Ireland should continue to grow and to be fostered in their midst'.[65] Devlin followed up this positive approach in a speech on St Patrick's Day, 1926: 'The dominant duty of every Irishman is to look forward, not to keep gazing back on the past … not to sulk over misfortunes that are no longer avoidable.'[66]

The new Ulster identity might have involved nationalists. In parliament on 9 March 1926, Devlin declared: 'We are all Ulstermen and proud to be Ulstermen. We want to further the welfare of our province. We are all Irishmen and want to see North and South working harmoniously together.'[67] Three years later, however, he objected that 'there is an ever-growing tendency here in the north of Ireland to draw us away … from our national attachments; to tell us that we are not Irishmen but Ulstermen, that we belong to something that is apart from Ireland'.[68] Nationalists were strongly opposed to abolition of proportional representation in 1929, which did not reduce their number of MPs but served to remove the possibility of effective Labour or independent MP allies (in the 1932 southern general election Fianna Fáil won only seventy-two out of 153 seats but gained power thanks to support from labour and others). Devlin and his colleagues now felt increasingly frustrated with their minority situation, with little influence in political affairs. By the early 1930s, in the face of this impotency and the growing dominance of the Ulster/British identity, most nationalist MPs withdrew from parliament. From 1934 until 1945 only two Belfast MPs attended on a regular basis.[69] Difficulties for nationalist politicians were compounded by rivalry with republicans.

Northern Catholics retained a keen sense of their Irish identity. In spite of its exclusion from the dominant ethos and political power, the northern Catholic community was large enough to be able to keep its own group solidarity around a strong nationalist and Catholic consciousness, unlike the southern Protestant minority whose numbers were smaller and whose unionism was now redundant. Organisations such as the Gaelic Athletic Association and the Ancient Order of Hibernians, and the Catholic school system, were important in maintaining an all-Ireland national identity. When the Catholic Truth Society conference met in Belfast in 1934, an editorial of the *Irish News* declared:

> North and south are forever tied by the unbreakable bonds of their common faith, which is their proudest heritage. The ceremonies which will take place in Belfast tomorrow, the first day of the Catholic Truth Society conference, will have a northern setting, and the majority of the vast multitude worshipping in Beechmount will be northern Catholics. But the glory will belong to the Catholic Irish nation … We leave it to the Catholics of Ulster to uphold their proud tradition … Because they are children of the Catholic nation which knows of division of soil but not of soul, they will, we are sure, demonstrate unswerving loyalty to the faith to which the mass rock gives testimony in the dark yesterdays of our history.[70]

Hopes that the arrival of de Valera and a Fianna Fáil government would somehow change their situation proved ill-founded. De Valera failed to honour an earlier pledge to allow northern representatives to sit in the Dáil. The Irish Nationality and Citizenship Act of 1935 placed restrictions on the eligibility of northerners to claim Irish citizenship.[71]

The movement in the northern Protestant community away from an Irish identity did not take place overnight and did not include all Protestants. J.M. Barkley recalled the events that followed his ordination as a Presbyterian minister in 1935:

Then came the reception in the High Street Café, Ballymoney, the meal being followed by the usual hearty toasts and speeches. The first toast, 'Prosperity to Ireland', was replied to by Mr W.V. McCleery MP, later minister of labour and afterwards of commerce. This toast, normally responded to by a prominent layman in the local community, remained the custom until about 1937. Following Éire's adoption of a new constitution, some began to use it for party political purposes, and when Éire became neutral in 1939, the custom fell into desuetude.[72]

In 1925, in protest at a decision to set up a separate medical register for the south, the Belfast unionist paper *Northern Whig* declared:

When Ulster declined to join the south in separating from Great Britain it did not surrender its title as part of Ireland, nor renounce its share in those Irish traditions in art, in learning, in arms, in song, in sport and in science that were worth preserving in a united form.[73]

In some areas, for many unionists a sense of Irish identity survived and there were those who still regarded themselves as Irish. The churches, various sporting organisations and some cultural bodies maintained their all-Ireland character. Northerners continued to attend Trinity College Dublin, which, given the Catholic bishops' ban on Catholics attending the college and the decline in the number of southern Protestants, probably helped its survival. *Irish Historical Studies*, established in 1938 to publish material embodying original research in Irish history, was run as a joint journal of the Irish Historical Society, based in Dublin, and the Ulster Historical Society, based in Belfast. A number of Irish national sports teams drew members from both sides of the border. In late 1938 the Irish Association for cultural, economic and social relations was founded, with influential public figures from north and south, to 'make reason and good-will take the place of passion and prejudice in determining the character of the relationship between north and south, no less than between each part of Ireland and Great Britain'.[74]

Sometimes unionist politicians still acknowledged an Irish dimension. On 5 March 1929, in a parliamentary debate, Lord Craigavon declared: 'We are Irishmen ... I always hold that Ulstermen are Irishmen and the best of

Irishmen – much the best.'[75] When he died, his successor as prime minister, J.M. Andrews, lauded him as 'a great Ulsterman, a great Irishman, a great imperialist'.[76] In 1949, at an Orange demonstration, in one of his first public speeches, Brian Faulkner, unionist MP, objected to the way in which the south had now adopted the title of Republic of Ireland: 'They have no right to the title Ireland, a name of which we are just as proud as they.'[77]

Nonetheless, it was clear that developments since 1921 had caused significant change in how Irish identity was perceived, north and south, by politicians and the public at large. In a radio interview in April 1949, Jack Sayers, editor of the *Belfast Telegraph*, surveyed identities in the two parts of Ireland, over the previous three decades. He observed: 'What has happened is that some differences have been accentuated, but others have sprung up that can hardly have been thought of when partition was first put forward as a remedy. And taking them all in all, I fear that by now they amount to a formidable total.'[78] In the new southern state, Irish identity had assumed certain prescriptive political, religious and political features that influenced many northern unionists to reconsider their Irishness. As Victor Griffin, a member of the Irish Association and a dean of St Patrick's Cathedral, Dublin, recalled, they reacted to these changes by saying: 'If that's what you mean by being Irish, then count us out. We are not Irish.'[79] At the same time, unionists were often keen to assert their British identity, at the expense of any sense of Irishness.

Republic of Ireland and Northern Ireland in the 1950s and 1960s

During the next two decades Irish identity in the Irish Republic retained a strong confessional dimension as well as a confrontational approach to northern unionists. Down to the 1970s there was strong identification of Irish nationality with Catholicism.[80] Des O'Malley, who became a TD in 1968, recalled how until the early 1960s southern nationalism was 'essentially an aggressive and negative nationalism. It was almost as if the terms "Irish" and "anti-British" were interchangeable … there was virtually no acceptance that the northern majority had any right to determine their own constitutional position.'[81] In the 1950s a number of voices challenged the prevailing nationalist narrative. Hubert Butler criticised how the Irish nation and society had departed from the non-sectarian goals of Wolfe Tone and challenged his Protestant fellow countrymen to speak out more to challenge the prevailing ethos, while Donal Barrington urged radical reforms in the southern state.[82] These voices had little influence at the time, certainly not on Éamon de Valera. In 1962, when Irish president, in an interview with the *New York Times*, he stated that if 'in the north there are people who spiritually want to be English [sic] rather than Irish, they can go and we will see that they get the adequate, right compensation for their property'.[83]

Nonetheless, the election of Sean Lemass as taoiseach in 1959 saw the beginning of efforts to modify southern Irish identity. Most book censorship was ended in the 1960s. Lemass also took a less confrontational position on Northern Ireland and encouraged north–south cooperation. In December 1967, a Dáil Éireann all-party committee, established by Lemass and on which he served after his retirement as taoiseach, produced a report that recommended changes to the constitution, with implications for Irish identity.[84] Unanimously, it was proposed that article 3 be replaced with a conciliatory statement that 'the Irish nation hereby proclaims its firm will that its territory be re-united in harmony and brotherly affection between all Irishmen'. It also proposed changes to the articles that prohibited divorce and recognised the 'special position' of the Catholic Church. This report, however, was not well received by the Cabinet, one of whose members, Kevin Boland, described it as a 'departure from republican principles'.[85] Due to an unwillingness to risk political divisions by challenging key assumptions of Irish identity, the government shelved this radical report except for the proposal for changes to the electoral system, which subsequently the electorate rejected.

British and Ulster identities remained dominant among Protestants and unionists in Northern Ireland during these decades, although significant numbers continued to value their Irishness. Obviously, Catholics and nationalists placed great emphasis on their Irish identity. Less obviously, there were unionists who still acknowledged their Irish identity. In 1959 it was suggested to the Northern Ireland Cabinet that the name of Ireland in the state should be dropped, but the idea was rejected due to objections raised by Brian Faulkner. He stated that he was not prepared to concede to the south a monopoly of the term 'Irish': he saw nothing incompatible with being Northern Irish and British.[86] In 1971 Faulkner wrote that, in the same way as Scots can be Scottish and British, 'the Northern Ireland citizen is Irish and British; it is a question of complement, not of conflict'.[87] Lord Brookeborough, Northern Ireland prime minister, 1943–63, took a different approach in an interview in October 1968, when he described himself as 'a Britisher and an Ulsterman'. He said: 'I'm not happy being called an Irishman because of the 1916 rebellion.'[88]

In 1968, just before the outbreak of the 'Troubles', Richard Rose conducted a survey in Northern Ireland about national identity.[89] Of the Protestants polled, 39 per cent saw themselves as British and 32 per cent as Ulster, but also 20 per cent viewed themselves as Irish, 6 per cent as sometimes British and sometimes Irish, and 2 per cent as Anglo-Irish. We can assume that most of these who defined their identity as Irish were unionists. He quoted the unionist MP and Stormont minister Robert Simpson, who described in 1970 his nationality as follows: 'Certainly we are Irish. When your forefathers have lived in Ireland for hundreds of years this is obvious. But we are also British. We are United Kingdom citizens paying United Kingdom taxes and electing representatives to the United Kingdom parliament.'[90] The Rose survey revealed that among Catholics, 76 per cent saw themselves as Irish, but also that 15 per cent viewed themselves as British, 5 per cent Ulster, 3 per cent sometimes British and sometimes Irish and 1 per cent Anglo-Irish.

The 'Troubles' and Identity Changes

Subsequent decades, due to the impact of the 'Troubles', saw important changes in national identities in both parts of Ireland. Ten years after the Rose study, Edward Moxon-Browne conducted another survey in Northern Ireland.[91] In 1968, some 20 per cent of Protestants had identified as Irish, but ten years later, he observed, 'after having borne the brunt of the IRA campaign, Protestants have swung more definitely towards adopting the label "British"'. He found that only 8 per cent still favoured an Irish identity. Those choosing an Ulster identity had also fallen to 20 per cent, while 67 per cent declared a British identity. Later surveys confirmed these trends.[92] By 1989, just 3 per cent identified as Irish, compared with 14 per cent for Ulster and 68 per cent for British. Among Catholics, the first decade saw limited change in identities. By 1989, however, having lost faith in 'the possibility of reform within existing institutions', those choosing a British identity had fallen to 8 per cent and an Ulster identity to 2 per cent, while support for an Irish identity stood at 60 per cent.[93] At the same time, these 1989 figures revealed significant support for a new identity in both communities, that of Northern Irish. The term was first offered in a survey of 1986. Identities of Anglo-Irish and sometimes Irish and sometimes British were dropped as choices. The 1989 survey recorded that 16 per cent of Protestants and 25 per cent of Catholics opted for a Northern Irish identity.

The 'Troubles' also impacted on identity in the south. Some responded in a traditional nationalist way, but others challenged aspects of contemporary national identity. In 1972, Conor Cruise O'Brien in his book, *States of Ireland*, 'tried to understand some of the feelings share by most Ulster Protestants and to communicate some notion of these feelings in the republic'.[94] That same year, Garrett Fitzgerald in his book, *Towards a New Ireland*, outlined those changes that he believed would 'have to be made in order to achieve a society which is acceptable to all Irishmen'.[95] During these decades, however, any such changes were minor. In 1970 the Catholic bishops withdrew their prohibition on Catholics attending Trinity College, while in 1971 the GAA removed its ban on 'foreign games'. Mention of the 'special position' of the Catholic Church in article 44 of the Irish constitution was removed in 1972. In the 1970s a pass in Irish was made no longer essential for the leaving certificate at schools and Irish was dropped as a mandatory requirement for the civil service. However, an attempt in 1974 to repeal the legal ban on the sale of contraceptives was unsuccessful, although in 1979 a compromise Health (Family Planning) Act was passed. A referendum in 1987 to change the country's divorce laws was unsuccessful. Writer Roddy Doyle has recalled about Ireland in the 1980s: 'It was the insistence that if you're Irish, you're white and you're Catholic as well, and if you're not both of these things then you're not fully Irish.'

Accession to the European Economic Community in January 1972 added a European dimension to Irish identity. In 1983 Fitzgerald and the Irish government established the New Ireland Forum to deliberate on the shape of a new Ireland. Significantly, in a new language for Irish nationalists, its report, published in 1984, talked of different traditions and identities and promised to recognise the 'unionist identity and ethos'.[96] In spite of such pluralist aims, however, as George Boyce has commented, 'its conclusions were entirely traditional'.[97] The root of the problem was identified as the 1920 arrangements that established partition. The report's main proposal was a thirty-two-county unitary state, while joint authority and a federal system were also presented as possible options, all of which unionists rejected outright as unacceptable to their British identity.[98] Suggestions to amend articles 2 and 3 of the Irish constitution, with their territorial claim over Northern Ireland, were rejected, especially by members of Fianna Fáil, and the first debate on the matter in the Dáil, instigated by a member of the Workers' Party, occurred only in 1991.

A New Diversity of Identities

The late 1980s and 1990s saw new efforts to appreciate diversity of identities in Ireland. In Northern Ireland, the Cultural Traditions Group ran conferences from 1989 looking at 'varieties' of Britishness and Irishness. Irish history and language now had a greater role than before, both in the schools and society at large. In 1989, the Ultach Trust was established to promote the Irish language, involving a strong cross-community outreach element. Some prominent unionists, including unionist councillor Chris McGimpsey and author Sam McAughtrey, called for a revised sense of Irishness. In 1994, McAughtrey wrote:

> I embrace my Irishness and am glad of it. I am a citizen of the United Kingdom and I want it to stay that way ... We, all of us in Northern Ireland, together with the people of the Irish Republic, are part of the Irish nation ... Unionists, in proclaiming their Irishness, should also proclaim that the nation and the state need not necessarily be enclosed within the same boundaries.[99]

That same year saw the first production of Marie Jones's one-person play, *A Night in November,* in which the Belfast character deals with issues of national identity during the soccer world cup games and concludes: 'I am a free man, I am a Protestant man, I am an Irish man.'[100]

In 1995 the leader of the Ulster Unionist Party, David Trimble, recorded his support for a pluralist British identity that involved an Irish dimension: 'The United Kingdom is a genuinely pluralist state in which it is possible to be Welsh or Scottish and British. Similarly one can be Irish or Ulster and British as well.'[101] Others found value in a Northern Irish identity. In early 1995 the novelist Glenn Patterson stated: 'I have no sense of myself as a Protestant. I do though have some sense of Northern Irishness of which I am proud – Northern Irishness free of political and constitutional absolutes – Northern Irishness in the way that I had of Northern Englishness when I lived in Manchester.'

This decade witnessed efforts to promote pluralism in southern society. There was increased questioning of links between Church and State. A referendum in 1995 permitted the removal of the ban on divorce in the Irish constitution. A number of scandals and court cases involving some members of the Catholic clergy and church-run institutions served to undermine clericalism in Irish society and also the relationship between Catholicism and Irish national identity. The election of Mary Robinson as president in 1990 was significant. She promised to 'encourage mutual understanding and tolerance between all the different communities sharing this island'.[102] Her election reflected the rise of an effective women's movement that challenged male dominance, not just in the workplace but also in politics and the prevailing national identity. A new recognition of the role of Irish soldiers in both world wars helped to create a more inclusive Irish identity. The Forum for Peace and Reconciliation was established in Dublin in 1995 to examine 'the steps required to remove barriers of distrust on the basis of promoting respect for the equal rights and validity of both traditions and identities'.[103] That same year President Robinson delivered an important speech to the two houses of the *Oireachtas* in Dublin, primarily on the Irish diaspora but also on Irishness. She declared: 'Irishness as a concept seems to me at its strongest when it reaches out to everyone on this island and shows itself capable of honouring and listening to those whose sense of identity, and whose cultural values, may be more British than Irish.'[104]

The Belfast/Good Friday Agreement established new agreed constitutional and institutional arrangements for Northern Ireland.[105] The principle of consent was firmly established, along with the right of self-determination. The agreement guaranteed the status of Northern Ireland as part of the United Kingdom, as reflecting the wishes of the majority, but accepted the right of a majority to change this status in the future. It also sought to acknowledge and respect different national aspirations and traditions. The agreement recognised the 'birthright of all the people of Northern Ireland to identify themselves and be accepted as Irish or British, or both, as they may so choose'. The right to identify as both Irish and British was an acknowledgement that there were those whose national identity did not fall into straightforward Irish and British opposites.

As part of the new arrangements, articles 2 and 3 in the Irish constitution with their claim over the six counties of Northern Ireland were changed. A new article 2 declared 'the entitlement and birthright of every person, born in the island of Ireland ... to be part of the Irish nation' and to be citizens of Ireland. It said that 'the Irish nation cherishes its special affinity with people of Irish ancestry living abroad'. Speaking in 2017, Maurice Hayes argued that the agreement 'had the "emancipatory merit" of unhitching the nation from the state, allowing national identities to flow across political boundaries, which become less significant'.[106] A new article 3 declared the 'firm will of the Irish nation, in harmony and friendship, to unite all the people who share the territory of Ireland, in all the diversity of their identities and traditions'. It recognised that a united Ireland 'shall be brought about only by peaceful means of a majority of the people, democratically elected, in both parts of Ireland'.

Changes Following the 1998 Agreement

Post the 1998 Agreement there have been ongoing changes in Irish identity in both parts of Ireland. Some sports and cultural bodies changed their rules. In 2001 the GAA abolished its ban on members of the British army and the Northern Ireland police playing Gaelic games. In 2008 the Gaelic League removed from its constitution support for 'a free and independent Ireland', an aim introduced in 1915 that had led to the resignation of its president, Douglas Hyde.[107] In 1998, President Mary McAleese hosted the first of a series of official receptions in July for southern Protestants, especially members of the Orange community in the border counties. On 27 November 2008, she visited Brakey Orange Hall, Bailieborough, Co. Cavan, the first such visit by an Irish president. She urged a new sense of inclusion, following the success of the Good Friday Agreement. 'It is possible,' she declared, 'to be both Irish and British, possible to be Orange and Irish.'[108]

In June 2011, President McAleese visited Rome, where she gave a very different view of the Irish people than that expressed in Rome by Éamon de Valera on a number of occasions.[109] She said that despite 'past political and religious conflicts' modern Ireland has emerged as 'a country, a family, which is at once Catholic, Protestant, agnostic, atheist, Islamic, Jewish'.[110] On 20 July that same year, in Dáil Éireann, following the issuing of a report on child abuse and its handling in the Cloyne diocese, Taoiseach Enda Kenny denounced clericalism and the role of the Vatican in the matter, which led to the closure of the Irish embassy in the Vatican for the next three years.[111] The visit of Queen Elizabeth II to the Irish Republic in 2011, the first of a British sovereign since the founding of the state, marked an important change in British–Irish relations.

Contemporary Irish identity in the Irish Republic was investigated by Fintan O'Toole in a series of articles in the *Irish Times* in August 2017.[112] He described not just a more pluralist sense of identity but also multiple identities. Twenty years ago Irish society was relatively homogeneous but at present some 17 per cent of those living in the state were born abroad, and many of these have retained their original identities alongside their Irishness. Thanks also to the changes of 1998, there is an awareness that the nation involves 'diversity of identities'. Catholicism and Gaelicisation are no longer primary features of Irishness. The Irish language, however, remains 'a crucial touchstone of Irish identity', and of importance for many, although the 2016 census revealed that only 73,803 spoke Irish daily outside the education system.[113] A European dimension is also widely valued – a point stressed in a speech at Queen's University Belfast in August 2017 by Taoiseach Leo Varadker: 'I passionately believe that being European is an essential part of the modern Irish identity, an enhancement not a dilution of who we are.'[114] At a popular level, Irish dance, music and Gaelic games are features of modern Irish identity.

Besides the new developments in Irish identity pointed out by O'Toole, we can observe other earlier elements that have continued, although in revised form. During 2016, the Irish state celebrated the hundredth anniversary of the 1916 Rising as the key founding moment of the Irish state, but important inclusive elements were brought into proceedings. For many, a united Ireland remains important but not in the irredentist sense of former years. In 2008, Taoiseach Bertie Ahern expressed hope for a united Ireland based on consent and people working together: 'If it doesn't prove possible, then it stays the way it is under the Good Friday Agreement, and people will just have to be tolerant of that if it's not possible to bring it any further.' In a press interview in January 2018, Taoiseach Leo Varadker declared: 'Our constitution aspires to there being a united Ireland. I share that aspiration. But only on the basis that it is done by consent, and when it does come about I would like it to command a degree of cross-community support.'[115] He talked of the need for an 'agreed Ireland'.

In Northern Ireland there have also been also important developments in Irish identity. Nationalists continue to value their Irish identity, which they see as enhanced by the 1998 Agreement. Many of the changes in Irish identity experienced by southern nationalists in this period have been shared by northern nationalists. Among unionists, British identity has remained a priority, but a sense of Irish identity has been seen sometimes. At his meeting with Taoiseach Bertie Ahern in Dublin in April 2007, DUP leader Ian Paisley remarked: 'I am proud to be an Ulsterman, but I am also proud of my Irish roots,' while on 30 May 2008, on UTV, he referred to himself as an 'Irish unionist'.[116] Nonetheless, surveys in the last two decades have shown only a small increase in the number of Protestants who identify as Irish. In part this may be because Irishness and Britishness are still viewed by many as diametrically opposed, and in part because some surveys do not allow for a joint Irish and British identity. The Irish state, although it comprises only twenty-six counties of the island of Ireland, is often referred to as Ireland by the Irish government and others, and this alienates northern unionists from wanting to associate with Ireland and Irish identity.

For the first time, in 2011 the UK census recorded national identity. It found that of the resident population of Northern Ireland, 40 per cent described their national identity as British only, 25 per cent as Irish only, 21 per cent as Northern Irish only, 6 per cent as British and Northern Irish only, and 8 per cent as other identities, including a combination of the above.[117] It also revealed that 94 per cent of people with an Irish-only national identity were or had been brought up as Catholics, while 81 per cent of those with a British-only national identity were or had been brought up as Protestants. Of those who identified as Irish only 4 per cent were Protestant, while of those who identified as British only 12 per cent were Catholic. Ulster is no longer a popular identity but many value an Ulster Scots dimension.

The Northern Irish identity deserves further comment. Edward Moxon-Browne has written: 'As a badge of identity, it is clearly less divisive than many others. Its attractiveness rests on an inherent ambiguity.'[118] For many Protestants the term Northern Irish probably derives from the name Northern Ireland, part of the UK, and includes some of those who earlier called themselves Irish. For many Catholics the term Northern Irish is probably a northern variant of Irish, part of Ireland. At the same time, as John Garry and Kevin McNicholl have recently observed: 'Northern Irishness does appear to be a real common in-group identity, inclusive of both Protestants and Catholics.'[119] It can be seen as a form of Irish identity. Among those in 2011 with a Northern Irish identity only, 58 per cent were from a Catholic background while 36 per cent were from a Protestant background. Of those who identified as British and Northern Irish only 87 per cent were protestant and 13 per cent Catholic.[120] It is very likely that the number of those who value this Northern Irish identity will grow in future.

The impact of devolution in the UK has led to a new appreciation that the UK is a multi-national state. In the 2011 British census for England and Wales, just 19.1 per cent associated themselves with a British identity only, with most others opting for English or Welsh identities.[121] The census reported an increase in 'national consciousness' and noted that national identity in the UK is now 'multi-dimensional'. Of course, people remain British citizens, that is citizens of the United Kingdom of Great Britain and Northern Ireland. At the October 2017 Conservative party conference, Prime Minister Theresa May talked of the 'British people' and referred to 'our precious union of nations – four nations that are stronger as one'.[122] These four nations refer to England, Wales, Scotland and Northern Ireland, that part of the Irish nation which remains in union with Great Britain. This development is likely to lead to more of those who opt for a British identity in Northern Ireland to choose to combine it with an Irish or Northern Irish identity. In the future, the movement towards enhanced national identities in Great Britain may make it possible for more unionists to acknowledge their Irishness and their place in the Irish nation, without feeling they are losing their Britishness or their unionism.

Over the last 100 years what it has meant to be Irish has changed considerably. In the early 1900s most people in Ireland shared a sense of Irishness, although underlying political, religious and cultural divisions meant that there were differences in how Irish identity was perceived. Important changes happened after 1921, due in large part to the dynamics affecting the establishment and running of the two new states in Ireland. Additional political, religious and cultural matters shaped Irish identity. The 'Troubles' introduced extra dynamics into how Irish identity was understood and expressed. Events of 1998 with the Belfast/Good Friday Agreement and changes to the Irish constitution represented an important effort to acknowledge a pluralist approach to identities in Ireland. Recent developments in the Irish Republic, Northern Ireland and Great Britain have introduced new and diverse ways in how people can acknowledge their Irishness. Brexit may lead to other changes. Clearly, the debate on Irish identity will continue.

'THE LOST TRIBES OF IRELAND': DIVERSITY, IDENTITY AND LOSS AMONG THE IRISH DIASPORA

St Patrick's Day, when Irish people celebrate their national saint, is one of the most widely marked national annual anniversaries in the world. This is not surprising when we consider that, although Ireland today has a population of around 6 million, it is reckoned that there are 70 million people around the globe who can claim Irish ancestry: in the USA, 40 million Americans are estimated to have Irish origins. As an indication of the significance of the international Irish dimension we may note that both former President Bill Clinton and former Prime Minister Tony Blair have important Irish roots. Although the story of Irish emigration is often associated primarily with the time of the Great Famine in the 1840s, in fact emigration has been a major factor of Irish life from the eighteenth to the twentieth centuries. It is reckoned that during the eighteenth century some 250,000 people went to the American colonies from Ulster. After Irish independence in 1921 emigration continued: between 1926 and 1966 nearly 900,000 people left the new state, chiefly for Britain.[1] This essay will examine the Irish diaspora by looking at the main recipient countries for this emigration. It will be concerned with exploring the diversity and identity of this group, looking in particular at significant absences in both the academic and public perceptions of the Irish diaspora.

My approach to the subject will be informed by comments from two important sources. The first comes from the leading historian of the Irish diaspora, Donald Akenson, who in his classic pioneering study of 1993 insisted that when we consider the Irish abroad what we mean is all those born in Ireland or their descendants, whatever their religion or politics.[2] The second comes from a notable address by President Mary Robinson, 'Cherishing the Irish diaspora', which she delivered to a special joint sitting of the two Irish houses of parliament in 1995. She stressed not only the spread of Irish people in the world but also the diversity of the country of Ireland that provided this flow of people. She reminded her listeners of the varied groups, including not only Celts but also English and Scottish settlers and others, which had inhabited Ireland over the centuries. She warned that 'if we expect that the mirror held up to us by Irish communities abroad will show a single familiar identity, or a pure strain of Irishness, we will be disappointed. We will overlook the fascinating diversity of culture and choice which looks back at us.'[3]

Such an approach may seem obvious. In practice, however, much of the material written on the Irish diaspora has not accepted this line of enquiry. It is fair to say that there has been wide acceptance of a single, unitary Irish diaspora and identity abroad that has encompassed primarily the Catholic and nationalist sections of the Irish overseas. In part this is because Irish identity has been expressed most conspicuously by some members of these groups and because today the population of the island of Ireland is around 80 per cent Catholic. In part also it is because public and academic appreciation of the Irish diaspora has not taken the broad approach advocated above. In recent years, however, there has been a growing awareness of the diversity of the Irish overseas and their different experiences, including the very sizeable number of Protestants and non-nationalists who make up this diaspora.[4] This study will examine the new academic and public understanding of the diverse character of the Irish diaspora that has emerged. It will show how various sections of the diaspora had been lost or ignored – hence the 'lost tribes of Ireland' in the title – and how this new approach is helping to lead to their recovery.

The United States of America

In 1976, Lawrence McCaffrey published his important book *The Irish Diaspora in America*, which dealt with the Irish American community. In 1997 he produced a second edition of the volume which was now retitled *The Irish Catholic Diaspora in America*.[5] The earlier work had taken for granted that the Catholic Irish American community was synonymous with the Irish in America. In his introduction to the later work, however, he acknowledged that the change in title was due to a new understanding that a majority of people in the USA who currently defined themselves as Irish or partly Irish were not Catholic, as had been very widely assumed, but in fact Protestant. This change had happened because of efforts for the first time in the USA to correlate ancestral background with religious affiliation. The evidence of a number of opinion polls in the 1970s and 1980s showed that of the 40 million or so Americans who identified their background as Irish, a majority were Protestant.[6] This new information caused considerable shock and even denial in some circles, in both Ireland and the USA.

To explain the new picture we must look closely at Irish emigration to America over the previous three centuries. The eighteenth century witnessed the first significant waves of emigration from Ireland. The majority of these people were Presbyterians and descendants of Scottish emigrants who had settled in Ulster during the seventeenth and early eighteenth centuries. Although some left for the American colonies in the seventeenth century, this movement really began in a substantial way around 1717–18. Economic factors as well as religious disabilities, which Presbyterians suffered in Ireland at the hands of the Anglican establishment, lay behind the emigration, as well as greater opportunities in the colonies. There has been a wide range of opinion among historians as to the extent of this migration from the early eighteenth century until the American Revolution, but the most recent estimate is that this period saw the exit of up to 200,000 from Ulster, of whom most were Presbyterians, although there were also other Irish Protestants (Church of Ireland) and Catholics.[7] This flow of emigrants from Ireland was interrupted by the American War of Independence, but picked up again afterwards and, it is believed, at least another 100,000 left Ulster in the next half-century, as did people from the other parts of Ireland. The numbers of Irish Catholic emigrants grew significantly and by the 1830s they formed, for the first time, the majority of Irish emigrants. From this time on, emigration from Ireland increased very considerably, especially during the Famine years, and the vast bulk of these emigrants were Catholic.

A number of observations can be made about the eighteenth- and early nineteenth-century Protestant emigrants from Ireland. The first matter relates to their numbers. The main explanation for the numerical predominance of their descendants in the Irish section of the American population today is a simple mathematical one. It is fair to say that of all the Irish emigrants to arrive in America over the last three centuries, a majority were Catholic. The Protestants, however, came earlier to the colonies and due primarily to a multiplier factor there are more people today from a Protestant than a Catholic background. The analyses of people in the 1970s found that 83 per cent of Protestants were at least fourth generation while only 41 per cent of Catholics had such early origins in America.[8]

Among these figures of eighteenth-century Protestants, we must include a number of Catholics who became Protestant.[9] Social conditions in the colonies and the early years of the republic witnessed changes in religion, not only of Catholics who became Protestant but also of many Presbyterians, who eventually joined the Baptist Church as this was better organised for frontier conditions than the other main denominations. A majority of the descendants of these emigrants today are Baptists. In addition, there were other Irish Protestants who did not have Scottish ancestry and were Episcopalian rather than Presbyterian. Joseph Lee has made the point that this group of Irish Protestants from a Church of Ireland background has often gone unnoticed in accounts of the Irish diaspora in America (a point that can be made about them elsewhere).[10] It is important also to recall that not insignificant numbers of Protestants – Presbyterian and Episcopalian – continued to emigrate to America from Ireland throughout the nineteenth and early twentieth centuries.[11]

A second matter concerns the identity of these Protestants from Ireland. In the case of many, their families had been settled in Ireland for only a few generations. Nonetheless, references in their correspondence and in contemporary material show that they called themselves, and were called by others, Irish. We also find references to some of them as Scotch-Irish. There has been debate among scholars as to the relative importance of these terms, Irish and Scotch-Irish, in the eighteenth century.[12] From the evidence that has been presented, it seems fair to say that the term Irish was used generally, especially from the mid-eighteenth century, but the term Scotch-Irish was sometimes used by contemporaries for the Scottish Presbyterian colonists from Ulster. Many of these people were heavily involved on the revolutionary side during the American War of Independence. Twentieth-century scholarship has shown the important role played by the Scotch-Irish communities in extending the American frontier and building the new republic in the early 1800s.[13] Among the American presidents of the nineteenth century, there were three (Jackson, Buchanan and Arthur) whose fathers were born in Ulster, while others had significant Ulster roots.

From the mid-nineteenth century onwards, however, there is little evidence of an acclaimed Irish identity among these Protestants. After the Great Famine, the term Irish refers very largely to the new Catholic Irish emigrants. There are various reasons for this change. In part, it is because these earlier Protestant emigrants had become integrated substantially into American society and so did not retain a strong Irish identity. In part also it was because religion remained a key identifying and dividing factor in American society.[14] Due to the massive influx of Irish Catholic emigrants, during and after the Famine, Irishness became associated with Catholicism. As David Doyle has pointed out, between 1845 and 1860 the number of Catholics in America trebled from 1.1 million to 3.1 million and Irish immigration accounted for roughly half the increase, and children of Irish parents for perhaps one-third of the balance.[15] Among these new Irish Catholic emigrants, who had sought to escape harsh conditions at home but who continued to experience tough circumstances, although greater opportunities, in the New World, a strong Irish nationalist and Catholic identity developed. During the second half of the nineteenth century we see the building of important Irish Catholic communities in places such as New York and Boston.[16] In common perception, Irish identity in America became linked very closely to members of the Catholic Irish community, who were known as Irish Americans, to the exclusion of the Protestant Irish.

What happened to these Irish Protestants and their descendants from the mid-nineteenth century onwards? In contrast to the eighteenth century, when their communities and identity have been well explored by historians, there has been very little research on their position after the early nineteenth century. In large part, however, this reflects the fact that they became part of American society in general. No doubt they retained an interest in and knowledge about Ireland, as we can tell from information about individuals. In a privately printed family history of 1885, banker Thomas Mellon of Pittsburgh acknowledged his Scotch-Irish background and spoke of his home in Co. Tyrone.[17] The paternal family of artist Jackson Pollock, originally called McCoy, arrived from Co. Donegal in the mid-eighteenth century and subsequent generations remained within a Scotch-Irish Presbyterian milieu and family grouping. An orphan, the artist's father took the name of Pollock from his new parents, probably also Scotch-Irish. His mother's grandparents were Presbyterian weavers who left Ireland in the 1840s.[18] On the death of Belfast-born medical doctor Dr David Walker in 1917 in Portland, Oregon, the press reported how every week he had received a copy of the weekly *Belfast News Letter*. Walker came from an Irish Episcopalian family and there was no reference in this or other press reports on him to an Ulster or Scotch-Irish background.[19]

These Irish Protestants, however, whether from Ulster or elsewhere, do not appear to have retained a heightened interest in Ireland, or formed a distinct political or ethnic community, although they seem to have maintained their own localised communities in many instances. In the late nineteenth and early twentieth centuries we should note a rise in the number of societies and organisations with an interest in the history and identity of the Scotch-Irish, but concern about this subject seems to have largely waned by the First World War.[20] In the introduction to his 1944 book on the Scotch-Irish of colonial Pennsylvania, historian W.F. Dunaway observed about their descendants that they 'have lost to a considerable degree their distinctive characteristics as they became merged with the general body of the people'. He commented: 'They have never been greatly concerned about traditions of fatherland, nor encumbered by these, in the manner of some.'[21]

We now return to the 1970s. The general assumption in America and Ireland was that the Irish Americans, with their Catholic and predominantly nationalist background, represented the Irish diaspora in America. There was some acknowledgement of the role of the Scotch-Irish in the eighteenth century, but their descendants were not regarded as an especially numerous or distinct group. The 1980 census return showed that 40 million Americans claimed to have Irish ancestry. This census material did not link ethnic background to religion, but work by a number of scholars, in particular Father Andrew Greeley, investigated this matter for the first time in a rigorous manner through the evidence of opinion polls. A study by the National Opinion Research Center of the University of Chicago in the 1970s revealed that of those Americans who said their primary ethnic group was Irish, 56 per cent were Protestant; a survey by the Gallup polling organisation in the 1980s put the figure at 54 per cent. The National Survey of Religious Identification, based on a random survey of 113,000 Americans, and published in 1991, confirmed that a majority of people who acknowledged an Irish background were Protestant.[22]

Other information emerged at this time about the Irish in America.[23] We now know that, very generally speaking, those with an Irish Protestant background are located mostly in the south and in the countryside, while those with an Irish Catholic background are found mainly in the north-east and north-central regions and in the cities. Another interesting matter is how these groups fare today in areas of social and financial attainment. Figures from the 1980s and early 1990s showed that Protestants of Irish descent experienced significantly lower levels of educational standards, family incomes and high-prestige jobs than Catholics of Irish ancestry. Protestants with an Irish background were more likely to be working class than were Catholics. The disparity in such standards has been attributed primarily to the different geographical locations of the two communities, with Catholics enjoying greater prosperity in the more affluent north and urban areas than Protestants in the less prosperous south and rural areas.

Attention has now shifted to efforts to identify further those Protestants with an Irish background. A popular book by James Webb,

Born Fighting: How the Scots-Irish Shaped America, has argued that many Scotch-Irish descendants have retained to the present their own particular Scotch-Irish identity, with its individualistic religious and political sense.[24] The author Tom Wolfe claimed that at the presidential elections in 2004 it was the Scotch-Irish of the south who formed the backbone of the Republican support for George Bush.[25] At the same time, we should note that, in November 2006, James Webb, a former Assistant Secretary of Defence and Secretary of the Navy during the Reagan administration, who regards himself as Scotch-Irish, was elected as a Democratic senator for Virginia, in strong opposition to Bush's war policies. Former President Bill Clinton has talked of his Irish background through his mother's family of Cassidy, who came from Co. Fermanagh in Ulster (but not, it is likely, of Scottish or Presbyterian origins). Variously called Irish Protestant, Scots-Irish or Scotch-Irish, this identity still retains for millions of people an acknowledgement of roots in Ireland, as indicated by all those from this background who continue to claim Ireland as their country of origin in the census returns. For many today, from all the different Irish strands in America, who hold a strong sense of identity with Ireland, their Irishness often involves a concern for Irish culture, as in the form of music, dance or drama.[26] There remains an active Irish American political lobby in relation to Ireland but it no longer represents a major constituency.

Australia

We also find important readjustments in academic and public perceptions of the Irish in Australia: by the early twenty-first century it was estimated that up to a third of the Australian population had some Irish ancestry.[27] In 1986 eminent Australian Church historian Patrick O'Farrell published *The Irish in Australia*, to be followed by a number of major chapters on the Irish in Australia and New Zealand in two volumes of *A New History of Ireland*.[28] This work pays only minor attention to Protestant emigrants in Australia. At the beginning of his chapter on the period 1870–1990 in volume six of *A New History of Ireland*, for example, he remarks that 'the usual means of tracing the Irish group is to take advantage of the strong correlation between Irishness and Catholicism'.[29] He then proceeds to devote almost the entire chapter to the Irish Catholic community in Australia. In a footnote he refers to 'the significant (up to 20 per cent) element of Irish in Australia who were Anglo Irish or Ulster Protestant', but he says very little about them.[30]

This approach, however, came under challenge from a number of younger Australian historians. In 1990 Gordon Forth protested that 'until recently most Australian historians ... seem to have regarded individual Anglo Irish as English who just happen to have been born in Ireland'.[31] In 1994 a major study by David Fitzpatrick appeared, entitled *Oceans of Consolation: Personal Accounts of Irish Migration to Australia*, which looked at correspondence from nineteenth-century emigrants, including Protestant as well as Catholic writers. In his introduction to this volume he stressed that 'no study of the Irish in Australia should ignore the experience of Protestant settlers including those of humble background whose performance in Australia probably differed little from that of Irish Catholics'.[32] His findings showed that in the nineteenth century the Protestant Irish had a very similar identification with their Irish home to the Catholic Irish.

Among the Irish emigrants to Australia it is clear that Catholics were the largest section, but Protestant numbers were still significant. It is reckoned that Protestants made up about 20 per cent of total Irish immigration; we may note that the 1911 census recorded that in that year nearly 30 per cent of Irish-born Australians were Protestant.[33] Among the Protestant Irish immigrants, Anglicans were the major single element; many came from Ulster but also from other parts of Ireland. In the course of the late nineteenth and early twentieth centuries, however, a new important, political and religious sense of Irish identity emerged in Australia, which did not include Irish Protestants. Home Rule for Ireland won enthusiastic supporters among the Catholic Irish and a strong Irish Catholic religious community developed, partly in response to the dominant Protestant culture and society in Australia. From the 1920s onwards this Irish Catholic community was identified with the Labour party in Australia. As regards Irish identity in Australia, Patrick O'Farrell has described how the Catholic Australian community of Irish descent that stabilised its character in the late 1920s 'was determined that it alone was "Irish" in Australia: for the job of being Irish no other than Catholics need apply'.[34]

Irish Protestants were not part of all this and became integrated into more mainstream Australian politics and community. Some Ulster societies were formed in the twentieth century and the Orange Order had a role in some places, but it is probably fair to say that these organisations had a limited part in maintaining a sense of Irish or Ulster connections. In recent times, there have been important changes in public perceptions of Irish identity in Australia. The identification of the Catholic Church with the Catholic Irish community has diminished, and cultural and less restrictive concepts of Irish identity have emerged. Most of the traditional St Patrick's Day parades had petered out by the early 1970s, but a number have been resurrected recently, with significantly less of their earlier religious and political overtones.[35] Various centres of Irish studies and history have been established, and there has been an effort to promote a more inclusive sense of Irishness among descendants of all Irish emigrants.

New Zealand

The situation as regards Irish emigrants in New Zealand (an approximate 15 per cent of all emigrants to the country in the nineteenth century) was different from that in Australia. In 1995 Patrick O'Farrell, who had been brought up in New Zealand, published an article entitled, 'How Irish was New Zealand?'[36] He questioned whether one could talk at all of an Irish presence in New Zealand, because from the mid-nineteenth century Irish emigrants had integrated successfully into New Zealand society. He dismissed Ulster and Anglo-Irish Protestant emigrants as 'invisible' in any history of Irish influence in New Zealand. As regards Irish Catholic emigrants, he stated: 'to speak of the New Zealand Irish is misleading.' Because they had blended well into local society (apart from some political upheavals in 1921), and did not have the solidarity and separate identity of the Irish Catholics in Australia or America, he argued that it was questionable whether even they could really be seen as evidence of an Irish presence or influence in New Zealand. O'Farrell attributed the high level of integration to the lower proportion of Irish emigrants in a much smaller total population in New Zealand, compared to Australia, as well as to the influence of French clergy in the New Zealand Catholic Church. O'Farrell's article not only drew attention to the particular experience of Irish emigrants to New Zealand but also illustrated an approach to the Irish diaspora, which saw it only in terms of a strongly articulated and separate Irish identity.

A different approach, however, was taken by Donald Akenson in his 1989 study of Irish emigrants to New Zealand.[37] His first premise was to look at all immigrants from Ireland, whatever their religion or background. He observed that between one-fifth and one-quarter of the entire Irish ethnic group was Protestant, mainly but not exclusively from Ulster, and including Presbyterians and Anglicans. Akenson noted how both Catholic and Protestant emigrants' groups became reasonably quickly and successfully involved in New Zealand society. The Protestant Irish were more easily integrated into the Protestant majority in New Zealand than the Catholic Irish, who retained a collective identity largely through their separate Catholic schooling system, but the latter also blended into the larger society. Whatever the degree or speed of integration, however, Akenson regarded both groups as part of the Irish diaspora and he urged further study of the special contribution of Irish emigrants to New Zealand. This challenge to examine the history of the Irish in New Zealand has been taken up by a number of historians, and their work includes a recent important collection of essays on the role of emigrants from Ulster.[38]

Canada

In both the historiography and the actual experiences of members of the Irish diaspora in Canada, the situation was very different not only from that in New Zealand but also from that in the USA and Australia. When in 1990 Cecil Houston and William Smyth produced their general survey, *Irish Emigration and Canadian Settlement: Patterns, Links and Letters*, they dealt in full and equal terms with both Catholics and Protestants among the substantial number of Irish emigrants to Canada.[39] This reflected the historical background in Canada where the two groups had been roughly equal in numbers and no one group dominated or monopolised Irish identity. Work by Donald Akenson and others in the previous two decades had brought out the main features of Irish immigration in Canada in general, and at the same time had examined the special contributions of the two sections.[40]

In the 1871 census, people of Irish origin made up 24.3 per cent of the Canadian population, the single largest European group after the French, but by 1961 the figure stood at 9.6 per cent.[41] In 1991 around 3.8 million Canadians claimed full or partial Irish ancestry.[42] It has been established that approximately 55 per cent of Irish settlers in Canada were Protestant. Among the Protestants, more were from an Anglican than a Presbyterian background; while a majority came from Ulster, significant numbers also arrived from the rest of Ireland.[43] During the nineteenth century these Irish emigrants usually continued to belong to their respective religious communities, within which Irish identity remained important. There was a strong tendency for Irish settlers to congregate among members of their own faith. For example, Irish Protestants were strongly based around Ontario, while Irish Catholics were very numerous in Newfoundland. Compared to Australia and the USA, strident public claims for a singular religious or nationalist sense of an Irish identity were rarely made in Canada.[44]

Both Irish communities retained a sense of Irish identity in their own manner. One way in which this Irish connection was experienced for many Protestants was through the Orange Order. In their 1980 book, *The Sash Canada Wore: A Historical Geography of the Orange Order in Canada*, Cecil Houston and William Smyth showed how Orangeism, which was a distinctly Irish creation, was brought to Canada in the early nineteenth century and spread not only among Irish Protestants but also the wider community as a movement for loyalism and Protestantism, until by the end of the nineteenth century it is reckoned that one in three Canadian Protestant males was a member.[45] The organisation continued to grow until the end of the First World War, since which time it declined until by the 1970s it ceased to be of much importance. For Irish Catholics, their sense of Irish identity was encouraged by organisations such as the Christian Brothers in the separate Catholic schooling system and the Ancient Order of Hibernians. By the last quarter of the twentieth century, however, denominational divisions mattered little in Canada. It has been claimed that the Irish became so well integrated into Canadian society that they are now 'invisible as an ethnic group'.[46]

Nonetheless, there remains an interest in Ireland that is concerned with both family links and an appreciation of cultural connections.

Great Britain

Irish emigration to Great Britain has been very extensive over the last two centuries and is second only to the USA as a destination for people from Ireland. Until the 1970s the Irish-born population was the largest immigrant group in Britain. There have been two major periods of Irish immigration, although throughout the two centuries there has been movement of population from Ireland to Britain. The first of these important periods ran from the 1840s until the 1860s. In 1861 the Irish-born section of the population stood at just over 800,000. Numbers fell but picked up again in the second important wave of Irish immigration, from the 1930s until the 1960s. By 1971 the total of Irish-born stood at around 952,000.[47] The 2001 census recorded a figure of 753,338 for the number of people in Britain born in Ireland.[48] The greater number of these emigrants came to England and Wales rather than Scotland, although Irish emigrants and their descendants make up a greater proportion of the current population in Scotland than in England and Wales. The bulk of these emigrants have been Catholic but a significant minority have been Protestant, from both north and south of Ireland. It has been argued that probably around 25 per cent of Irish emigrants to Britain in the twentieth century have been Protestant.[49]

Recently new research has been carried out on the experiences of these Protestant Irish immigrants, who, as Roger Swift pointed out in 2000, 'have for too long been conspicuous by their relative absence from the historiography of the Irish in Britain'.[50] This past neglect was partly due to the tendency of many of the Protestants to integrate easily into mainstream British society, given the absence of religious barriers for them. In Scotland, of course, there have been important concentrations of Irish Protestants, particularly from Ulster (between a quarter and a third of nineteenth-century Irish emigrants to Scotland are reckoned to have been Protestant).[51] In England also there have been some areas, such as Liverpool, which especially attracted Protestant Irish-born emigrants, and organisations such as the Orange Order played a role in maintaining a sense of solidarity among them.[52] By the last decades of the twentieth century, however, among these Protestant Irish and their descendants there was little evidence of any distinct sense of community. Among Catholic emigrants in England and Wales there was a greater tendency to create separate communities thanks to their larger numbers and the impact of religious division in society, and an Irish identity was often an important part of this sense of community in a number of areas, although rarely in the overt political sense seen in America. Here also, by the end of the twentieth century, few such communities had survived, and even in areas that continued to have substantial numbers of people with an Irish ethnic background they still made up a 'relatively small proportion of the population'.[53]

The question of the extent of Irish identity today in Britain among these people of Irish birth or descent, Catholic and Protestant, is an interesting and controversial one. In 2001, for the first time, the census gave people the option to register Irish as their ethnic identity. The outcome of this, however, was that, in spite of massive Irish immigration over two centuries, the number who chose to declare this identity was much lower than had been expected. Out of a population of 57,103,927, only 691,000 (just over 1 per cent), of whom nearly three-quarters were born in Ireland, recorded an Irish ethnic background.[54] Although the picture is not a full one, some of the other findings from this census material reveal a view of Irish people in Britain strongly at odds with earlier surveys that had stressed discrimination against, and marginalisation of, the Irish in Britain.[55] Analysis of the census returns in relation to the Irish ethnic group in 2001 showed that 'the historical stereotype of the Irish manual labourer bears no relation to the factual evidence about occupational structure of the White Irish population'.[56] It was revealed that the proportion of Irish men in a routine or manual occupational group (29 per cent) was smaller not only than all other immigrant groups but also than 'White British', while 'more than one in three men and women of working age belonged to a managerial or professional occupational group, the highest proportion for any ethnic group'. In nearly half the Irish households, Irish people shared with partners or children who were British.[57] Almost one-third of the Irish population lived in London.

Various explanations have been given for the low numbers to record an Irish ethnic identity, such as people's failure to understand the question or an unwillingness to declare an Irish identity on official British forms.[58] A better reason, however, lies in the high degree of integration of Irish-born people and their descendants into general British society, and a consequent decline in Irish identity. By the end of the twentieth century, people with an Irish background were fully involved and successful at all levels of society in Britain. For example, this success can be seen in the leadership of the British political system. When Prime Minister Tony Blair addressed Dáil Éireann in 1998 he stated:

> Ireland … is in my blood. My mother was born in the flat above her grandmother's hardware shop in the main street of Ballyshannon in Donegal. She lived there as a child, started school there and only moved when her father died, her mother remarried and they crossed the water to Glasgow. We spent virtually every childhood summer holiday, up to when the troubles really took hold, in Ireland …[59]

Other Labour politicians with an Irish background include Ruth Kelly, former education minister, and Michael Martin, former speaker of the House of Commons. John Major, the former prime minister, has recorded how one of his grandfathers 'married a young Irish girl, Sarah Anne Marrah; illiterate, my grandmother signed my father's birth certificate with an "x"'.[60] Chris Patten, a Major minister, and former governor of Hong Kong, has remarked on the irony of his role, as the great grandson of an Irish potato farmer, in serving as 'the last governor of the British Empire'.[61] Curiously, it seems that James Callaghan cannot be included in a list of British statesmen with an Irish background, in spite of his popular Cork name. His father (originally called Garoghan) assumed the name and a false date of birth in the 1890s when he joined the navy and sought to hide his whereabouts from his family; his son only discovered this in 1976, after he became prime minister.[62] We can note, however, that the father of Denis Healey, his deputy prime minister, was born at Kiltyclogher, Co. Leitrim.[63]

The high degree of Irish integration into mainstream British society today is the main reason for the diminution of acclaimed Irish identity, as revealed in the low figures for Irish ethnic identity in Britain. The decision to include Irish as an ethnic identity came as a result of lobbying from various groups that believed that the Irish were a discriminated, marginalised minority, like some other ethnic minorities, and required special attention and resources.[64] No doubt some Irish groups still face particular problems, but this picture of marginalisation and deprivation did not fit in with the experience of the vast majority today with Irish links, many of whom see themselves as belonging to mainstream society rather than a minority group. The background to the decision, and the decision itself, to include Irish as a minority ethnic category, probably played a part in why some people with Irish roots decided not to declare themselves in this category. Another factor that probably affected people in their approach to this issue was the impact of Irish Republican bombing in Britain over the previous thirty years. In the late 1960s around 20 per cent of Protestants in Northern Ireland (most of whom were also unionists and carried British passports) saw themselves as Irish. Over the next two decades, however, as a reaction to Irish Republican violence this sense of Irish identity among unionists fell dramatically, so that by 1989 the figure stood at 3 per cent.[65] It is very likely that the same happened in Britain, and that, because of such violence, many people with an Irish background chose to identify strongly with Britain rather than Ireland. In addition, in the census, people could not choose a dual Irish British background or identity, and, faced with a choice between the two, the vast majority selected British.

While the number of those from an Irish background who decided to acclaim an Irish identity in the 2001 census was low, this is not to say that the many others, who did not register, felt no affinity with Ireland or had lost all their Irish identity. Under new circumstances, which have arisen from the peace process in Northern Ireland, it is likely that more people in Britain will feel keener to acclaim an Irish identity, although not necessarily on their census returns as part of a minority. There are good relations between the British and Irish governments. Recent reports have indicated that the peoples of Britain and Ireland have very positive attitudes towards each other.[66] Changes in understanding of the many components that have made up British society and identity may allow for a greater acceptance of the Irish role, as part of or alongside British identity. All this may cause many Irish in Britain to be happier to acknowledge an Irish identity. Recognition of a dual British Irish identify is now more likely. Writing in 2006, Marianne Elliott has described how 'in England it is now fashionable to be Irish, second- and third-generation Irish in their teens and twenties displaying none of the sensitivities of those in their fifties and older'.[67] The success of centres of Irish Studies and Irish cultural programmes in Britain reflect this growing interest in Ireland and Irish identity.

Observations

The creation of the Irish diaspora involved a long time period in which the Famine exodus was only one episode. These Irish emigrants came from all parts of Ireland and from a wide range of backgrounds. As Enda Delaney has commented: 'the Irish diaspora ... never was and is not now a homogeneous unit.'[68] Nowhere is this more apparent than in the diversity of Irish identity held by the different groups abroad. In the past, however, the Irish diaspora was often viewed as very largely a single religious and political entity with a special Irish identity. This reflected not only the experiences of many of the Irish abroad but also a widespread perception of what the Irish diaspora and identity had come to mean. While this view related to reality on the ground in many places, a narrow understanding of the Irish abroad emerged as conforming to a largely Catholic, nationalist stereotype with a heightened sense of Irish identity. This concept of the Irish diaspora often meant the absence or loss of groups such as Scotch-Irish/Irish Protestants in America, Irish Protestants in Canada and Australia, Irish Protestants and Catholics in New Zealand, and, if applied today, all those non-affirming Irish in Britain. Under this limited approach, the numbers who make up the Irish diaspora would be a lot fewer than the 70 million that are understood to belong to it – perhaps even fewer than half. The picture changes, however, when we accept the new, more inclusive perspective of Mary Robinson and Donald Akenson, put forward at the beginning of this paper, that the Irish diaspora should mean all those abroad who were born in Ireland, or their descendants, regardless of background, politics or religion. In this case, it is possible to talk of an Irish diaspora of 70 million.

This new approach has important implications for what we mean by Irish identity, as revealed by the wide spectrum of Irish people abroad. Irish identity has been expressed by these people in a whole range of ways. Obviously it involves the Irish American or Irish Australian who sees or used to see this Irish identity in a strong Catholic and nationalist light, but it also involves the Canadian Irish Protestant for whom it means none of these things, but who sees or used to see Irish identity through a Protestant and British standpoint. For many, in all countries, Irish identity has meant primarily attachments of family or sentiment, which is just as valid as any other form of identity with Ireland. Among the Irish diaspora, until recently, religious divisions continued to be very important for their communities and their different senses of identity. It was not simply that the Irish brought these denominational divisions with them. In the mainstream societies in all the host countries, from America to Canada, Australia, New Zealand and Britain, religion and associated religious divisions remained significant throughout the nineteenth and much of the twentieth centuries. This meant that religious division continued to differentiate the Irish abroad and to have a great influence on the nature of the Irish identity that groups held. The character of Irishness, Irish identity and the Irish diaspora in these countries was affected not only by the Irish emigrants themselves but also by the particular circumstances that the different groups faced in each country.

At present, the new, broader, more inclusive sense of the Irish diaspora, which acknowledges this diversity, can be seen in some but not all the popular literature and commentary on the diaspora. It has also been incorporated into much of the academic writing on the subject, although, while there is a new awareness of the variety of this diaspora, there is sometimes an inability to see how it alters the total picture and to appreciate how some previous generalisations about the Irish abroad do not work when these other groups are brought into the picture. Among many members of the diaspora there is a new awareness of the larger, more diverse picture, and also an effort to create a more inclusive identity. Thanks in large part to a diminution in denominational division in the Christian world, the successful integration of most Irish emigrants into their new countries, and a concern for the peace process in Northern Ireland, there has been a considerable reduction in religious and political links to identity. Irish identity among the diaspora has undergone and continues to undergo great change. There is now a widespread attempt to see this identity in cultural, non-denominational and non-political ways that have the potential to embrace all, not just a section, of the Irish diaspora. The strong support in many countries for the Ireland Funds is one example of new non-partisan identification with Ireland among the members of the Irish diaspora.

These changes may have important implications for Northern Ireland. At the beginning of the twentieth century, most unionists in Ulster still retained a sense of Irish identity alongside their position as British citizens.[69] In the new Northern Ireland, however, there was a retreat from this idea of Irishness, as they sought to build up their own exclusive Ulster/British identity, which was in part a response to the exclusive sense of Irish identity that developed in the new Irish Free State/Irish Republic and among many parts of the Irish diaspora. By the late 1960s it was reckoned that only some 20 per cent of Northern unionists still retained an Irish identity but over the following period even this disappeared almost entirely (although we should note the rise of a 'Northern Irish' identity). Today, however, it is possible that the broader, more tolerant understanding of the Irish diaspora and Irish identity, as promoted by Mary Robinson and others in Ireland and now seen among members of the diaspora, will allow unionists to value an Irish identity again, alongside their Britishness. The legitimacy of such a joint identity was accepted by the Belfast/Good Friday Agreement of 1998, which recognised the 'birthright of all the people of Northern Ireland to identify themselves and be accepted as Irish or British or both, as they may so choose'.[70] For unionists as well as nationalists, Protestants as well as Catholics, in

Northern Ireland, acknowledgement of their links to the Irish diaspora admits them to a global network made up of tens of millions of people, many of whom are descendants of their own families, groups and communities. Changes in the Irish diaspora and Irish identity abroad may well have important consequences for changes in Northern Ireland.

PRESIDENT BARACK OBAMA, FULMOUTH KEARNEY AND THE IRISH IN AMERICA TODAY

The visit in 2011 of President Barack Obama to the home of his Irish ancestor, Fulmouth Kearney, in Co. Offaly, Ireland, served to remind us once again of the strong links between Ireland and America. At the same time, his connection with Ireland helps to answer some of the important questions about the Irish in modern America. First, how do we explain their very large numbers? Ireland today has a population of just over 6 million. Between 1820 and 1920 almost 5 million people are estimated to have gone from Ireland to America. And yet, in 2013 a colossal figure of some 34 million people in America claimed Irish ancestry. Another 3 million self-identified as Scotch-Irish.[1] Secondly, how do we explain the fact that a majority of these people are Protestant or from a Protestant background? In Ireland today Protestants are a minority of around 3 per cent of the population of the Irish Republic, about 55 per cent of the population of Northern Ireland and some 20 per cent of the total population of the island of Ireland of around 6 million. In America, however, Catholics are a minority among the Irish, numbering in 2006 just under 30 per cent of the very much greater figure with Irish ancestry. Protestants are nearly 50 per cent, while those of no or other religion count for slightly over 20 per cent.[2] Most Scotch-Irish are Protestant. Thirdly, how is it that we have only become aware of these facts in recent decades? Fifty years ago there was very little understanding in either Ireland or America of the real size and composition of the Irish in America. President Obama's Irish roots help to cast light on these questions, especially concerning the place of the Protestant majority among those of Irish ancestry in America today.

Views Fifty Years Ago About the Irish Americans and Scotch-Irish

Half a century ago, most people believed that they had a good idea of the number and make-up of those in America with an Irish background. In his 1961 book, *The Making of the President*, about John F. Kennedy's presidential election the previous year, Theodore White wrote that there were an estimated 14 million Americans of Irish descent.[3] An article by Patrick J. Blessing on the Irish in the *Harvard Encyclopedia of American Ethnic Groups*, published in 1980, reported a 1972 survey that stated some 16.4 million Americans claimed Irish descent.[4] An article in the *New York Times*, as late as May 1981, declared that 'more than 13 million are estimated to be of Irish ancestry'.[5] The general assumption was that these people were Irish Americans, that is Catholic Irish or descendants of Catholic Irish who arrived in America in large numbers from the time of the Great Irish Famine onwards. For example, L.J. McCaffrey's important book of 1976, called *The Irish Diaspora in America*, dealt exclusively with the Catholic Irish Americans who were regarded as synonymous with the Irish in America.[6]

What can we say about the Scotch-Irish, the name sometimes given to eighteenth-century Ulster immigrants whose families had originally come from Scotland, and their descendants? Unlike the Irish Americans who were an easily identified, well-organised and influential community, the Scotch-Irish were not greatly in evidence fifty years ago. In his 1962 study, *The Scotch Irish: A Social History*, J.G. Leyburn noted that the last general history of the Scotch-Irish had appeared in 1915, and although 'millions of Americans' had Scotch-Irish ancestors, he believed that little was known about them – hence the need for his book.[7] Leyburn's study, however, dealt almost entirely with the Scotch-Irish in the eighteenth century, because he believed that after the Revolution the Scotch-Irish, mostly Presbyterians, were 'integral parts of the American nation, making no distinction between themselves and any other Americans'.[8] In the 1980 *Harvard Encyclopedia of American Ethnic Groups*, the entry on the Scotch-Irish by Maldwyn A. Jones traced their activities into the nineteenth century but claimed that 'Today the Scotch-Irish are widely dispersed and are not easily identifiable'.[9] At the same time, he ventured a guess that by 1980 there were probably some 8 million Americans with Scotch-Irish forebears.

New Evidence About the Irish in America

All these assumptions were now to be challenged dramatically by new evidence that emerged in the 1970s and 1980s. For the first time, the American census of 1980 carried a question about ancestry. The outcome was that the census recorded a massive figure of 40.2 million people who declared an Irish ancestry.[10] There was no return for numbers of Scotch-Irish. Journalist Niall O'Dowd has written of the great amazement over the figures when they were announced. He has recorded a conversation at the time with Edward Fernandez, head of the population division of the census.[11] Fernandez remarked that the figures were 'surprisingly high' and added, jokingly, that the census was 'not taken around St Patrick's Day'. This high figure served to give greatly added confidence to the Irish American community. Other evidence, however, was now emerging that served to cast a new light on the composition of these people with Irish ancestry.

In the 1970s, a series of opinion polls and surveys by the National Opinion Research Centre (NORC) of the University of Chicago investigated the religious, social, economic and educational attainments of different ethnic groups, including the Irish. From this the surprising picture that emerged was that, of those Americans who said their primary ethnic group was Irish, 56 per cent were Protestant.[12] In 1981, Andrew Greeley, in association with NORC, published his book *The Irish Americans: The Rise to Money and Power* and in the introduction made clear that his study of the Irish in America covered the Irish Catholics and not the more numerous Irish Protestants. He declared:

'Irish Protestants and Irish Catholics in the United States have had very different cultural and historical experiences in American life, live in different geographic settings, and, in most respects, are very different from one another.'[13] Other surveys from the 1980s confirmed that a majority of the Irish were Protestant. A study by the Gallup polling organisation put the figure of Protestants among the Irish at 54 per cent.[14] When L.J. McCaffrey published a new edition of his study of the Irish American community in 1997 he entitled it *The Irish Catholic Diaspora in America* in acknowledgement of the new understanding of the Irish and Scotch-Irish in America.[15]

Explanations for the New Picture

To understand the new picture, we must be clear about the nature of the evidence from the 1980 census. Although this census was the first time that respondents were asked their ancestry, the subject was one that the census authorities had been interested in for some time. Starting in 1969, the annual publication of the Current Population Survey, based on a very large national sample, had contained a section on 'ethnic origin' based on self-identification that was determined by 'a report on what persons perceive their origin to be'.[16] This proved to be very unsatisfactory, for all groups not just the Irish, because numbers would fluctuate considerably between years, due to members of the sample changing their minds. Also, many refused to give a single identity, or said they were American, and all these were placed in a general 'other' category. Those who declared they were Scotch-Irish were not recorded separately, and the enumerators were instructed to add them, along with Scots and Welsh, into the English group.[17] We can note that the 1972 return reported 16.4 million Irish and 85 million as under 'other'; the 1978 return revealed that the Irish figure had fallen to 8.4 million and the figure under 'other' had risen to 147 million.[18] Then, in a radical shift, the survey in 1979 changed the question to ask people their ancestry and it was decided to accept not only single-identity entries but also multiple identities. As a result the 1979 survey reported a single Irish ancestry figure of 9.76 million, and a multiple Irish and other ancestry group of 34 million, which gave a grand total of some 44 million Irish.[19]

The 1980 census reflected this new approach, when a novel question on ancestry replaced the question on parents' place of birth that had been requested since 1870. The census asked: 'What is this person's ancestry?' Instructions with the census form explained that: 'Ancestry (or origin or descent) may be viewed as the nationality group, the lineage, or the country in which the person or the person's parents or ancestors were born before their arrival in the United States.'[20] Crucially, people were allowed to indicate a multiple ancestry. From 1990 the question asked: 'What is this person's ancestry or ethnic origin?'[21] The 1980 census reported a total of 40 million Irish, a figure that has often been quoted. When we look at the results more closely, however, we find this total consisted of 10.3 million who indicated a single Irish ancestry, while 29.8 million stated Irish as part of a multiple ancestry.[22] The 1990 census recorded a total of 39 million, consisting of 12.3 million who gave a single Irish identity, 10.4 million who stated their first ancestry as Irish and 16 million who recorded their second ancestry as Irish.[23] The figures for 2000 were 19.3 million single and with a first ancestry Irish and 11.2 million second ancestry, a total of 30.5 million.[24] It should be noted that a majority of those who acknowledge Irish ancestry also claim at least one other ancestry.

What about Scotch-Irish ancestry? The 1980 census did not give a number for Scotch-Irish. In fact, many people returned Scotch-Irish as their ancestry, but the census authorities treated the term as a multiple-origin term and added these figures into both the Irish and Scottish figures. Later it would be revealed that just over 3 million recorded Scotch-Irish.[25] In 1990, following protests over this matter, the term Scotch-Irish was recorded separately. The 1990 census recorded the number of Scotch-Irish as 5.6 million, including 3 million single ancestry, 1.3 million first ancestry and 1.3 million second ancestry.[26] Their separate entry explains in large part the fall in numbers between 1980 and 1990 of Irish and Scots (from 10 million to 5 million). By 2000, the figure for Scotch-Irish had dropped to 3.2 million single and first ancestry and 1 million second ancestry, totalling 4 million.[27] The fall in numbers of both Irish and Scotch-Irish between 1990 and 2000 has been put down mainly to more people describing themselves as American.

Clearly, the particular approach taken by the census authorities from 1980 had a strong influence on how the Irish in modern America were identified and counted. The decision to link ethnic identity to ancestry created a broad sense of identity that helped to embrace many millions from a Protestant Irish background (and no doubt many also from a Catholic Irish background). The new willingness to allow for double or multiple identities was also important because for many of these people whose roots in America went back a long time their families had often intermarried with other immigrant groups. After the 2000 census, the US Census Bureau published commentary on some frequently asked questions about the ancestry entry in the census.[28] The point was emphasised that the intent of the ancestry question was not to measure the degree of attachment the respondent had to a particular ethnicity, and the Irish case was used to demonstrate the point: 'For example, a response of Irish might reflect total involvement in an "Irish" community or only a memory of ancestors several generations removed from the individual.' For most Protestant Irish it is likely that their response to this question arose from personal awareness of their Irish roots, rather than involvement in ethnic Irish organisations, unlike many of those from an Irish Catholic background.

It seems that most of those with an Irish Protestant background are fully involved in their local churches, societies and organisations, and are not usually concerned greatly about Irish associations or networks. Recent research on Irish organisations in Savannah, Georgia, has shown how in spite of the city having a reputation for Protestant–Catholic Irish organisations in the nineteenth century, this is no longer the case. W.L. Smith has written: 'While the Irish population of the South is overwhelmingly Protestant, more than 90 per cent of the members of Savannah's Irish organisations identify themselves as Catholic (although only 3 per cent of the population in South Georgia is Catholic).'[29] The census for Georgia in 1990 revealed nearly 1 million people who recorded an Irish ancestry and nearly 200,000 who acknowledged a Scotch-Irish ancestry, but the vast majority of Protestants among these people do not play a part in ethnic Irish organisations.[30] And yet, in census returns and opinion polls they are happy to acknowledge their roots with Ireland.

Why so Many Protestant Irish and Scotch-Irish?

Important questions remain. How do we explain the very large numbers of these Protestant Irish and Scotch-Irish? Where exactly do we find them in modern-day America? The first historian to explore these matters fully was Donald Akenson in a series of important publications in the 1980s and 1990s, especially his 1993 classic study of the Irish diaspora throughout the world, including the USA.[31] The basic premise of this book was to investigate all those who came from Ireland, regardless of religious or political background. He put forward three main explanations for the very significant numbers of Irish in America with a Protestant background.[32] First, he drew attention to the initial wave of Irish emigrants who arrived in America in the eighteenth and early nineteenth centuries. Because of their early arrival and due to a multiplier factor, there are now very large numbers of their descendants. This is the single most important factor behind the large number of Americans with Irish ancestry. David Doyle has pointed out: 'From 1700 to 1820, between a quarter of a million and half a million immigrants came from Ireland to America. They accounted for 30 per cent of all European immigrants in that period (and 50 per cent between 1776 and 1820).'[33] A majority of these were Ulster Presbyterians of Scottish origin. Many played a significant role in the American revolutionary wars and in the early pioneering years of the new republic.

The second point put forward by Akenson to explain the substantial number of Protestant Irish in America was that during the nineteenth and early twentieth centuries large numbers of Protestants from all parts of Ireland, Presbyterian and members of the Church of Ireland (Episcopalian), continued to emigrate to America. The presence of these people, especially Church of Ireland members, has often been ignored in the past. His third point was that in predominantly Protestant America, there was an important stream of people from an Irish Catholic background who became Protestant. The eighteenth-century immigrants from Ireland contained a not insignificant number of Catholics (and also members of the Church of Ireland).[34] Catholic Church structures in the American colonies were very weak for much of the century. It was not until after the Revolution that the first Catholic bishop was appointed and previously Church affairs had been administered by a vicar–general operating out of London. In the absence of effective Catholic diocesan organisation, it seems that many Catholics became Protestant.[35] In the nineteenth century strong Catholic structures were established in America, but still, in predominantly Protestant America society, there were Catholics who became Protestant. Most of these people joined Baptist or Methodist churches, as did many Irish Presbyterians and Church of Ireland members.

Where do we find most of the descendants of this first wave of emigrants from Ireland? The answer is that they are located all over America, but especially in the South. Figures from the 1990 census showed how the 38.8 million of Irish ancestry were distributed across the four main regions of America. Surprisingly, the largest number of Irish were to be found, not in the north-east with 24 per cent, including New York and Boston, but in the South with 33 per cent, while the West had 17 per cent and the Midwest 25 per cent of the total.[36] In the South there were nearly 13 million who declared an Irish ancestry and another 2.6 million who stated a Scotch-Irish ancestry. We know where most Irish emigrants from the Great Famine and after went, due to a return of the 1890 census that gives the birth place of all first and second generation respondents.[37] Out of a total of some 4 million born in Ireland or the offspring of parents born in Ireland, only 5 per cent were in the South compared to 64 per cent in the north-east. So clearly few of the Famine emigrants went to the South.

In 1990, for example, people who declared an Irish ancestry numbered 875,155 in Tennessee and 485,804 in South Carolina, while a century earlier just under 11,000 in the former and just over 3,000 in the latter had been born or had parents born in Ireland. In 1990 there were another 197,942 in Tennessee and 159,534 in South Carolina who declared a Scotch-Irish ancestry. Irish Catholics did arrive in fairly significant numbers in the South in the early nineteenth century and in the past half-century people, including those of Irish Catholic ancestry, moved from north to south, especially Florida and Texas.[38] Nonetheless, it is clear that the bulk of the people today in the South with Irish ancestry must be descendants of the early waves of Protestant Irish emigrants, mainly from Ulster, rather than the later Famine emigrants, and a majority call themselves Irish rather than Scotch-Irish. Opinion poll figures for the last decade of the twentieth century indicated that of those in the South who identified as Irish, 73 per cent were Protestant, 19 per cent were Catholic and 9 per cent were other or none.[39]

Who are the Protestant Irish Today?

In regard to the first immigrants from Ireland in the eighteenth century, we can identify a number of modern-day American politicians who acknowledge this ancestral background. Democratic Senator Jim Webb, a former combat marine and later Secretary of the Navy during the Reagan administration, in his 2004 book *Born Fighting: How the Scots-Irish Shaped America*, has described how his ancestors came in 1748 from Ulster to Pennsylvania. They then moved to the West Virginia mountains. Family members later travelled west and south to settlements in North Carolina, Tennessee and Kentucky, before moving to California in the twentieth century.[40] In his case, he uses the term Scots-Irish to explain his origins and identity, referring to the family's earlier links with Scotland. Republican Senator John McCain, a former presidential candidate, also had an eighteenth-century Ulster background. His ancestor, Hugh Young, of Scottish Presbyterian origins, went from Co. Antrim to Virginia in the eighteenth century.[41] During the 2008 presidential election, Senator McCain's wife, Cindy, who has this Ulster background as well, responded to a question about race by saying: 'Yes, you know, Mr Obama is an African American man, and yes, we're Irish. And isn't that a wonderful thing for America.'[42]

Another example of these early Irish immigrants and their descendants is William James, Presbyterian grandfather of the writer Henry James.[43] From a small farm in Bailieborough, Co. Cavan, he emigrated to Albany in the 1790s. The 1832 epitaph on the tombstone at his grave in Albany Rural Cemetery describes him as 'a native of Ireland'. In the last decades of the nineteenth century, his grandson visited Ireland a number of times. For some people whose roots went back to these early years, it is likely that such Irish links were remembered but were not a matter of great concern or interest. In his 1960s autobiography, the journalist Ralph McGill described growing up in east Tennessee in the early years of the twentieth century in a poor, entirely Presbyterian farming community, imbued with 'stern Welsh-Scottish Calvinism'. He noted that all the children had biblical names, although 'there was an occasional William to commemorate William of Orange' – a reference to King William III, the seventeenth-century Dutch hero of Irish Protestants. He also observed: 'In an old family bible it is written that my father's great-great grandfather had been born on one of the two sailing ships which left North Ireland [sic] in 1753.'[44] McGill visited Northern Ireland as a war correspondent in 1942.

In his explanation for the large number of those in America with a Protestant Irish background, the second factor that Akenson highlighted was the importance of continued Protestant emigration from Ireland during the nineteenth and early twentieth centuries, including the period of the Great Famine. This is where the example of President Obama's ancestor, Fulmouth Kearney, from whom his mother is descended, casts an important light. His family were impoverished members of the Church of Ireland (Episcopalian) from Moneygall, Co. Offaly, in the south of Ireland. A shoemaker by trade, Kearney emigrated to America in 1850. His parents and siblings also came to America in the 1849–54 period.[45] Kearney reminds us of the many Protestants who left Ireland, including southern parts and not just Ulster, and whose background was Church of Ireland rather than Presbyterian. Other Irish Protestant emigrants from this famine period include Church of Ireland member John Ford, who emigrated from Co. Cork to Michigan in 1847 with his son; his wife did not survive the voyage. John Ford's grandson, America's most successful industrialist, Henry Ford, established in Cork a tractor factory in 1917 and a major car manufacturing plant in the 1920s.[46] Very few other Irish emigrant families were able or willing to return and provide employment in their home country until late in the twentieth century. In April 2017 Bill Ford, executive chairman of the Ford Motor Company, and family, returned to the ancestral home Ballinascarty, West Cork, to celebrate 100 years of Ford in Ireland.[47]

At the age of 17, Presbyterian farmer's son Samuel Hamilton left from near Ballykelly, Co. Derry, in 1847 to travel to New York and then to California. In August 1952 Hamilton's grandson, the writer John Steinbeck, returned to the family homestead and later described his trip in *Collier's Magazine*. He wrote: 'Every Irishman – and that means anyone with one drop of Irish blood – sooner or later makes a pilgrimage to the home of his ancestors. I have just made such a pilgrimage. I am half Irish, the rest of my blood being watered down with German and Massachusetts English. But Irish blood doesn't water down very well; the strain must be very strong.'[48] This Protestant emigration continued, as we can note from the example of both sets of grandparents of actor Burt Lancaster, who left Belfast for New York in the second half of the nineteenth century.[49]

In 1865 E.L. Godkin, born in Co. Wicklow and a student at Queen's College Belfast, became the founding editor of the radical magazine *The Nation* in New York (still in existence today). From Co. Antrim, Samuel S. McClure, described by film-maker Michael Moore as the 'godfather of the muckrakers', launched in 1893 *McClure's Magazine* with its hard-hitting, investigative articles.[50] It is likely that this nineteenth- and early twentieth-century Protestant emigration is the main factor in the significant Protestant Irish presence outside the South in today's America. Opinion poll figures for the last decade of the twentieth century in the 'non-South' indicated that of those Americans who identified as Irish, 45 per cent were Catholic, 39 per cent Protestant and 16 per cent other or none.[51]

Thirdly, Akenson drew attention to people from a Catholic background who became Protestant. In the case of Ronald Reagan, his Irish links are believed to go back to Ballyboreen, Co. Tipperary, although the details are not fully clear. His Catholic father married a Scottish Presbyterian and their son Ronald was brought up in the faith of his mother. Former President Bill Clinton has an Irish connection through his mother, who was a Cassidy and whose family is believed to have come originally from Co. Fermanagh, probably in the eighteenth century. In July 2004 in an interview on BBC television, in reference to the unionist leader David Trimble, Clinton declared: 'He's a Scots-Irish Presbyterian and so am I, I guess mostly by background but my state of mind, I'm more like the Irish Catholics, more sort of rosy and loquacious.'[52] In fact, the name Cassidy is Gaelic rather than Scots and most, although not all, Cassidys in Fermanagh are Catholic. Vice-President Mike Pence is from a Catholic Irish American background but is now an evangelical Protestant. We may note that a recent Pew survey of religion in the US found that 28 per cent of people had left the faith in which they were raised, in favour of another religion or no religion at all.[53]

Characteristics of Protestant Irish

Other features of these Protestant Irish can be noted. Unlike nineteenth-century Catholic Irish emigrants, who in many places retained their Irish Catholic communities in face of a predominantly Protestant, and often hostile, American society, Protestant Irish emigrants intermarried and integrated very easily with members of other groups, 'bending them to their "characteristics and traditions" while also accepting them as equals in their communities'.[54] This aided their growth in numbers, as several writers have noted.[55] An obituary for the Irish American Notre Dame academic Ralph McInerny, 1929–2010, noted how he once wrote: 'My mother was fond of telling her children that they were all Irish, no tainted blood in our veins.' (In spite of this, his wife, whom he married in 1953, was of German Catholic origin.)[56] In contrast, from the early period these Protestant Irish intermarried with other communities, such as English, Scots and German, as well as former Catholic Irish.[57] We know this to be the case with members of Fulmouth Kearney's family in America.[58] In his autobiography, President Obama mentions the English and Scots forebears of his mother's family but not the Irish, showing how in his case the Irish connection became forgotten, until revealed by genealogists when he ran for the presidency.[59] On St Patrick's Day, 2009, President Obama joked at the White House with his guests from Ireland that if he had only known sooner about his Irish heritage, this fact 'would have been very helpful in Chicago'.[60] Other family members, however, were more aware of the Irish link.[61]

In addition, this factor of intermarriage and integration assists to account both for why these Protestant immigrants have been so influential in the past and also for why there was so little awareness of their existence fifty years ago. Unlike many Irish Americans, they rarely belonged to Irish ethnic social or political organisations. Instead, they were members of local churches and political societies. They were very much part of mainstream American society. This explains why so many American presidents have had Protestant ancestral links to Ireland, especially Ulster. Of the nineteenth-century American presidents, three (Jackson, Buchanan and Arthur) had one or two parents who were born in Ulster. Woodrow Wilson had a special Scotch-Irish background in the sense that his mother was Scottish while his paternal grandparents had come from Ireland in the early nineteenth century (Co. Tyrone and Co. Down). At the same time, in 1912 he protested against 'speaking of German-Americans, or Irish-Americans' and urged instead to 'drop out the first words, cut out the hyphens and call them American'.[62]

In the late nineteenth and early twentieth centuries, partly in response to the emergence of a strong Irish American community and political lobby around the Catholic Irish, there was a rise in interest among members of the Protestant Irish in creating a separate Scotch-Irish identity and community. A number of Scotch-Irish societies were formed and a series of conferences and publications were organised. By the 1920s, however, interest in this idea had largely waned. In a 1944 history of the Scotch-Irish in colonial Pennsylvania, W.F. Dunaway observed about their descendants that they 'have lost to a considerable degree their distinctive characteristics as they became merged with the general body of the people'. He commented: 'They have never been greatly concerned about traditions of fatherland, nor encumbered by these, in the manner of some … Once an isolated group, they are no longer so, being characteristic Americans in thought, word and deed.'[63] Nonetheless, evidence from census returns in the late twentieth century revealed that millions of Protestant Americans were still happy to acknowledge their Scotch-Irish ancestry.

What do we know about the socio-economic position of these Protestant Irish in modern America? Some of the wealthiest American families, such as the Gettys (from Co. Derry), the Hearsts (from

Co. Monaghan) and the Mellons (from Co. Tyrone), have Protestant Irish roots.[64] Nonetheless, the information that emerges about the bulk of people from this background reveals a very different picture, especially when we compare it to the position of Irish Catholics. The surveys conducted by NORC from the 1970s onwards have shown major divergences in the fortunes of Protestant Irish and Catholic Irish in twentieth-century America.[65] They revealed that on a table of key socio-economic indicators, such as education and income, for all European immigrant groups, the Protestant Irish were among those at the bottom while Catholic Irish were among those at the top.

The reason for this is explained by their contrasting geographical locations. Many Protestant Irish are located in less prosperous, southern and rural areas, while many Catholic Irish are located in more prosperous, northern and central, industrial and urban areas. Andrew Greeley in 1999 pointed out that, when Irish Protestants and Irish Catholics who live in the large cities in the north are compared, there is no difference in the economic and social measures: 'Region and urbanity account for the differences, not religious faith.'[66] We should also remember that while the largest concentration of these Irish Protestants is to be found in the South, significant numbers of those with Irish Protestant ancestry are to be found in the other areas.[67]

T.J. Meagher has described how the settlement of Irish Catholic emigrants in northern metropolitan regions in very tough circumstances in the nineteenth century, nonetheless, 'permitted their children, grandchildren and great grandchildren to take advantages offered by the dynamic centres of the world's most dynamic economy'.[68] In addition, because of their tendency to create major urban communities around a strong Irish Catholic identity, Irish Americans achieved a very visible and influential political place in twentieth-century America. This helps to explain why they were more easily observed in modern times than the Protestant Irish, whose presence and influence were more diffuse and integrated, although still influential in a general sense. It is important to note, however, that in recent decades, due to the passage of time and changes in American society and among Irish Americans, the Irish American community has also experienced considerable intermarriage and integration, as Reginald Byron has shown in his study of the Irish in Albany, New York.[69] It has been observed that there is no longer a monolithic Irish America or a significant Irish American voting bloc or influence.[70]

Figures for Irish and Scotch-Irish in the twenty-first century can be noted. The report of the 2013 American Community Survey recorded that all those who claimed an Irish ancestry numbered 33,996,484, including 9,492,676 who stated Irish as a single ancestry. The number who claimed a Scotch-Irish ancestry was put at 3,075,045, of whom 1,401,794 chose a single Scotch-Irish ancestry.[71] The report survey for 2009 showed that of the 36,915,000 who opted for a single or multiple Irish ancestry, 32 per cent were from the South, 24 per cent from the north-east, 24 per cent from the Midwest and 18 per cent from the West. Of the 3,570,000 who chose a single or multiple Scotch-Irish ancestry, 51 per cent were from the South, 20 per cent from the West, 17 per cent from the Midwest and 12 per cent from the north-east.[72] As regards their religious background, we can note that the 2006 NORC survey reported that of those who described their first ancestry as Irish, 48 per cent were Protestant, 29 per cent were Catholic and 23 per cent were other or no religion.[73] Most Scotch-Irish are Protestant.

It is important that these figures are interpreted correctly. There is still a widespread tendency, in America and Ireland, to assume that in the US there are some 3 million with a Scotch-Irish background and then another 30–40 million who are nearly all Irish Americans. This is not correct, as a majority of those 30–40 million who claim Irish ancestry are Protestants or are from a Protestant background and do not usually describe themselves as Irish Americans (or Scotch-Irish). A number of writers, including Andrew Greeley and Kevin Kenny, have used the term American Irish to refer to all people of Irish origin in America, regard-less of religion or regional background.[74]

Final Observations

Our knowledge of the Irish in America has changed greatly in recent decades. This relates not only to the size and composition of this group but also to how Irish identity is shared. Numbers are much greater and more diverse than understood before, thanks to evidence from the census reports and opinion surveys. This new picture was met with considerable surprise in both America and Ireland. In Irish American and Irish academic circles there was a deep reluctance to embrace the fact that a majority of those who claimed Irish ancestry were and always have been Protestant.[75] For many commentators the centre of attention for the story of the Irish in America remained the Irish Americans. At the same time, there has been a rise in research and published work on the importance of the Protestant Irish and Scotch-Irish role in eighteenth- and early nineteenth-century America.[76] David Doyle has written: 'In this era, 1763–1800, the Scots-Irish properly hold a place in "world history" as a key component in the first of the great modern revolutions.'[77]

Their descendants, however, have received much less attention. In 1993 Don Akenson's book, *The Irish Diaspora*, discussed the new findings on all the Irish in late twentieth-century America. *The Encyclopedia of the Irish in America*, edited by Michael Glazier and published in 1999, included work on the 'neglected' Scotch-Irish in earlier times and a valuable essay on the contemporary Irish, Protestant and Catholic, by Andrew Greeley.[78] Rankin Sherling has written on Protestant Irish immigrants in nineteenth- and early twentieth-century Ireland.[79] In 2000 the *Journal of Scotch-Irish Studies* was established, under the editorship of Joyce Alexander and Richard McMaster, to encourage scholarly studies on the Scotch-Irish, past and present. Nonetheless, many recent books and articles on the Irish diaspora and the Irish in America continue to give only cursory treatment to the majority Protestant section of those with Irish ancestry in America today.

The use of the term 'Scotch-Irish' has been a matter of debate, both in the past and the present. Writing in 1962, J.G. Leyburn claimed that the appellation Scotch-Irish had been used rarely in the eighteenth century, but was a 'useful term' to distinguish Presbyterians from Ulster of Scottish origin from other emigrants, from Ireland and Scotland.[80] Recently a number of historians have agreed that the name was seldom used in this earlier period, but they have differed in their views as to whether it was in the late eighteenth and early nineteenth centuries or the late nineteenth century that the term took on a special significance for some Irish Protestants to differentiate them from Irish Catholics, now defined widely as Irish Americans.[81] They prefer to use the name Scots-Irish or Ulster Scots. On the other hand, in 2004 Michael Montgomery wrote that the appellation Scotch-Irish had 'considerable currency' before the nineteenth century and recorded some twenty-four examples of references to its use in seventeenth- and eighteenth-century America. He believes the term has long been and still is meaningful for 'people of Presbyterian heritage with Ulster foreparents'.[82] He rejects the name Scots-Irish and insists on Scotch-Irish, citing 'the privilege, granted routinely to groups in modern society, to name themselves'. At the same time, it seems that while the term was used in the eighteenth century, it was more common for these emigrants from Ulster to be called Irish. Today a majority of their descendants self-identify in census returns as Irish, rather than Scotch-Irish or Scots-Irish.

The new figures for the Irish in America raise interesting issues about identity today, especially among those Protestants who claim Irish or Scotch-Irish ancestry. Probably, for many the acknowledgement of their ancestry is primarily a matter of record, describing simply their place of origin or their ancestral roots, as they understand or recall them. For others, however, this background has a special significance. Published in 2004, Senator Jim Webb's best-selling book, *Born Fighting: How the Scots-Irish Shaped America*, raised a new awareness of the Scots-Irish/Scotch-Irish heritage. He chose the term Scots-Irish as a more appropriate modern term than Scotch-Irish, although he accepts the latter name was valid in earlier times. Webb argued that, rather than blending completely into American society, many Scots-Irish descendants have retained to the present their own particular Scots-Irish identity.[83] He emphasised their military and musical traditions.[84] He believes that the Scots-Irish are an underestimated and unrecognised group, and that many who self-identify as Irish are also of Scots-Irish background. In a 2006 article, Michael Carroll asked why so many people, especially in the South, still claimed an Irish identity. He argued that they did so because they 'are likely associating themselves with the character traits stereotypically associated with the Scotch-Irish', who are seen as an independent, individualistic and religious people, at the forefront of the American Revolution, and whose values came to dominate American culture. He stated that 'For American Protestants … to be Irish is to present yourself as someone who embodies the continuing spirit of the American Revolution'.[85]

In 2016 J.D.Vance's *Hillbilly Elegy: A Memoir of a Family and Culture in Crisis* was published. He explained that he identified with 'the millions of working-class white Americans of Scots-Irish descent who have no college degree. To these folks, poverty is the family tradition.'[86] He stated: 'Their ancestors were day labourers in the Southern slave economy, sharecroppers after that, and machinists and millworkers during more recent times.' From their first arrival in the eighteenth century, these people were attracted to the extensive Greater Appalachian region. Later many moved and became blue-collar workers in other states. Vance reckons that 'the Scots-Irish are one of the most distinctive subgroups in America', with their own cultural, social and political traditions. In recent times, however, many of these people have suffered job losses and social disintegration, due to changes in the American economy and society. Vance told his story as a member of this group. The book became a bestseller because it was seen as giving a special insight into the white American working class whose members took on a special significance during the presidential election. Also it helps to illuminate one strand of the descendants of these eighteenth-century Ulster immigrants.

On 28 July 2016 the *Washington Post* carried an article with a headline that read: 'Our first black president plays up his Scots-Irish heritage – and it has everything to do with Trump.' This referred to a speech at the Democratic National Convention, when President Barack Obama recalled his Kansas grandparents and their predecessors. Although his Kearney ancestors were Episcopalians from the south of Ireland, he declared: 'They were Scotch-Irish mostly farmers, teachers, ranch hands, pharmacists, oil rig workers ... Some were Democrats, but a lot of them, maybe even most of them, were Republicans.'[87] The article warned: 'Politicians ignore the Scots-Irish at their peril.' It noted that those who self-identified as Scots-Irish in the census were relatively small in number but acknowledged that they had strong historical and cultural links to a much larger group, especially in the Greater Appalachian region. Some now describe themselves as 'American', but, as we have seen, most from this Scots-Irish background identify as Irish in the census. Both Obama and Vance chose to employ the terms Scots-Irish or Scotch-Irish, rather than Irish, perhaps on these occasions to avoid popular confusion with the term Irish American. Their use here in 2016 reveals that they retain a contemporary resonance.

The picture that has emerged of the current numbers and identities of the descendants of people who left Ireland for America challenges some of our traditional assumptions. The example of Barack Obama and his Kearney family connections has helped to cast light on such matters. Not only are there far more from a Protestant background among these people than expected, but most of them acknowledge an Irish rather that a Scotch-Irish/Scots-Irish identity. We should avoid viewing these identities as prescriptive or exclusive. At present such identities are often fluid and interrelated, as they probably were in the eighteenth century.[88] Currently, some 3 million identify as Scotch-Irish. But around 34 million acknowledge an Irish ancestry, and of these a majority are from a Protestant or former Protestant background, due in large part to eighteenth-century emigration from Ulster. Most of these Protestants have always described their background as Irish, although sometimes they will acknowledge a Scots-Irish/Scotch-Irish dimension. At the same time, especially outside the South, there are many others with Irish ancestry who are Protestant, but do not have these eighteenth-century Ulster origins, such as Barack Obama. The new information about the American Irish that has emerged in recent decades challenges ideas of an exclusive Irish identity or a pure strain of Irishness based around one religious or ancestral section. The tens of millions who acknowledge their Irish ancestry – Irish Americans, Scotch-Irish/Scots-Irish and Protestant Irish – reflect different historical experiences. For all these people, with their family roots in Ireland, and in their various ways, an Irish identity remains of value.

PART 4

POLITICS, 1885–1923

THE 1885 AND 1886 GENERAL ELECTIONS: A MILESTONE IN IRISH HISTORY

In the recent history of Ireland, both north and south, certain events are seen in retrospect to have been crucial in establishing the basis of our parties and political divisions. Modern politics in the republic are viewed as rooted in the 1916 Rising in Dublin and in the Civil War of the early 1920s, while politics in Northern Ireland are regarded as based on the outcome of the events of 1912–14 and the Government of Ireland Act of 1920. Undoubtedly these episodes were very important, but it should be realised that they influenced a political situation that had already emerged in its essential form at the general elections of 1885 and 1886.[1] These elections saw the birth of modern political parties based on a new mass electorate that embraced nearly every household in the country. Even more significantly, these years witnessed the emergence, for the first time throughout Ireland, of distinct nationalist/unionist politics linked to a clear Protestant/Catholic division. Later events of 1912–23 would determine the final shape of the territorial and constitutional structures for the two new political units of modern Ireland, but the outcome of these two crucial elections established the basic character of late nineteenth- and early twentieth-century politics in both parts of the country.

Politics, Pre-1885

Conflict over nationalism was not new to elections in 1885–86, but in the past there had usually been a wide range of political opinion and swings in popular support often occurred. Daniel O'Connell's Repeal party and the Young Irelanders had laid the grounds for a nationalist movement. In the 1850s and 1860s, however, the political scene in Ireland had been dominated by the liberal and conservative parties, which accepted the United Kingdom framework. It was not until the general election of 1874, with the appearance of the home rule movement, linked to the issues of land and educational reform, that constitutional nationalism became again an important political force. Even so, the general election of 1880 returned not only sixty-two Home Rule party MPs, but also fifteen liberals and twenty-six conservatives. There were important regional variations. On the eve of the 1885 general election, three Home Rulers only, plus nine liberals and seventeen conservatives, represented the nine counties of Ulster, compared with sixty-two Home Rulers, seven liberals and nine conservatives for the rest of Ireland.[2]

Rivalry between denominations was also not new to Irish politics in 1885, but at previous elections the influence of religious division in relation to political matters was rarely clear cut. While Protestants tended to vote conservative and Catholics were likely to vote liberal, there were times of noticeable exception, such as the general election of 1859 when many Catholics voted conservative, and the general elections of 1868–80 when many Protestants, in particular northern Presbyterians, backed the liberal cause. The Home Rule party won largely Catholic support, although in 1874 and 1880 there were considerable numbers of Protestant Home Rule MPs. Elections before 1885 reflected reasonably well changes in political attitudes, although the franchise was restricted to limited categories of property owners and occupiers. There were some well-run local political associations in Ireland before 1885, especially in Ulster, but party organisation in the constituencies was for the most part conducted on an ad hoc basis.

From 1885–86 onwards, however, conflict over the national issue, based very largely on a Protestant/Catholic divide, remained at the centre of Irish elections right up to 1921 and significantly affected the nature of politics that emerged after 1921 in Northern Ireland and the Irish Free State. These political divisions were strongly felt throughout the whole community owing to the new household vote and effective political organisations, both local and central. The first part of this study will look at the social, economic and religious background. The second part will be concerned with analysis of the changes to the electoral law, growth of new party organisations and an account of the two election campaigns, followed by an analysis of the polling. Finally, the impact of political developments in these two years must be examined and an explanation given as to why the outcome of these two general elections has proved to have had such a lasting significance.

The Social, Economic and Religious Background

To understand the significance of the elections of 1885 and 1886 it is essential that the political events surrounding them should not be viewed in isolation. Social and economic factors formed an important background to the rise of nationalism and unionism in Ireland. In 1841 the population of Ireland was three times that of Scotland and more than half that of England and Wales.[3] Fifty years later, however, after the Famine and continuous emigration in Ireland and massive industrialisation in Great Britain, the picture was very different. By 1891, Ireland's population had fallen to slightly less than that of Scotland and one-eighth of the population of England and Wales.[4] Such developments helped to encourage nationalism. To many nationalists this population decline was seen as linked to the union. In November 1885 Parnell's lieutenant, Thomas Sexton, declared: 'We look back to the year of the union, along that level plain of years to see the shameful, the miserable results of English rule in Ireland ... The population of Ireland was greater than now, the comfort of the people was greater.'[5]

In Ulster the nineteenth-century social and economic experience was rather different. Although parts of Ulster witnessed population decline similar to that elsewhere in Ireland, other parts, especially in the northeast, experienced considerable prosperity, as a result of industrialisation.

In 1841 Ulster's population was 29 per cent of that of the whole of Ireland, but by 1891 it stood at 34 per cent. In 1841 Belfast's population was 75,308, or one-third of Dublin's population of 232,726, but by 1891 Belfast's figure was 255,950 compared with Dublin's 245,001.[6] Belfast grew faster than any other urban centre in the British Isles in the second half of the nineteenth century. The Grand Trades Arch in Donegall Place in Belfast for the royal visit of 1885 captured well the spirit of Victorian Belfast with slogans such as 'Trade is the golden girdle of the globe' and 'Employment is nature's physician'.[7] Industrialisation around shipbuilding, engineering and linen linked Belfast and the region to the markets of Great Britain and the empire. For many unionists in Ulster the period of the union was seen as a time of rising prosperity.

The land question was another source of division between Ireland and Great Britain and between Ulster and the rest of Ireland. The Great Famine, with its enormous human toll, affected north-east Ulster less than elsewhere in Ireland, thanks to northern industrialisation and the availability of crops other than the potato. After the Famine, rising agricultural prices brought a growth in prosperity throughout the Irish countryside.[8] Nonetheless, the question of tenure continued as a major source of discontent until the reforms of the 1880s that followed the land war of 1879–81. In Ulster, however, farmers benefited from the 'Ulster custom', which gave certain rights to farmers. While this custom had weaknesses, which were to help cause tenant unrest at various points in the nineteenth century, it gave greater security to Ulster farmers than elsewhere and, as a result, the question of land reform, whether in the early 1850s or the 1870s, seems to have caused less bitterness in the north than elsewhere.

Such major social and economic divisions, which influenced the rise of Irish nationalism, could have helped to create a straightforward split between a totally unionist Ulster and the rest of Ireland, which was entirely nationalist. To understand why this did not happen it is essential to look at the religious factor. In 1881, Catholics formed 76.54 per cent of the Irish population while in Great Britain the population was predominantly Protestant. Within Ireland Protestants were 23.46 per cent of the total population, and only 9 per cent outside Ulster, but they were in a small majority in the whole province of Ulster and a substantial majority in the north-east. Three-quarters of Irish Protestants were to be found in Ulster, but Catholics in Ulster were only one-fifth of their whole community in Ireland.[9] For Catholics and Protestants in nineteenth-century Ireland both religious conflict and the strength of denominational bonds had an important impact on their political positions. Religious division was important not only between Ireland and Britain but within Irish society.

Religious issues such as Catholic emancipation had been the cause of considerable political unrest in the first half of the nineteenth century. Although most specifically religious issues were settled by the 1870s, this denominational factor still coloured people's views on broader political matters, including the question of the link with Great Britain and community relations within Ireland. Religious controversies, particularly over education, continued to cause Catholic disillusionment with Westminster, a feeling not experienced by Protestants. The strengthening of denominational ties and identities in Ireland, influenced greatly by the revivalism that occurred among all the main denominations in the second half of the nineteenth century, meant that for most people in Ireland, the links with their respective religious groups were very important.[10] Until the mid-1880s, nonetheless, the correlation between religious and political divisions was far from complete. There were sharp divisions in voting behaviour between Presbyterians and members of the Church of Ireland in Ulster, and there were differences between Catholics in Ulster and elsewhere in how they voted.

During 1885–86, however, denominational ties and identities emerged as the main determining factor in political behaviour, regardless of regional or class differences. In these years nearly all Ulster Catholics, of every social rank, identified with the political aspirations of their co-religionists elsewhere in Ireland and voted nationalist. In March 1886, Patrick MacAllister, the new Catholic bishop of Down and Connor, expressed his satisfaction at 'seeing the Catholics of Belfast working in harmony with those of the rest of Ireland in the cause of nationality'.[11] Most Protestants, Presbyterians as well as members of the Church of Ireland, in Ulster and in the rest of Ireland, came together in support of the union, although only in Ulster were they able to elect unionist MPs. Social and economic differences between Ulster and the rest of Ireland go part of the way to help explain the rise of nationalism and unionism, but in the new political alignments that finally emerged in 1885–86, the division between Protestant and Catholic proved of great importance.

Economic and social tensions between Protestant and Catholic played some part in the rise of the opposing camps of unionist and nationalist, but their importance should not be exaggerated, chiefly because the other main divisions and conflicts in society did not correlate to a simple Protestant/Catholic divide. Members of the Church of Ireland owned most of the land and dominated official positions, at the expense not just of Catholics but also of Presbyterians. In many parts of Ulster, Catholics were over-represented among unskilled labourers and small farmers, while Presbyterians dominated the skilled jobs and the larger farm sector. However, many ordinary members of the Church of Ireland had little or no special advantage in these latter areas.[12] Social divisions in Ireland often crossed religious divisions. Nonetheless, in the long run religion served not only to provide a key source of grievance, namely education, but it united people on a denominational community basis. The new political arrangements of 1885–86 now established firmly the link between parties and religious division.

Franchise Changes, Party Organisations and Political Campaigns

In addition to the underlying social, economic and religious factors affecting Irish life in the 1880s, changes in electoral law provided important new conditions for the crucial general elections of 1885 and 1886. As a result of the 1883 Corrupt and Illegal Practices Act, the amount of money that candidates could spend on their election campaigns was restricted, and so new, voluntary party organisations were now required. Throughout the country, constituencies of roughly equal size were established by the 1885 Redistribution of Seats Act, which also expanded the number of constituencies from 64 to 101. The Third Reform Act of 1884 extended the vote to adult male householders and thus increased the number of Irish voters by more than 200 per cent between 1884 and 1885: important sections of the population, in particular labourers and small farmers, were now enfranchised for the first time.[13] A parliamentary return of 1884–85 showed Catholic majorities in all constituencies except for half the Ulster divisions. These changes presented the existing parties with considerable problems and opportunities.

Other challenges also faced the parties on the eve of the 1885 general election. Throughout the community there was a heightened sense of political consciousness, aroused originally over the land question. Agrarian protest had not only resulted in the 1881 Second Irish Land Act, which gave farmers new rights, but it had also undermined the landlords, who had traditionally played a key role in Irish politics. After the 1881 Tyrone by-election one observer commented: 'The fact is that Protestants as well as the Roman Catholics do not want an Orangeman or even a Fenian if he is a gentleman or a landlord.'[14] By 1885 landlord–tenant relations were no longer the major issue, which meant that other divisions such as between farmers and labourers, urban and rural interests, and Protestant and Catholic, assumed new importance for the parties, as did interest groups and internal conflicts.

The various parties responded in different ways to these new challenges. After the 1880 general election C.S. Parnell had taken over the leadership of the Home Rule party, the largest party in Ireland with sixty-three seats, but until 1885 it remained a loosely organised body with little discipline among the members in parliament and ad hoc organisational structures in the constituencies. In early 1885 it was reckoned that Parnell could count on the wholehearted support of only some twenty to thirty MPs of his Home Rule group, and he also had to deal with both agrarian activists and radical nationalist elements.[15] Parnell, however, was also head of the National League, which had been set up to harness agrarian and nationalist protest after the suppression of the Land League. During 1885 the Home Rule movement underwent marked reorganisation and growth under the direction of Parnell and his followers in the National League.

In common parlance the term 'home-ruler' gave way to 'nationalist'. The National League provided for the nationalist party an effective organisation through its local branches, which expanded rapidly in

1885. County conventions selected parliamentary candidates, under the supervision of representatives from the organising committee of the League, which was controlled by Parnell. A pledge was introduced to bind the MPs together into a tightly disciplined party. Thus, as Conor Cruise O'Brien remarked, the National League turned the Home Rule movement from a loose grouping of independent elements into a 'well-knit political party of a modern type ... effectively monopolising the political expression of national sentiment'.[16] This reorganisation allowed the nationalist party to face the general election very effectively. The National League embraced small farmers and labourers as well as larger farmers and so helped to mitigate chances of social division. Efforts by Michael Davitt and others to radicalise the movement, in particular to organise the labourers, were thwarted and the influence of nationalist radicals was largely destroyed.

Vital for this socially cohesive, countrywide organisation was the forging of a 'very effective, if informal, clerical nationalist alliance', as Emmet Larkin called it.[17] Acceptance of Catholic claims on education won the party the approval of the hierarchy in mid-1885. The intervention of Archbishop William Walsh of Dublin ensured that all Catholic clergy should have the right to attend nationalist conventions to select parliamentary candidates.[18] Catholic clergy now played an important role at these conventions as well as in many cases, such as in Co. Westmeath, providing local leadership for National League branches.[19] In the months immediately preceding the election, candidates were selected for every constituency, except those Ulster divisions with a Protestant majority. So successful was the party in capturing the nationalist electorate that only in one Irish constituency did an independent nationalist stand. In early October Parnell declared that the party platform would consist of a single plank, 'the plank of legislative independence'.[20]

In response to this nationalist reorganisation, the Irish Loyal and Patriotic Union (ILPU) was formed in Dublin in May 1885 by a number of southern businessmen, landowners and academics. It sought to organise opposition in the three southern provinces to the nationalists, and to unite liberals and conservatives on a common platform of maintenance of the union. The ILPU also published pamphlets and leaflets that were circulated widely. In its aim of bringing together liberals and conservatives the ILPU was successful, and in some cases candidates came forward in the election simply as 'loyalists'. A total of fifty-four of the southern seats were contested by anti-Home Rule candidates.[21]

In Ulster, however, appeals for unity between supporters of the union went unheeded and the liberal and conservative parties continued to operate separately. The election of 1885 in Ulster involved not only nationalists against supporters of the union but rivalry between liberal and conservative. Before the general election, the Ulster liberals, whose support lay chiefly with the tenant farmers, and included both Catholics and Presbyterians, held nine seats. With an impressive headquarters at the recently built Reform Club in Belfast, they sought to develop new local divisional associations. In spite of a good central office, however, and contrary to later claims of a strong liberal effort, the evidence of liberal activity at the registration courts and in the constituencies during the campaign reflected lack of vitality and effective local organisation.[22] Attempts were made to embrace labourers in their new divisional associations, though with little success, partly because of the identification of the liberals with the farmers' cause. On the eve of the 1885 general election, the liberals still retained considerable support among Presbyterian farmers, even if it was clear that the nationalist movement was proving very attractive to Catholic farmers in Ulster who had formerly voted liberal. Liberal candidates declared their support for the union between Great Britain and Ireland and also called for further land reform.

Before the 1885 general election the conservatives held seventeen seats in Ulster. They were widely regarded as the former landlord party, and because of this their electoral prospects must have appeared poor. Conservative party organisation had developed to some extent in the province over the previous ten years with the growth of a number of county and borough conservative associations, but these bodies had a limited popular involvement. Historians have sometimes painted a bleak picture of conservative organisation during 1885, but this picture relies on the evidence of party apathy and disunity in Counties Armagh and Fermanagh.[23] Elsewhere, however, matters were very different, especially in the north-east of Ulster. Under the energetic leadership of E.S. Finnigan, a full-time party organiser based in Belfast, the conservatives extensively reorganised in 1885. Finnigan helped to set up, with strong local participation, many divisional associations, especially in the key areas of Belfast and Counties Antrim and Down.[24]

A vital aspect of these new branches was the involvement of the Orange Order. Local lodges were given special positions in many of the new organisations. For example, speaking in Ballynahinch, Co. Down, on 7 May 1885, Finnigan described proposals to set up a broadly based local committee: 'The Orange Association would have a well-defined position. The district master and district officers ... would be appointed upon each committee.'[25] At this stage the Order was a minority movement among Protestants, but it embraced many of the newly enfranchised labourers and was therefore an important means of integrating the working class into the conservative party. Such arrangements went smoothly in Counties Antrim and Down, but ran into trouble in Belfast and Counties Armagh and Derry, where Orange labourers felt that they were being given no influence in the new conservative machine: in the latter areas they rebelled against the local conservative organisers and either forced them to accept candidates agreeable to them or, as in the case of two of the four Belfast seats, ran independent candidates of their own. In a number of cases in addition, conservative party organisers co-operated secretly with nationalist party organisers to undermine the liberals and the middle ground. Conservative candidates emphasised their support for the union.

In Ulster the nationalist party had started the election campaign in a weak position. Only three of the former Ulster MPs were Home Rulers, thanks to a weak Home Rule organisation in the past and to the success of the Ulster liberals in attracting the anti-conservative vote. During 1885, however, the National League expanded considerably in many parts of Ulster. A government report on National League activity over the period 1 January–30 June 1885 commented: 'The most noteworthy feature is the progress that the League is making in Ulster, especially in Armagh, Down, Fermanagh, Tyrone and Monaghan; three new branches have even been started in Co. Antrim.'[26] League organisers from Dublin, such as Timothy Harrington, played an important role in the spread of the movement and in its preparations for the elections. Conventions, under the chairmanship of a representative of the party leadership, were held to select candidates for those constituencies with a Catholic majority. Mid-Armagh was the only division with a Protestant majority contested by a nationalist (see paragraph below). In both the conventions and the National League branches, Catholic clergy played an important part in most constituencies. Only in Co. Derry was there an effort, among both clergy and party leaders, to avoid a clerical image.[27]

Early in the campaign strong efforts were made to promote nationalist unity. National League branches in Belfast, favourable to Michael Davitt, were closed down in late 1884 and early 1885, and other steps were taken to weaken his influence, including the removal of the editor of the *Morning News*, C.J. Dempsey, a supporter of Davitt's, who later commented to John Pinkerton: 'I am too great a disciple of Davitt's ... the MPs want me effaced from Ulster politics.'[28] In some areas nationalist organisers co-operated secretly with conservative organisers to keep all Catholics together in the nationalist movement and also to undermine the liberals. For example, to thwart Dempsey standing for South Armagh, the local convention under the chairmanship of T.M. Healy had picked a compromise candidate, Alex Blane, a tailor by trade. Since, in Healy's words, 'nobody knew him and snobbery was rampant', this aroused the threat of an independent nationalist splitting the Catholic vote – a danger only averted by Healy secretly arranging for a conservative to come forward in South Armagh, which obliged the independent to step down; in return for this conservative favour, Healy agreed to put forward a nationalist candidate in Mid-Armagh to damage the liberal candidate's chances.[29] In other areas where there was no nationalist candidate, the Catholic vote was given to the conservatives to help destroy the liberals and any potential cross-community electoral support they might command.[30]

Results of Elections

The outcome of the 1885 general election was a resounding victory for the nationalist party, which won eighty-five seats throughout Ireland, plus a seat in Liverpool; in Ulster the party held seventeen out of the thirty-three constituencies. Apart from two Dublin University seats, held by the conservatives, pro-union candidates were successful only in Ulster, where the conservative party took sixteen seats, while the liberal party failed to win a single division. These conservative figures include two successful independent candidates in Belfast who were subsequently adopted by the official conservative associations. Out of eighty-five nationalists, eighty were Catholic; all Ulster nationalist MPs were Catholic. All the eighteen conservatives were members of the Church of Ireland, except for three Presbyterians and one Methodist; most of the unsuccessful liberals had been Presbyterian. Parnell now returned to parliament with a strong, disciplined nationalist party. For their part, the Ulster conservatives had emerged as the clear leaders of pro-union support in Ireland.

An analysis of the voting for the two sides shows a high degree of religious polarisation in the constituencies. It is clear that nearly all Catholics who voted backed the nationalist party, except in some northern constituencies where there were no nationalist candidates and where Catholics voted conservative for tactical reasons. In perhaps as many as six divisions, last-minute Catholic support for the conservative against the liberal proved significant.[31] In a few southern constituencies small numbers of Catholics may have voted for pro-union candidates. It is also evident that nearly all Protestants who voted supported pro-union candidates. Although Protestants were 10 per cent of the population outside Ulster, they were too widely dispersed to win any seats. In Co. Derry there is evidence of some Protestants voting for a nationalist (partly because of the candidate's reputation on the land question, and efforts in the county to present a non-sectarian image). Generally, however, it is clear that the electorate had polarised sharply along denominational lines throughout the country. Protestant nationalists such as C.S. Parnell, or Jeremiah Jordan from Co. Fermanagh, and Catholic unionists such as Daniel O'Connell, son of the Liberator, and W.T. McGrath from Belfast were rare exceptions.

Within nine months there occurred another general election, which would serve to copper-fasten the outcome of the 1885 general election. Early in 1886 Gladstone announced his support for Home Rule, and in April the First Home Rule Bill was introduced but defeated. Gladstone's action now caused a split among the liberals. In Ulster the vast majority of liberals became liberal unionists and in the general election of mid-1886 joined with the conservatives in a common pro-union front. Various social and denominational differences between the former liberals and conservatives were ignored in the new unionist movement. A small group of pro-Gladstone supporters fought the election as Gladstonian liberals. There also appeared a new organisation called the Irish Protestant Home Rule Association with the aim of promoting the principle of Home Rule among Protestants.[32]

At the 1886 general election only thirty-three constituencies in Ireland were contested, compared with seventy-nine in 1885; outside Ulster a mere seven divisions out of sixty-eight saw a poll. Out of seventy nationalist candidates, sixty-two were returned unopposed in the southern provinces; the eight who were opposed were returned with large majorities. Most Ulster divisions were contested.[33] In seventeen of these contests, conservatives faced nationalists (including some Protestant nationalist candidates), in five liberal unionists fought nationalists and in another five Gladstonian liberals opposed conservatives. The bulk of former liberals in the main unionist constituencies in the northeast played little active part in the election, leaving the unionist political organisations to be effectively controlled by the conservative victors of 1885. The outcome in Ulster was the election of fifteen conservatives, two liberal unionists and sixteen nationalists. Overall, the nationalists won eighty-four seats, plus a seat in Liverpool. The conservatives won seventeen (including two Dublin University seats) and the liberal unionists two – a result that reflected accurately the comparative strength of the two groups in the new unionist movement.

Viewed broadly, it is evident that again most Catholic voters supported nationalist candidates and most Protestant voters backed unionist candidates. Some Protestants did vote for nationalists, although it is difficult to put a precise figure on their numbers. Probably it is fair to say that only around 3,000 Protestants (mainly former liberals) voted for Gladstonian liberals and nationalist candidates. Under the unionist flag were now former conservatives and liberals. The latter would survive as a minor grouping within the unionist family until the full incorporation of the Ulster Liberal Unionist Society into the unionist party in 1911. The nationalist party would split over the Parnell divorce but eventually would succeed in realigning itself within the broad framework established in 1885. These two crucial years, therefore, saw the emergence of nationalism and unionism in Ireland and the polarisation of politics on the basis of religious affiliation. In spite of later attempts at accommodation, the divisions that emerged at this time with Catholic and nationalist on one side and Protestant and unionist on the other remained central to Irish politics up to 1921 and formed a basic background to the politics that emerged thereafter.

Consequences of these Elections

The political developments of 1885–86 had a vital effect on how nationalism and unionism emerged finally in their particular forms. These two years were the climax to a period of great political change and mobilisation in the whole country. The extension of the franchise and changes in electoral law, as well as the high degree of popular excitement over the issues that now held the public attention, meant that entirely new demands were placed on party organisations and leaders. Their response to this situation not only affected immediate party fortunes but also influenced greatly the whole nature of politics to emerge at this time. The structure and spirit of the new party organisations had a very important bearing on the type of politics and society to develop. These parties reflected certain divisions in society, and particular elements (such as the Orange Order and the Catholic clergy) had key roles in the new organisational structures. The religious divisions in Irish society had often had some bearing on party divisions but in 1885–86 the two victorious parties based firmly their respective movements on denominational differences. The decisions by both the nationalist and conservative party leadership to adapt their organisations in the way they did (important in the first instance to meet the challenges of 1885–86 and to win the elections) had a far-reaching influence on the new political and social confrontations that materialised at these elections.

Many special features of nationalism and unionism were the result of developments that occurred in these years. The new nationalist movement that emerged had support from throughout the island of Ireland, but in practice it represented only the Catholic community.[34]

The events of this period ensured that Irish nationalism emerged as a Catholic movement with strong clerical support. There had been connections in the past between Irish nationalism and Catholicism but events of the mid-1880s established the link in a formal and thorough way. Ironically, it was a Protestant leader of the nationalist party, C.S. Parnell, who was responsible for the 'alliance' of 1884–85 between nationalism and the Catholic Church in Ireland that played a vital part in the electoral success of his party in 1885. Undoubtedly, as Emmet Larkin argued, this link had democratic benefits in that it prevented the emergence of an all-powerful central party, but it did help to give Irish nationalism a strong denominational character.[35]

The new unionist movement was concerned with defending the union but because of the events of 1885–86 it represented only Protestants and won seats only in Ulster. The failure of the Ulster liberals to hold Catholic support meant that the new combination of former liberals and conservatives represented just one part of the Ulster population. This new unionist movement, furthermore, was dominated by the conservative, Orange-backed element in Ulster society, with the gentry still prominent, at the expense of the more radical, liberal section. Ironically, the tactical support given by nationalists to conservative candidates in 1885 played a vital role in moving power in the pro-union community to conservative elements. The link between the Orange lodges and the new unionist associations did introduce a populist, democratic element into unionist politics but it also served to reinforce the denominational nature of unionism. The individual responsible for this Orange/unionist link was E.S. Finnigan and not, as is often alleged, Lord Randolph Churchill, whose well-known 'Orange card' speech was made only in 1886 (after the link was well established) and related primarily to English power politics. Outside of Ulster, unionists formed an important minority but their only parliamentary representation came from the two Dublin University seats.

The 1885–86 general elections marked the birth of modern politics in both parts of Ireland.[36] In the succeeding three and a half decades up to 1923 there would be significant developments that would affect the new territorial and constitutional arrangements to emerge in the early 1920s, but which would not alter the essentials of the conflict that materialised in 1885–86. Unionism would move from a concern to maintain all Ireland for the union, to a defence of Ulster, and then to support for only six of the Ulster counties. Nationalism would witness the collapse of the parliamentary Nationalist party and the triumph of Sinn Féin. Support from the main parties in Britain affected the fortunes of both nationalists and unionists. The threat or use of violence played an important role. The two new states would be marked by the turmoil of their establishment in the years 1920–23. All these developments, however, took place within the basic framework established in 1885–86 and served to modify but not to replace the fundamental confrontations and alliances that emerged at that time. The results of the 1918 general election served only to confirm the outcome of these crucial earlier general elections.

Conflict over nationalism remained the key factor, whether between nationalist and unionist before 1921, between pro-treaty and anti-treaty nationalists in the Civil War or between unionists and nationalists in Northern Ireland after 1921. The new party systems to emerge in both the Irish Free State and Northern Ireland were greatly influenced by this conflict, which effectively diminished the importance of other social and regional divisions. The connection between politics and religious division remained very strong. Both sides could sometimes win supporters across the denominational barriers, such as the Catholic unionist MP Denis Henry, or the Protestant Sinn Féin MP and TD Ernest Blythe. Nonetheless, unionism and nationalism were rooted firmly in their respective religious camps. After 1921 most Protestants in the south were politically marginalised outside the main parties, while in the north political and religious divisions remained strongly linked. The creation of two new political units in Ireland in 1921, and the political systems 'without social bases', that emerged in both parts thereafter, are directly linked to the outcome of the 1885–86 general elections.

Explanations for the Importance of these Elections

Why were these elections so important? Other elections in the nineteenth century had witnessed significant events, but none had such obvious lasting relevance. Part of the answer to this question lies in the nature of some of the broader changes that occurred. Key social and economic developments, in particular the main resolution of the land question, the enormous growth of Belfast and the strengthening of religious identities, all of which set the scene for modern Ireland, occurred in the preceding period. This, it should also be remembered, was the era when for the first time the vast majority of the people were able to read and write. The other part of the answer lies in the very significant extension of the franchise and the rise of modern political parties that took place in these years of mass political mobilisation and electoral change. Although universal suffrage was still a thing of the future, most households had a vote. There was now an extensive network of local political associations with popular involvement, and, especially in the nationalist case, a strong central party organisation.

The importance of such developments has been noted elsewhere by political scientists.[37] In many parts of Europe the particular divisions that emerged as important at the end of the nineteenth and the beginning of the twentieth centuries have remained significant throughout the succeeding years. Party systems have continued remarkably true to the traditions and shape of the politics established at this point where broad-based modern parties, with a wide franchise, came into being for the first time. People have subsequently voted simply for the same parties as their parents. Even when particular parties have collapsed and new ones have arisen, they have often remained within the basic framework of the party system established at this earlier stage. Nationalism and unionism, along with religious divisions, emerged at this key formative period to dominate modern politics in Ireland.

Neither the polarisation of politics along denominational lines nor the emergence of nationalism were unique to Ireland, but have strong parallels in contemporary Europe. Although it was no longer a major factor in politics in Great Britain by this stage, religious conflict remained important in other parts of Western Europe. In Germany, Switzerland and Holland there were significant divisions between Protestant and Catholic parties.[38] Various European countries, such as Norway and Italy, also experienced the rise of nationalist politics with important consequences for party cleavages.[39] The situation in Ireland, however, differed from the situation in these countries in that, besides religious differences, there was also a split over the national question and, because of the changes we have witnessed, each division powerfully reinforced the other.

These general elections of 1885–86 saw the emergence of two distinct political movements, based firmly on particular religious groupings, with strongly opposed views on the nature of the nation, the state and the central issue of sovereignty. Both sides would claim ancient historical roots for their position, but in fact the conflict that emerged was greatly influenced by contemporary political and social developments. At this key period, party leaders, organisers and supporters, influenced and aided by the social, economic and religious developments of their age, created a new order of politics where the religious and national divisions were firmly related in a form that would prove long lasting. Later political events would influence the final territorial and constitutional shape of the new political units to emerge in 1921 but the outcome of the events surrounding the general elections of 1885 and 1886 decided the basic character of political conflict in the country. These crucial years set the scene for the rivalry between unionist and nationalist in the north and between different nationalist groups in the south that has dominated all subsequent political development in both parts of Ireland.

SOUTHERN PROTESTANT VOICES DURING THE IRISH WAR OF INDEPENDENCE AND THE CIVIL WAR: REPORTS FROM CHURCH OF IRELAND SYNODS

The subject of the experiences of southern Protestants, 1919–23, has just recently attracted the attention of historians. In the past most books on the Irish War of Independence and the Civil War avoided mention of their position. When we turn to histories of the Church of Ireland we find only the briefest account of the impact of this period. For example, in W. Alison Phillips's edited three-volume history of the Church of Ireland, published in the 1930s, there are whole chapters devoted to the early Patrician period, but events of a decade previously are covered in one page where the author writes: 'It could give no pleasure to the present writer to recall for others the dark and terrible deeds done in Ireland during one of the darkest periods in her history.'[1]

More recently, the subject has attracted greater attention. In particular, the work of the late Peter Hart included an examination of the position of southern Protestants in these years.[2] The murder of ten Protestants in the Dunmanway area of West Cork in April 1922 has become an issue of considerable interest and controversy.[3] In the last few years a number of important articles have studied the fate of Protestants in the revolutionary period.[4] What is agreed is that during these years Protestants in the twenty-six counties that became the Irish Free State experienced a drastic fall in numbers. What is not agreed is why this happened, and explanations for the decline have ranged widely from ethnic cleansing to voluntary emigration and demographic factors. In this study the experiences of southern Protestants during the period 1919–23 will be charted through contemporary accounts in the form of speeches from annual synods of the Church of Ireland, a source that hitherto has been largely ignored.

Church Members, Synods and Bishops

Throughout these turbulent years a general synod of church members continued to meet in Dublin each May, after which local diocesan synods were held in various locations, covering the whole country. Members of the Church of Ireland comprised the largest section of the Protestant population in the twenty-six counties that became the Irish Free State. In 1911 members of the Church of Ireland numbered just under 250,000, slightly over three-quarters of the Protestant population, and nearly 8 per cent of the total population.[5] At this time in the twenty-six counties there were twenty-nine dioceses, but only ten bishops and two archbishops, each of whom, apart from the archbishop of Armagh, the bishop of Meath and the bishop of Clogher, was responsible for a number of dioceses. In some cases joint synods were held while in others there were separate synods. To assist in identifying the geographical location of the dioceses, the places where the synods took place have been recorded in this text. Consisting of elected lay and clerical members, the synods were concerned primarily with general Church matters, but during this time contemporary political issues intruded. These events began with a speech by the bishop, who acted as president, and it is their speeches that were reported in the press, especially the *Irish Times*.[6] As both leaders and observers of their dioceses, the bishops in these speeches reflected many of the concerns and anxieties of their community. Through these contemporary voices we can gain a valuable insight into the experiences of southern Protestants during the revolutionary period. Sometimes they are outspoken in their comments while other times they are restrained, perhaps reflecting the dangerous times they lived in or concern not to cause panic.

A brief commentary can be made about the bishops, who numbered fourteen over these critical years. All were born and educated in the south, except for the northerner A.E. Ross, bishop of Tuam and Killala, and J.A.F. Gregg, bishop of Ferns, Ossory and Leighlin, later archbishop of Dublin, and finally archbishop of Armagh, born and brought up in England, but with strong Cork clerical antecedents and connections. Ross also served as a chaplain in the First World War, 1916–18, and was the recipient of the Military Cross for bravery. All except two were graduates of Trinity College Dublin and the Divinity School at Trinity. In the cases of the archbishop of Armagh, the bishop of Clogher and the bishop of Derry and Raphoe, their dioceses were cross border after 1920. All had extensive parochial experience, except for J.H. Bernard, archbishop of Dublin, who resigned in June 1919 to become provost of Trinity. After Bernard's resignation, C.F. D'Arcy became archbishop of Dublin. Following the death in April 1920 of J.B. Crozier, the primate and archbishop of Armagh, D'Arcy was elected to succeed him in June 1920, after which Gregg became archbishop of Dublin in September 1920. In 1919 their average age was 58.

Before 1921 all were unionist in their politics. In May 1917, however, while remaining unionist, J.A.F. Gregg, then bishop of Ossory, B.J. Plunket, bishop of Tuam and Killala, and later bishop of Meath, and Thomas Sterling Berry, bishop of Killaloe and Clonfert, had broken ranks with their fellow bishops to sign a declaration against partition, along with seventeen Catholic bishops.[7] This led to a counter-declaration from the archbishop of Armagh, J.B. Crozier, and the four Ulster bishops, but caused no long-term schism among the bishops. Bishops Plunket and Sterling Berry joined the general committee of the Irish White Cross Association, set up in 1921 to distribute funds raised by the American Committee for Relief in Ireland, which led to criticism in the press from Lord Ashdown on the grounds that the committee members included Michael Collins and 'other notorious republicans'.[8] C.R. Dowse, bishop of Cork, Cloyne and Ross, was one of four patrons of the Tomás MacCurtain memorial fund and one of two clerical patrons, along with the Catholic bishop of Cork, Daniel Cohalan, of the Cork Distress Committee, set up to deal with distress and unemployment following the burning of the city.[9]

The First Synods after the War, 1919

The first general synod of the Church of Ireland after the Great War opened in Dublin on 12 May 1919. In his speech the primate, Archbishop J.B. Crozier, began by saying that 'the awful cloud of war, as far as the Central Powers are concerned, has passed away'. He concluded with 'an eloquent reference' to the debt everyone owed to the 'Contemptible Little Army', under Lord French, which 'so nobly and bravely resisted the German onslaught in 1914'.[10] At this general synod and subsequent diocesan synods the main subject of concern was reform of the parochial structures and the deployment and stipends of clergy in light of population changes in Ireland since disestablishment. In early June at the Kilmore synod in Cavan, Bishop W.R. Moore pointed out that the Church of Ireland had experienced a fall in numbers over the previous forty years that necessitated a reorganisation of parishes. He noted that their decrease countrywide was less in proportion than the decrease among Roman Catholics over this period, and in the decade 1901–11 was only some 5,000, but 'on account of the fewness of their numbers they felt it more'.[11] Church of Ireland members were widely dispersed and in many parts of the country were in small numbers, which created special problems.

The bishops' speeches at synods in June and July contained little or no reference to current political problems. At the very end of July 1919, however, at the Killaloe synod, held at Nenagh, Co. Tipperary, Bishop Thomas Sterling Berry declared: 'The policy adopted by the British government in its treatment of Ireland in recent years has been disastrous to the peace of the country. The policy has been a combination of vacillation and irritation.' He continued: 'But no policy, however misguided, could justify crimes which make all true lovers of Ireland hang their heads in sorrow and shame.' He denounced the murder of policemen.[12] At the synod of the united dioceses of Cork, Cloyne and Ross on 22 October 1919 in Cork Bishop C.R. Dowse stated: 'Murder, robbery and crime stain our native land, and call forth our sternest and most uncompromising condemnation.'[13] He expressed strong sympathy and admiration for the police 'who are serving their country with such splendid loyalty, and who, in the discharge of their duties and in their efforts to maintain law and order, are brutally attacked, and often foully murdered. We owe them a deep sense of gratitude, far beyond anything words can convey.' In the years 1919–21 a total of ninety members of the Royal Irish Constabulary lost their lives in Cork county and city.[14]

Reforms and Concerns at Synods, 1920

Reports from synods in 1920 reveal concern about a deteriorating situation in Ireland. At the general synod in May 1920, the new archbishop of Dublin, C.F. D'Arcy, in place of the recently deceased primate, gave the president's address. He described how 'the issues were so confused, the outlook so obscure' and how they had been horrified by 'the deeds of bloodshed which had in the past few months stained the records of their country'.[15] The question of reform of the Church in the face of falling numbers in parts of Ireland and growth in others, in particular Belfast, was the main issue of discussion at the synod. In November 1920 a special general synod of the Church was convened in Dublin to deal with the question of parish amalgamations and revised stipends for clergy.[16] In the speeches of the bishops at diocesan synods during 1920 there was often mention, usually brief, of the troubled times they lived in. At the Elphin synod at Boyle, Co. Roscommon, on 9 June, sympathy was expressed by Bishop W.R. Moore with 'the men of that splendid force, the Royal Irish Constabulary' and with 'the many, both of their own communion and others, who had been the victims of outrage either against their person or their property'.[17]

Similar views were expressed at other June synods. At the Tuam synod at Tuam, Co. Galway, Bishop A.E. Ross referred to the murder of Frank Shawe-Taylor, apparently over a land dispute, and stated: 'Disorder and lawlessness have gone very far. We feel very impotent.'[18] Bishop R.D'A. Orpen, who presided at the Limerick synod in Limerick city, declared that 'the country must suffer intensely while strife between brethren, which was the saddest of all strife, continued'.[19] Addressing the Cashel synod at Cashel, Co. Tipperary, Bishop Robert Miller talked of 'events which are taking place all around us, so full of callous cruelty, of extreme inhumanity, of utter indifference to the laws of God'. A meeting of the Dublin diocesan synod in July was mainly concerned with electing a new archbishop, and the only comment about the situation by the acting president, C.R. Dowse, bishop of Cork, apart from stressing the importance of choosing 'a fit and proper person to serve his church in this great crisis', was that 'the land they loved so well was rent asunder and stained with terrible crime'.[20]

In October 1920 a number of synods were held. At the synod for Cork and Ross, in Cork city, Bishop C.R. Dowse noted briefly that 'the past year had been marked by some unpleasant events, both within their united diocese and also within its bounds', but stated that 'amid the various disturbances and disorders which had taken place amongst them, the ordinary ministrations of their church had been uninterrupted'.[21] A second synod of Dublin diocese heard their new archbishop, Dr J.A.F. Gregg, briefly deplore the violence and call for reconciliation.[22] The longest comments on the political situation came from Bishop Thomas Sterling Berry at the Clonfert and Kilmacduagh synod in Ballinasloe, Co. Galway. He remarked: 'Things have drifted into a state of anarchy and strife.' He then declared: 'Ireland can never work out her salvation through murder and bloodshed. But, on the other hand, England cannot maintain her hold on Ireland by bringing the weapon of coercive legislation and coercive actions upon the attenuated population of this little island.' He urged 'better understanding between Great Britain and Ireland'.[23]

Sterling Berry also talked about the need to reorganise parishes with small numbers, a subject raised by the archdeacon of Dublin, Rev. T.S. Lindsay, in an article in the *Irish Times* at the end of December 1920. He pointed to diminishing membership of the Church over a long time, a process 'shared with all the other religious denominations'. However, he stated that this was now advancing at a more rapid rate for their Church, 'as large numbers of her members are leaving the country and settling in England due to the terrible condition of things that prevails here'. He claimed that 'in hundreds of country parishes the congregations are reduced'.[24] Nonetheless, A.F. Maude, secretary of the Representative Church Body, the central financial trustee body of the Church, in his annual report for 1920, produced in May 1921, remained positive. He wrote of 'much unrest' and 'times of adversity', but he also reported 'increased financial stability' for the Church nationally during the year in spite of the political difficulties.[25]

Gloom and Hope at Synods, 1921

Reports from synods in 1921 painted a much gloomier picture, although some also carried messages of hope. In his address to the general synod in May 1921, the new primate, Archbishop C.F. D'Arcy, spoke at length about the violent state of the country: 'The things that had happened in their country during the past year had been so terrible, so disastrous, so fateful, in relation to the social and moral life of the whole country as to be paralysing.' He referred to several members of the synod who had been murdered. He then declared: 'Members of our church, and others, in several parts of the country – quiet, defenceless farmers for the most part – have been most cruelly killed. We do not know for what reasons, and can but conjecture that it was because their political views were not acceptable.'[26] In early July 1921, at the Limerick diocesan synod, in place of the bishop who had resigned, Dean T.A.P. Hackett spoke of how 'murder and destruction of property went unchecked'. He hoped that 'religious strife might not aggravate the present troubles' and stated his opinion that 'where their people had suffered it was not because of their religious opinions, and, as the present representative of the city and county clergy, he was glad to say that never in their experience had the relations between all religions been more harmonious'.[27]

At a number of synods reference was made to church members and others who had been murdered by republicans. In his address to the Ardagh synod in Longford in late July, Bishop W.R. Moore referred to 'the death of Mr William Latimer, who was so cruelly murdered, which reminded them of the dreadful times through which they had been passing. One of their most highly esteemed clergymen had had to leave the country simply because he acted as a loyal citizen.' He thought that 'it would serve no good purpose to dwell at length on the awful state of their country, which had been especially bad in parts of their diocese – Ballinalea and Ballina – except to express his deep sympathy with those who had had so much to endure'.[28] A few days later at the Kilmore synod at Cavan, Bishop Moore expressed great shock at the murder of the elderly Rev. John Finlay, former dean of Leighlin, who had been killed in June outside his burned-out home in Co. Cavan. Both the Belfast and Dublin press carried a letter from four local Catholic parish priests, expressing their 'horror and indignation at the crime commit-ted by the murder' of Dean Finlay.[29] Bishop Moore observed that their numbers were becoming fewer: 'Very large numbers of their church people had left the south and west during the last two years, and they knew not what the future had in store for them.'[30]

At the Tuam synod in Tuam, Co. Galway, and the Killala synod in Ballina, Co. Mayo, Bishop A.E. Ross was both brief and guarded in his addresses. He spoke of 'this time of lawlessness and strife and hatred' but hoped that 'a spirit of conciliation may save us from still worse things'.[31] At the Waterford synod in August, Bishop Robert Miller referred to the killing of the 60-year-old Mary Lindsay, 'a personal friend of my own', from Coachford, Co. Cork, who had alerted the authorities to a planned IRA ambush.[32] Subsequently, she and her driver were kidnapped, held prisoners for over four months and then executed.[33] Besides such fatali-ties, the period from early 1920 to mid-1921 included sectarian attacks against members of the Protestant community, such as the burning of three Church of Ireland churches in Co. Clare in 1920 and threats and outrages against Protestant farmers in various parts of the country.[34]

The truce of mid-July 1921 created hope. At the Killaloe synod at Nenagh, Co. Tipperary, in August 1921, Bishop Thomas Sterling Berry commented: 'We have been living through dark days – days of trouble, days of mourning – here in our land. Now there comes the dawn of a new hope.'[35] In October at the Ferns synod, Bishop J.G.F. Day spoke of 'an intense longing for peace'. He described how 'A real spirit of tolerance prevailed since the treaty. Protestant and Roman Catholic farmers were living side by side in perfect friendliness … such a thing as religious bitter-ness or intolerance, was almost unknown in that part of Ireland.'[36] Later that month at the Ossory synod at Kilkenny, Bishop Day recorded his concern that the rights of the minority in the new political arrangements in south-ern Ireland would be protected: 'they are real Irishmen, with just as strong and patriotic a love for their country as any other portion of the country.'[37]

At the united synod of Cork and Ross in Cork at the end of October, Bishop C.R. Dowse spoke briefly and cautiously about how 'for their country, especially for their own diocese, the year had been one of fearful happenings and tragic events'.[38] At the 1910 December general election the two Cork city seats and six out of seven county seats had been won by the All-for-Ireland League led by William O'Brien and his policies of reconciliation between former landlords and tenants and between north and south.[39] In contrast to such moderation, however, an estimated fifty 'big houses' or suburban villas in Cork city and county, most owned by members of the Church of Ireland, were destroyed by the IRA during the War of Independence.[40] Later, an IRA commander in West Cork, Tom Barry, described targeting the homes of 'loyalists' in reprisal for the activities of the British army: 'Our only fear was that, as time went on, there would be no more loyalist homes to destroy.'[41] After referring to the deaths of Major George O'Connor, Tom Bradfield and Mary Lindsay, Bishop Dowse declared: 'We must hope on.'[42] Then he stated: 'We thankfully recognise that throughout our diocese so many churchmen and Roman Catholics live side by side in terms of friendship and goodwill.'

On 18 October 1921, J.A.F. Gregg, the new archbishop of Dublin, spoke at the Dublin diocesan synod. He expressed thanks that there was 'a truce from bloodshed', but voiced worries about the safeguarding of their rights in any new settlement. Gregg declared that, as a minority, 'we differ from the majority in religion, in politics, in *ethos* generally', and referred to their aloofness from 'the political movement directed against the British connection, in so far as the methods adopted by its supporters seem to us to be wrong'. He said: 'Although we are as truly Irish as are many in the other camp, the differences are so marked as to cause us to seem alien in sympathy from the more extreme of our countrymen.' He insisted: 'Whatever our religious or political outlook may be, here is our home, and we have every right to be here.' Gregg then stated that it would be a very bad day if large numbers left, but if they were to stay they needed to have confidence for the future. He asked, not for 'preferential treatment', but that they be 'assured of a fair chance'. He observed: 'A good many people have already left Ireland, just because they can choose where they live, and they refuse to remain in so disturbed an atmosphere.'[43]

In October at the Ferns synod in Enniscorthy, referring to political talks, Bishop J.G.F. Day expressed hope that 'in spite of difficulties, an honourable compromise might be arrived at'. He also observed that 'A real spirit of tolerance prevailed since the truce. Protestant and Roman Catholic farmers were living side by side in perfect friendliness

... such a thing as bitterness or intolerance, was almost unknown in that part of Ireland.'[44] At the Clonfert synod at Ballinasloe, Co. Galway, in late October 1921, Bishop Thomas Sterling Berry warned: 'Do not share the action of those who in timid apprehension are already quitting the homes of their forefathers and the land of their birth.'[45] A week later, probably in response to these comments, at the synod of Ardfert and Aghadoe, at Tralee, Co. Kerry, Bishop H.V. White stated: 'If hundreds of my fellow countrymen are leaving the country, they are doing so for no light cause, and are certainly not urged by unmanly panic. They know why they go, and they go to the great and permanent loss of Ireland.'[46] He also pleaded for toleration, arguing that in the past there had been toleration between Christians, but now it was implied that the minority should be grateful 'that we are allowed to share any of the rights and liberties of ordinary citizens'. He declared that he 'refused to be grateful to anyone but the Almighty for permission to breathe the air of my native land'. On Sunday, 11 December 1921, at the conclusion of a sermon in Dublin, Archbishop J.A.F. Gregg spoke of the prospects for peace, following negotiations in London between Sinn Féin representatives and the British government. He declared: 'We may not all like the facts: many of us had no desire for a change of our constitution. But it will be our wisdom to acknowledge them and reckon with them ... it concerns us all to offer to the Irish Free State, as shortly to be constituted, our loyalty and good-will.'[47]

A Deteriorating Situation and the General Synod, May 1922

When the next general synod was held in May 1922, however, these hopes for a peaceful future had not materialised. In early 1922 the RIC was disbanded and members of the British army were withdrawn, with the result that much of the countryside was subject to considerable lawlessness. Enlistment for a new police force began in February but the Garda Síochána was not established until 1923. In addition, the situation in Northern Ireland in early 1922 had deteriorated, with attacks by the IRA and tough government countermeasures. Sectarian conflict in Belfast included the murder on 23 March of five members of the Catholic McMahon family, and large numbers of Belfast Catholics fled south.[48] In March and early April a series of meetings of southern Protestants in Cork, Limerick and elsewhere condemned the outrages in Belfast, often stressing good Church relations in the south.[49] One such meeting at Nenagh, Co. Tipperary, heard Bishop Thomas Sterling Berry of Killaloe declare: 'We have come together, not from any sense of foreboding – not because we wish to ward off disaster from ourselves. We come together as Irishmen, deeply aggrieved at occurrences which bring reproach and dishonour upon our country.'[50]

At the end of April 1922, however, republicans were responsible for the killing in the Dunmanway district of Co. Cork of ten Protestants, of whom all but one were members of the Church of Ireland.[51] These murders, which were viewed by many as reprisals or revenge for what had happened in the north, were strongly condemned by Catholic and government spokesmen.[52] The attacks raised great concerns among the Protestant community. In a sermon shortly afterwards, the bishop of Limerick, Dr H.V. White, a personal friend of one of the victims, declared: 'We scattered, disarmed members of the Church in the south of Ireland have had in the murders of last week a grim reminder of our helplessness.'[53] What made the situation worse was that such events were not seen in isolation but as part of a much wider picture of intimidation experienced by many members of the Church of Ireland at this time. During the early months of 1922 the press reported many other examples of intimidation of Protestant families and businesses (often viewed as reprisals for violence in the north), which forced large numbers to leave.[54] Agrarian outrages affected the property of many Protestant landowners and farmers, while Protestant businesses were also seized or destroyed.[55] Although the War of Independence was over, those seen as loyalists, including not just Protestants but also Catholic ex-members of the RIC, were subject to widespread intimidation. In early May 1922, the archbishop of Dublin, J.A.F. Gregg, recorded in his diary: 'A week of v. great anxiety as to the church's future. News of evictions, ejections and intimidations everywhere. Where is it all to lead to? Is it beginning of end, or short term? Prol. Govt so far seems powerless to intervene.'[56]

On 9 May 1922 the general synod of the Church of Ireland met for its usual annual meeting. In his speech, the primate, Archbishop C.F. D'Arcy, began by saying that it was impossible to meet there that day 'without some reflection upon the present condition of the country'. He confessed that, personally, he 'remained, after all that had happened, and in spite of the disastrous blunders of a succession of British governments, a firm believer in the principles which they had been accustomed to describe as unionism'. 'However,' he declared, 'we must face things as they are, we have to prepare to meet a new order in this country.' He then went on to state that the clergy and laity of the Church, in southern Ireland and in Northern Ireland were prepared to do their duty as Irishmen 'to obey the law of the state to which they belong' and were 'most anxious to live in terms of goodwill with all classes and creeds among our fellow country-men'. He talked of the 'veritable nightmare of violence and bloodshed, which has been in existence for some time in parts of our country, north and south'. He spoke of their deep sorrow over 'the shocking deaths recently afflicted on some members of our church and the expulsion of many others'. He referred to Dunmanway, noting all the victims were Protestant. D'Arcy warned: 'Nothing more awful could happen than that the political strife in the country should become a war of religion.'[57]

That evening, after a special meeting of all southern synod members, a deputation, consisting of the archbishop of Dublin, the bishop of Cashel and Sir William Goulding, was chosen to meet the government 'to lay before them the dangers to which Protestants in the twenty-six counties are daily exposed'.[58] Two days later the members of this deputation met Michael Collins and W.T. Cosgrave. They told Collins that they were will-ing and anxious to remain 'as loyal citizens of the government of Ireland', brought to his attention 'many cases in which their co-religionists had suffered persecution in various parts of the country', and asked for assur-ances that the government desired to retain them. Collins replied to them that 'the government would protect its citizens, and would ensure civil and religious freedom in Ireland, and that spoliation and confiscation would not be countenanced by the Irish government'.[59]

On the same day that the Church of Ireland deputation met Collins, a well-attended convention of southern Protestants, mostly members of the Church of Ireland, from the south and west of the country, was held at the Mansion House in Dublin. Speeches denounced attacks on both Catholics in Belfast and Protestants in Cork and elsewhere. Speakers sought to demonstrate southern Protestant sympathy for the plight of northern Catholics and to emphasise good relations between Protestants and Catholics in the past and present. Many saw attacks on Protestants in the south primarily as a result of general lawlessness and a response to northern outrages.[60] These efforts brought little or no improvement to the situation. On 23 June 1922, the *Church of Ireland Gazette* reported that 'in certain districts in southern Ireland inoffensive Protestants of all classes are being driven from their homes, their shops and their farms in such numbers that many of our little communities are in danger of being entirely wiped out'. Whatever the concerns of the government about the Protestant minority it faced other major political issues, leading to civil war in June 1922. The next nine months in the country saw more deaths, destruction and lawlessness than in the previous three years.

Diocesan Synods During the Civil War

There continued to be annual meetings of Church of Ireland synods, although some were cancelled, postponed or not reported on, thanks to dangers and destruction caused by the Civil War. At the end of May 1922 at the Dublin diocesan synod, the archbishop of Dublin, J.A.F. Gregg, talked of losses in their ranks: 'The changing circumstances of our country have led some of our synodsmen to leave Ireland, while others have been transferred officially to the service of the northern government.' He expressed hope that 'the movements which have taken place against the members of our church, and which have, undoubtedly, tended to assume a complexion of a sectarian kind' would not continue. He believed these actions against church members occurred 'partly because they possess what other people covet, partly because they are weak and have few friends, and partly because they do not profess the same political or religious views as the majority'. He was certain that public opinion in Ireland would be shocked if it was made 'fully aware of all the sufferings which have been inflicted on innocent protestants living quietly in various parts of the twenty-six counties'. The archbishop expressed his belief in the good intentions of the government and appealed for its support: 'In the name of my co-religionists, I ask for fair play from our fellow countrymen.'[61] A few days later, at the Kildare synod, at Kildare, Archbishop Gregg referred to the demographic impact on Kildare parish and cathedral of the withdrawal of British troops from the Curragh, and also mentioned the need to appoint chaplains to the new Irish army, as 'already members of our church are entering the service of the Free State'.[62]

At the Limerick diocesan synod in Limerick on 5 July 1922, Bishop H.V. White spoke of how their numbers had fallen over the last half-century, and then went on to say: 'It is far from satisfactory to have to face the fact that Ireland is losing many of her best, most patriotic and pro-gressive citizens, who are forced to leave their native land by economic causes or by political and religious intolerance.'[63] The press reported that 'owing to the disturbed condition of the country' Bishop White could not attend the synod of Ardfert and Aghadoe at Tralee, Co. Kerry, in September.[64] At the end of summer 1922, Bishop W.R. Moore spoke at the Elphin synod at Boyle, Co. Roscommon, where he declared that 'many of their people had suffered, and were suffering, cruel wrongs both in person and property, and some of their parishes had been thereby sadly depleted, notably the parish of Mount Talbot'. Shortly afterwards at the Kilmore synod at Cavan, he stated that the church had suffered severely: 'Even in their own diocese a considerable number of people had left the country, and in the more southern and western dioceses the exodus of their people had been calamitous. Many had suffered and were suffering the most cruel wrongs in person and property.' He expressed regret at the deaths of Michael Collins and Arthur Griffith.[65]

In October 1922, Bishop J.G.F. Day addressed the Leighlin synod at Carlow. He referred to the lawless conditions: 'Many of our people have suffered severely under these conditions. Some of them have been driven from their homes and lands. I suppose there are few, if any, of our people who entirely escaped molestation.'[66] He still continued to hope for the best: 'The vast majority of the people are quiet and law-abiding, and the members of different religious denominations are living side by side on the best of terms, and doing all they can to help one another.' That same month at the Ferns synod in Enniscorthy, Co. Wexford, Bishop Day spoke of great uncertainty and anxiety. He declared: 'Their hearts were heavy as they thought of the sufferings of their people of all classes.' He paid special tribute to the clergy, who he said had stuck to their posts 'living in loneliness and in an atmosphere of open or veiled hostility.

They had discharged their duty in danger and distress. Many had seen their flocks dwindle to almost vanishing point.'[67] At the Meath October synod in Dublin, Bishop B.J. Plunket referred to the suffering of church members: 'Some having lost their homes have left our shores; others, with no security for life or property, or with no prospect of employment, are, for the moment at any rate, exiled from their native land.'[68]

Twice postponed, the synod of Killaloe, Kilfenora, Clonfert and Kilmacduagh was held at Nenagh, Co. Tipperary, on 14 October 1922, where 'the business was expeditiously despatched'. Bishop Thomas Sterling Berry delivered a brief address in which 'sympathetic reference was made to the misfortunes recently sustained by members of the diocese', but the only detail mentioned in the press report was a short reference to the burning of a church at Ahascragh in July (which led to a protest of Catholic people in the area against the destruction).[69] These brief comments undoubtedly reflect caution on the part of the bishop, or concern not to cause alarm. In the archives of the Department of Justice in Dublin, however, is a letter dated 10 June 1922, written by Bishop Sterling Berry to draw attention to the state of affairs in north Tipperary. He wrote: 'There is scarcely a Protestant family in the district which has escaped molestation. One of my clergy has had his motor car and a portion of his house burned … Some other houses have been burned. Cattle have been driven off farms. Protestant families have been warned to leave the neighbourhood. Altogether a state of terrorism exists.'[70] About such conditions he added: 'Happily they stand in glaring contrast to the state of things here and elsewhere in the diocese of which I have charge.'

In spite of this positive remark about 'elsewhere', other clergy and members of his dioceses were subjected to serious violence of person and property, that were not – whether through pragmatism or lack of information – mentioned at the synods.[71] The most shocking of such incidents occurred a week later on 16 June, as revealed in another record in the Department of Justice papers. A gang of armed republicans broke into the Biggs family home at Hazelpoint, Dromineer, Nenagh, Co. Tipperary. They consumed a large quantity of alcohol, and the young Mrs Harriett Biggs was raped. The Biggs then fled to Dublin, where Mrs Biggs entered hospital. The police document reported: 'In view of the serious condition of Mrs Biggs, it is not inconceivable that the guilty party may be charged with manslaughter.'[72] She survived and later in August two men were charged in a local court with the crime and released on bail. It seems that in the end no action was taken against them.

Attempts to hold synods for the dioceses of Tuam and Killala during 1922 were unsuccessful, due to prevailing lawless conditions. Incidents in these dioceses included the burning in late June of Ballycronree orphanage, Clifden, Co. Galway, run by the Irish Church Mission, and the destruction and looting in November of the Church of Ireland church at Moyrus, Co. Galway.[73] On 25 October 1922, Bishop C.R. Dowse spoke to the united Cork synod in Cork city. He asked: 'Who can adequately describe the times through which our people have passed during the last few months? The memories of those ghastly massacres in West Cork can never pass away.' He acknowledged the messages of support his community had received, from organisations such as the Cork Corporation and Cork Roman Catholic Young Men's Association. He insisted that they were entitled to full rights of citizenship, not as favours but as fundamental rights.[74]

Synods for the cross-border dioceses were held in September/October 1922. At the Clogher synod at Enniskillen, Co. Fermanagh, referring to the south, Bishop Maurice Day described 'families broken up, their residences burned over their heads, they themselves, or those of them who were allowed to survive, fugitives from their native land, or trying to remain, living in daily terror of further outrage and death'.[75] Addressing the annual synod of Derry and Raphoe, in Derry city, Bishop C.I. Peacocke stated that he 'need not dwell on the awful crimes that defiled their land during the last twelve months', especially against those who were members of his Church, 'namely, in the south and west, but to some extent at least in parts of his own diocese in County Donegal'.[76] At the diocesan synod of Armagh, in Armagh, Archbishop C.F. D'Arcy referred to the terror and misery experienced by populations elsewhere at the time, such as in Eastern Europe. He then declared: 'Of our own land it is difficult to speak. Anarchy and outrage have left terrible scars. Many of the very best of our people have been driven from our shores. The sufferings which have been endured can never be told.' He expressed hope that in the south 'the forces of order will succeed in overcoming the forces of anarchy. The anarchy which has prevailed over great tracts of this country has placed members of our church in these parts in a position of the utmost difficulty.'[77]

The last synods of the year were addressed in early November by Bishop Robert Miller. Earlier, on 8 October 1922, at Christ Church, Leeson Park, Dublin, Bishop Miller had preached on behalf of poorer parishes in the south and west. He spoke of how 'during the past few years the whole church has passed through experiences which caused grave apprehension regarding our future in this country. Many of our people were driven from their homes, many others left through fear of violence, with the result that many of our parishes, especially where the numbers are small, are unable to meet their financial responsibilities.' Nonetheless, he said that they had been encouraged by the 'broad spirit of toleration' that was shown by the members of parliament. His advice to Church members was 'live in the land of your birth and work for its highest good'.[78] In early November Bishop Miller addressed synods at Cashel, Co. Tipperary, for Cashel and Emly, and at Waterford city for Waterford and Lismore. At both he declared that, besides interference with property, 'dreadful and unspeakable crimes have been committed'. He went on: 'Honest, brave men will face physical violence, the destruction of their property, but such deeds as we are now speaking of chill the hearts of strong men and fill them with an overwhelming desire to get away from a country where, in their opinion, civilisation is losing its hold.'[79] He acknowledged the good intentions of the government, but he urged them to take greater steps to protect its citizens.

The following months witnessed further deterioration in the situation. The new Irish Free State constitution did not provide specific safeguards for the Protestant minority, but in December 1922 a large number of Protestants and former unionists, more than twenty, mostly members of the Church of Ireland, were nominated by the government or elected to the new Irish senate, in an effort to acknowledge the role of the minority in the new state. This was an important gesture of reconciliation and tolerance by the new Irish government, which was acknowledged as such by Church of Ireland sources.[80] Unfortunately, it proved to be a double-edged sword. Whereas during the War of Independence and earlier in 1922 homes of loyalists had been deliberately targeted by republicans because their owners were seen as supporters or former supporters of the British government, now the homes of Protestant senators were targeted by anti-treaty forces because their owners were viewed as supporters of the Free State government, while other country houses continued to be destroyed in an effort to create chaos to undermine the state.

In late 1923, W. Alison Phillips estimated that fifty country houses were burned between January and November 1922, while another eighty-nine were torched between the beginning of November 1922 and the ceasefire of early spring 1923, which he described as 'the worst and most ruinous period of destruction'.[81] Recently Terence Dooley has put the total figure at 199.[82] A majority of these houses were owned by members of the Church of Ireland. Intimidation of Church members during the Civil War extended well beyond owners of country houses.[83] An editorial in the *Irish Times* on 3 October 1922 described 'losses which have fallen with peculiar severity upon the ex-unionists of the south and west – upon farmers and shopkeepers as well as upon the owners of great estates and lordly mansions' and stated that 'the exodus from Southern Ireland will continue so long as the campaign of destruction flourishes'. It rejected the idea that there was any 'well organised system' in this campaign of destruction and violence but also claimed that the southern minority were the 'foremost sufferers' in the current disorders, and called for support from government.[84]

Most fatalities during the Civil War involved combatants from the two sides.[85] However, members of the Protestant community endured widespread violence for a mixture of political, economic and sectarian reasons, as we know from evidence later given by many of them to the Irish Grants Committee, which offered compensation to loyalists for the loss suffered in the period after the truce.[86] People were intimidated because they were seen as ex-unionists or loyalists. R.B. McDowell has noted that Catholic loyalists were attacked as well as Protestants, but 'Protestants were singled out for harassment because religion was the easiest way of identifying a person's politics'.[87] Land agitation, including boycott and seizure of property, affected many Protestant farmers and landowners. In her study of violence during the Civil War in Counties Waterford, Limerick and Tipperary, Gemma Clark has concluded that, for members of the Protestant community, 'no one, and nowhere, was completely safe'. Protestant-owned shops and businesses were boycotted. She has written: 'Threatening letters, many issued on behalf of the anti-Treaty IRA, made specific threats against the Protestant community. The compensation evidence suggests that the victim's denomination was important to the perpetrator. Attacks on Protestant institutions and religious personnel leave even less room for doubt about the attacker's sectarian agenda.'[88]

Comments by two Catholic bishops at the time confirm the harsh treatment of Protestants. They also show their strong condemnation of these events. In February 1923 the Catholic bishop of Cork, Daniel Cohalan, described how 'Protestants have suffered severely during the period of the civil war in the south', and urged that 'charity knows no exclusion of creed'.[89] Speaking at Nenagh in north Tipperary in May 1923, the Catholic bishop of Killaloe, Michael Fogarty, appealed to a higher sense of patriotism, noting that 'their Protestant fellow country-men – he regretted to have to say it – were persecuted and dealt with in a cruel and coarse manner'.[90] In the last week of May 1923, a ceasefire was declared in the Civil War, which brought an end to most if not all the violence against members of the Protestant community.

In the conclusion to his report for the Representative Church Body on 21 March 1923, for the year of 1922, A.F. Maude, the secretary, painted a very different picture to that for the year of 1920. On the ear-lier occasion he could remain positive 'in the midst of much unrest', and draw attention to evidence in the report of increased financial stability in the Church generally. In the conclusion for the year 1922, however, he stated: 'The Church of Ireland cannot escape its part in the fortunes of the whole country; and our people have borne perhaps even more than their fair share of the losses and disappointments of the past year.' He continued: 'The serious drop in the payments of parochial assess-ments ... is an indication of a diminished church population in large districts, and of inability on the part of those who remain to make up the sums needed for the maintenance of public worship in many parishes. Numbers of the most generous friends of the church have left Ireland.'[91] Behind this stark financial picture of the fortunes of the Church of Ireland lay the reality that in a short period their numbers had dropped drastically in every one of the twenty-six counties that made up the new Irish Free State.

Synods in the Aftermath, 1923

On 16 May 1923 the general synod of the Church of Ireland met in Dublin. The previous evening, the bishop of Derry and Raphoe, J.I. Peacocke, in a sermon at St Patrick's Cathedral, Dublin, spoke of the ordeal that people had endured for several years: 'For whatever reason – some because of their religion, often for political or social causes – the members of their church had been much the worst sufferers in this time of disturbance.' He continued: 'Very many of them, who would have been good and loyal subjects of the Free State, and who only asked to be allowed to live quietly in their homes, had been driven from home and everything, out of the country. The country was the poorer for their loss, no less than the church.'[92]

The next day, the primate, Archbishop D'Arcy, took a more cautious and broader approach. He declared that it was not an easy task to address the synod at present, 'when silence and quiet, steady work were better than speech'. He spoke very briefly about a 'very anxious and terrible year of suspense and trouble. Tens of thousands of all classes and creeds had fled from the land; many of the very best were gone.' 'Their church,' he declared, 'had suffered especially, although all churches had been impoverished. The restraints of religion and morality had been relaxed in the general confusion.'[93] He was now hopeful that order and peace would be restored. The following day, 18 May 1923, an editorial in the *Irish Times* declared that members of the Church of Ireland had 'suffered more than the members of any other community in Ireland from the recent disorders because, for a variety of reasons, they were exposed peculiarly to the greed and violence of lawless men'. Nonetheless, the paper believed that, for the Church, 'there had been no slackening of her spiritual efforts' and she was 'calmly confident of her capacity for service to the new Ireland'.

Two other synods were held in Dublin in late May 1923. At the Dublin diocesan synod, the archbishop of Dublin, J.A.F. Gregg, talked of events in the diocese over the previous year: burnings, shootings and various forms of intimidation had produced their effect, he suggested, and had caused people to leave. He stated that not all who had moved elsewhere had had to do so, but they left in many cases because they wanted 'security and tranquillity'. Others, 'in various walks of life', and 'their number was not small', were forced to go. At the same time, he pointed out that 'there were very large numbers of them still there, and that very large numbers of them went about their affairs just as they used to'.[94] The following week the archbishop addressed the Glendalough and Kildare diocesan synod in Dublin. He talked of grievous havoc in the two dioceses in the last year, and he mentioned a number of stately homes that had been destroyed. One parish had lost three such homes.[95]

The united Cork diocesan synod occurred in Cork on 13 June 1923. In his address Bishop C.R. Dowse referred to the decrease of the Church of Ireland population in Cork:

> During the last two and a half years our church population has decreased by 8 per cent. It is serious but does not call for despair. Many of our people have gone. Neither we nor our country could afford to lose them. Their houses have been burned. Destruction has marched through the land. The ruins of Ireland may well make all who really love her weep.[96]

In fact, the 1926 census report showed a considerably higher figure of Church of Ireland decrease, after excluding army and navy figures, of around 30 per cent for the whole period, 1911–26. The underestimate by Dowse may be due to an effort not to be pessimistic, lack of knowledge of the full picture, or partly the result of subsequent decline in 1923–26.[97] He continued: 'But, notwithstanding all our losses we are not going to be chilled into inactivity, or to give way to depression. That way lies disaster.' He referred to the clergy and their wives: 'In loneliness and danger, in trial and distress, they have remained steadfast and have stood by their people, helping them, and being helped by them.' He acknowledged that 'during these trying days they have acted as good citizens. They have lived in friendliness and good fellowship with their

Roman Catholic neighbours, and Roman Catholic and Churchmen have proved mutually helpful to each other all over the diocese.'

Also in mid-June 1923, Bishop H.V. White, at the Limerick synod, asked: 'Why have hundreds of industrious protestant Irishmen and women left their native land?' To this he answered: 'Because they felt that they were not welcome here, and that satisfactory careers could not be secured for their boys and girls in their own country.' Nonetheless, he stated: 'I believe that anything like a protestant exodus from the Irish Free State would be deplored by our present rulers.' He urged harmonious relations between the clergy of the two Churches.[98] A month later, Bishop White at Tralee, Co. Kerry, addressed the annual synod of the dioceses of Ardfert and Aghadoe. He referred to positive changes in conditions since last year and also changes in the clergy. He mentioned how 'Canon Wade and his wife bravely stood months of persecution, camping, rather than living in a house stripped of its furniture'. They had now moved, as had Rev. Jumeux of Ardfert, 'due to the exodus of his people from Ardfert'. He mentioned other parishes whose numbers had been greatly reduced: 'The parish of Sneem, by a series of outrages and burnings had lost many of its chief supporters.'[99]

On 3 July 1923, Bishop Robert Miller spoke in Waterford at the Waterford diocesan synod. He declared: 'We have had many losses through removals from the diocese, but yet those of our people who remain have shown their love for the church to a remarkable degree.' He pointed out how there had recently been 'a campaign against the constituted authorities, resulting in terrible outrages upon the properties of supporters of the Free State Government'.[100] A resolution was passed expressing horror at the murder of farmer Henry Colclough, Clogheen, Cahir, Co. Tipperary, on 30 May, after the end of the Civil War. Speaking two days later to the Cashel diocesan synod at Cashel, Bishop Miller noted how since the last synod the diocese had passed through a time of great anxiety, 'but we are here today with hopeful hearts'.[101] On 5 July 1923 Bishop W.R. Moore addressed Elphin synod at Boyle, Co. Roscommon. He talked of the 'very dreadful condition of things' since they last met, but acknowledged improvements of the last few months due to the success of the Free State army. He stated: 'One of the saddest features of the situation is that so many of our communion

have been driven from the country. By their expulsion such citizens …
are now much fewer than they were.' Moore continued: 'Not a few in
our diocese have suffered most grievous wrongs, both in person and
property, and the numbers that have suffered in other parts of the country are even much greater … many parishes in the south and west are
almost derelict, because of the numbers which have been driven from
their homes.' He concluded: 'Yet we see signs on all sides of the loyalty of
our people to their church.'[102]

At the very end of July, Bishop Thomas Sterling Berry spoke to the
Killaloe diocesan synod at Nenagh, Co. Tipperary. Referring to the
last two years in the diocese, he said that there had been much suffering and loss and expressed deep sympathy with all who had personally
suffered: 'We miss today many who were always present at our synod.'
Nonetheless, he stated that he was convinced that 'it is better to think
of the present and of the future than of the past … To forget the things
that are behind is one great help towards reaching forth into the things
that are before.' He warned: 'One of the worst results of civil strife is
the risk that it may leave behind it antagonisms which will endure for
many generations.' He praised the 'ideal of a generous forgiveness and
forgetfulness of the past'.[103] Clearly, for the sake of the future, Sterling
Berry chose not to dwell on what had happened. He resigned in March
1924. On 4 April a synod to elect a new bishop for the united dioceses of Killaloe and Kilfenora, Clonfert and Kilmacduagh was held in
Limerick, presided over by J.A.F. Gregg, archbishop of Dublin. Gregg
was not so reticent. He paid tribute to Sterling Berry: 'the last years of
whose episcopacy had been saddened ones for Ireland.' He declared: 'In
the unsettled conditions of Europe during these years Ireland had not
escaped, and there was perhaps no part of the country more unsettled
than within the boundaries of the united dioceses.' Gregg then stated:

> Dreadful deeds had been committed, and the destruction of life and
> property was widespread and happy homes were broken up through
> violence. Some people in comfortable circumstances had been reduced
> to poverty, and the population of the dioceses, as far as the Church of
> Ireland was concerned, had suffered very considerably.[104]

The synods of the three cross-border dioceses in October 1923 have little comment on southern conditions, apart from educational matters. At the synod for the diocese of Meath, held in Dublin on 12 October, Bishop B.J. Plunket referred to those 'who cannot be with us today, because they have been exiled from their native land. Driven from their homes, they have been forced to seek safety and shelter across the channel.' He recorded that, among the synodsmen, 'no less than seven, have had their homes destroyed – burnt and desecrated at the hands of their fellow countrymen'.[105] During October 1923, Bishop J.D.F. Day spoke at three synods for the south-eastern dioceses of Ossory, Ferns and Leighlin. At each he mentioned the names of families whose homes had been destroyed. He expressed concern that many men and women had left because of these attacks and he feared they would not return. At the same time he warned against pessimism.[106]

Also in October, Bishop John Orr, who replaced the deceased Bishop Ross, addressed the Tuam diocesan synod at Tuam, Co. Galway. He declared:

> We of the Church of Ireland love our country. We would not be true members of the Church of Ireland if we did not. Our very name, of which we are justly proud, betokens our lineage. We are the church of the whole, and not of a part of Ireland, and no power on earth will ever, please God, partition our church, whatever it may do with our country.[107]

At the Killala and Achonry synod two weeks later at Killala, Co. Mayo, Bishop Orr stated: 'Many of our people have left our shores to seek new homes elsewhere. We hope they will be happy in the lands of their adoption, and we ask them not to forget us who remain, and who are endeavouring, amidst many discouragements to keep afloat the banner of the church.'[108]

Numerical Decline of Church Members

In this chapter we have heard the contemporary voices of some of those who lived during this troubled period. The subject and tenor of the bishops' speeches varied greatly, from descriptions of violence and expulsions to more cautious and guarded comments, and to efforts to find hope for the future, with references to shared troubles and instances of good inter-denominational relations. Through the evidence of these eyewitnesses we have learned something about the trials endured by many members of the Church of Ireland during these revolutionary years. The Church experienced what many described at the time as the 'exodus' of large numbers of its members, a term with strong Old Testament connotations. Publication of the 1926 census in 1929 revealed that in a short period numbers of members of the Church of Ireland had dropped in every one of the twenty-six counties that made up the new Irish Free State. An *Irish Times* editorial in 1929 attributed the decline in Protestant numbers over the period 1911–26 partly to the departure of British forces and to the ravages of the Great War, and then declared that 'the principal cause seems to have been the "troubles" which drove large numbers of Protestants from the country'.[109] The *Irish Independent* noted that 'many Protestants left the country during the internal troubles between 1918 and 1923'.[110]

The drop in numbers of members of the Church of Ireland can be set in the context of changes in Irish population figures. In the half-century before 1911, all denominational groups in Ireland showed a sizeable decline. Between 1861 and 1911 the Church of Ireland population on the island of Ireland fell from 693,357 to 576,611, but the proportion of Church members within the total population increased from 11.96 to 13.13 per cent, thanks primarily to the growth of Belfast, with its large and growing Church of Ireland working class. The Catholic proportion of the population fell from 77.69 per cent to 73.86 per cent in this period.[111] In the twenty-six counties that became the Irish Free State, over the period 1861–1911, numbers of Catholics increased only slightly from 89.3 per cent in 1861 to 89.58 per cent in 1911, while members of the Church of Ireland decreased marginally from 8.47 per cent to 7.95 per cent and total other persons, including all Protestants, altered merely from 10.64 per cent to 10.42 per cent. Over this period Church of Ireland numbers fell by 33 per cent, total other persons by 30.2 per cent and Catholics by 28 per cent.[112]

These figures challenge the views held by some of the 'inexorable decline' or the special long-term decline of southern Protestants.[113] The decrease of 5.6 per cent for Church of Ireland members in the period 1901–11 for the twenty-six counties was the lowest rate of decline in fifty years.[114] What followed in the next census period, 1911–26, was very different from what had happened before. In this fifteen-year period, numbers of members of the Church of Ireland in the south fell sharply by 85,320 from 249,535 to 164,215 – a decline of 34 per cent, compared with a fall of 33 per cent over the previous half-century. This ranged from a 24 per cent drop in the three Ulster counties and 34 per cent in Leinster to 35 per cent in Connacht and 43 per cent in Munster.

Explanations for Decline in Numbers

How do we explain this dramatic drop in the Church of Ireland population? World war losses and the transfer of British armed forces and their dependants out of Ireland after 1921 were commonly regarded as important at the time. There has been debate as to the total number of Irish wartime fatalities, but the latest estimate puts the figure of deaths of people from the island of Ireland at some 40,000.[115] Given the percentage of southern members of the Church of Ireland in the population, and allowing for a proportionally higher level of enlistment and deaths, this would come to a total of around 3,300 deaths of members of the Church of Ireland, representing 4 per cent of the fall in the Church of Ireland population.[116] The 1926 census attributed about 25 per cent of the decrease in Protestant numbers from 1911 to the withdrawal of the British army and navy and the disbandment of the police forces, as well as the emigration of their dependants.[117] The 1911 census figures contain many non-Irish-born members of the British army and Royal Navy who were classified as Episcopalians/Church of Ireland. In 1911 Church of Ireland members of the army, navy and police in the twenty-six counties numbered 18,404, to which we can add another twenty-eight dependants per hundred to give a total of some 23,577.[118] This figure represents 28 per cent of the drop in members of the Church of Ireland between 1911 and 1926. The military were important but only in a minority of counties, because army garrisons were based in a small number of areas. Together, these figures of war dead and departed armed services personnel and their dependants come to some 26,877, or 31 per cent of the fall in the Church of Ireland population over this period. Some civil servants, especially at the top level, transferred to Northern Ireland or Britain but most stayed in their positions.[119]

Two other factors that must be examined are emigration and demographic change. Some members of the Church of Ireland emigrated for normal economic reasons, as in the years 1911–14, but this movement cannot be regarded as especially significant, particularly as emigration largely stopped during the Great War. Attention has been drawn to the Protestant 11.2 percentage of all emigration for the period, 1926–36, and it has been argued that this figure can be applied to the estimated total emigration for the 1911–26 years to give a total of some 45,000 or over for economic and voluntary emigration by Protestants for the earlier period.[120] Taking this into account, along with other factors such as war losses and British withdrawal of service personnel, it has been claimed that only some 2,000 to 16,000, or under 15 per cent, left because of revolutionary violence.[121] A problem of double accounting arises with these figures, however, in that the total for all 1911–26 emigrants includes British military and world war dead, which are then included again in the table of figures to determine the number and type of Protestant departures: in other words, the method employed has a percentage of British military and world war dead departing twice.[122] Correcting this calculation, the figure for estimated involuntary Protestant emigrants according to the above argument should be about 9,000 to 23,000 and not 2,000 to 16,000.[123]

There is another more serious problem with this approach to economic and voluntary emigration. The later high Protestant emigration figure for 1926–36 reflects the new conditions of the fledgling Irish state, which increasingly alienated many Protestants.[124] Also, because of the violence against members of their community, 1919–23, others will have felt unhappy to remain in Ireland after 1926. It is important to note that in the preceding period, 1901–11, under 'normal conditions', including emigration, numbers of members of the Church of Ireland in the twenty-six counties fell by only 5.6 per cent, a figure of merely 15,729.[125] If, in the years, 1911–26, the fall in the Church of Ireland civilian population had been similar to the 5.6 per cent decline in the previous decade, the loss would have numbered nearly 19,000. This figure can be used to try to estimate roughly losses due to voluntary emigration, although it exaggerates the numbers involved because it does not take into account either those who died in the war rather than emigrated in normal circumstances or the drop in emigration due to wartime restrictions. In the decades before 1911, Protestant population decline generally due to emigration was on much the same scale as Catholic decline.[126] In this fifteen-year period the decline in Catholic numbers was only 2.2 per cent.[127] Suggestions that closure of wartime factories, or other post-war economic factors, were important, can be discounted as they should also have affected Catholic numbers, which they did not.

It has been argued that low fertility, along with the effects of mixed marriages, were important demographic factors that were the main cause of this population decline, rather than forced emigration.[128] Certainly there was a fall in the number of births among the Church of Ireland population, as reflected in a reduction in number of schoolchildren recorded in diocesan synod education reports, but this did not necessarily mean a falling population. Elsewhere in the British Isles, there was also a sharp decline in birth rates and fertility in the years 1901–26, but this was more than compensated by a significant increase in life expectancy, resulting in a growing population in these places.[129] For example, in Scotland the number of legitimate births per 1,000 married women, aged 15–44, fell from 272 in 1901 to 184 in 1926; in spite of this and massive war losses the Scottish population increased from 4,479,104 to 4,864,259 between 1901 and 1926. A fall in the birth rate of southern Protestants cannot be regarded as relevant for the decline in their overall numbers. Mixed marriages were significant for the later fall in Protestant numbers, due to the Vatican's Ne Temere decree of 1908, but the decree was not mentioned at synods in this period and it appears to have had little effect in these early years.[130] Whatever demographic problems affected members of the Church of Ireland at this stage or later, the decline in their numbers in the period 1901–11 was just 5.6 per cent, very much lower than the subsequent fall of 34.2 per cent.[131] Anyhow, it seems unlikely that demographic changes could have caused this drastic decrease in such a short period.

It has been observed, drawing on evidence particularly from County Cork, that southern Methodist membership fell significantly in the ten years before 1921 and it has been suggested that this was likely to have been the case also for Church of Ireland membership.[132] Apart from absences at the war, however, such decline does not appear to have been a significant, widespread problem for the Church of Ireland during this time. Comparisons between Methodists and members of the Church of Ireland are not meaningful because of important differences between the two denominations, as seen especially in the fact that in the twenty-six counties in 1911 Methodists numbered merely 16,444 compared with 249,535 for members of the Church of Ireland.[133] Voluntary and economic emigration and demographic matters were important for the subsequent fall in Protestant numbers, which continued until 1991, but they should not be accorded special significance in this earlier period.[134]

Impact of Violence

Critical for the decline in the Church of Ireland population at this time was violence arising from a number of political, economic and religious/sectarian factors that forced large numbers to leave. Members of the Church of Ireland suffered in the War of Independence because they were often identified as unionists/loyalists or with the interests of the British government, and in the Civil War because they were still seen as loyalists or were identified with the Free State government, with the result that they became political targets. While some left because they did not approve of the new political arrangements, speeches at the synods demonstrate the acceptance of the new settlement and government by Church leaders. Frequently, speakers counselled against people leaving, but the very obvious evidence of forced departures as recorded in these public statements, especially 1922–23, reveals how people saw themselves under attack or serious threat, and were not merely unhappy with the changes. In the years 1923–26, additional emigrants were probably influenced to leave by worries over government policies such as compulsory Irish in education and land redistribution, but it is likely that such concerns were greatly heightened by the violence inflicted previously upon members of their community.

During these years of conflict, many members of the Church of Ireland endured attacks on their person and property, which reflected underlying economic and social tensions over agrarian issues, exacerbated by contemporary violence. As well, in spite of efforts to maintain good denominational relations in the south, by Church of Ireland clergy, members of the government and Catholic bishops and laity, sectarian factors were significant.[135] There were examples of sectarianism during the War of Independence, but, curiously, the problem became more acute after the truce of July 1921. During early 1922, Protestants suffered in the form of reprisals and revenge for violence against northern Catholics and nationalists, which was nothing of their doing but for which they were seen to be associated and blamed. Later, during the Civil War, sectarianism was one of the major factors behind intimidation of members of the Church of Ireland that caused many to leave. In these years, thousands of Belfast Catholics were also forced to leave their homes and many came south, but most seem to have returned to the north; between 1911 and 1926 the number of Catholics in Belfast went up, although their proportion of the population fell slightly.[136] Figures for the decline in southern Protestant numbers indicate that few who left returned.

Besides those who fled because they had personally suffered serious intimidation or threats and boycott, the violence directed against members of their community caused others to decide not to remain in Ireland and these should be included in the forced movement of people from Ireland at this time. Gemma Clark has written: 'Individuals and families who had seen their neighbours attacked or received a threatening letter … did not have to experience actual physical harm to feel frightened enough to leave.'[137] Violence affected not just proprietors of country houses but also farmers, business people and shopkeepers. After the Civil War, many were compensated for their losses by either the British or Irish governments, but as John Whyte pointed out: 'It was no comfort to the religious minority to know that some, at least, of their fellow countrymen had regarded them as being automatically enemies.'[138]

As these statements from synods in every part of the country have revealed, members of the Church of Ireland community were adversely affected by revolutionary violence in all regions, not just in some, such as Counties Cork or Tipperary. The 1926 census showed that since 1911 every county had experienced a drop of at least 20 per cent in their Church of Ireland population, while sixteen had witnessed a fall of at least 30 per cent.[139] First World War deaths and removal of service personnel account for some 26,877 or 31 per cent of the total fall in numbers of 85,320. A figure for 'normal' decline, similar to the 1901–11 figure, would account for a fall of at most some 19,000 or another 22 per cent. This leaves 40,643 or nearly half. Some left because they did not like the new arrangements, but it seems reasonable to say that for most their departure was 'involuntary' and they were forced to leave because of violence, or the threat of violence.

During the War of Independence many members of the Church of Ireland suffered intimidation and loss, but speeches at the synods indicate that the worst experience for most came afterwards, during the first half of 1922 and throughout the Civil War from June 1922 until the end of May 1923. The term 'ethnic cleansing' is inappropriate to describe what happened countrywide because it does not compare fairly with events elsewhere in this era when ethnic and religious minorities were attacked and expelled in very large numbers, such as the Greeks in Asia Minor. At the same time, these revolutionary years, as well as the immediate aftermath, saw the exodus of substantial numbers of members of the Church of Ireland, due primarily to the widespread violence that their community suffered. In light of evidence from the statements of these Church leaders, and the highly abnormal level of decline, it is reasonable to conclude that their forced displacement was a major reason for the fall in numbers, rather than other causes such as voluntary or economic emigration, or demographic matters.

Final Observations

Through these contemporary accounts, we have heard the story of the many southern members of the Church of Ireland who were forced to leave Ireland at this time. Of course, it is also the narrative of the greater number of members of the Church who stayed, in spite of the extremely severe pressures on their community. While speakers at the synods told of violence against members, they spoke as well of efforts to maintain good relations between denominations and they urged their own people to stay. They acknowledged that during these turbulent years others also endured violence and destruction. Members of the government, and Catholic clergy and laity, denounced such attacks on the Protestant community. The majority of members of the Church of Ireland did not join this exodus. Many who suffered attack and loss, or fear of attack and loss, chose to stay, in part, no doubt, because they would not give up their only means of livelihood, but also, in part, out of a sense of patriotism and a desire to contribute to the new state and society.[140] In the professions and business they continued to take a major role. Members of the Church of Ireland played a prominent part in both Dáil Éireann and the Irish senate, at least over the next decade.[141]

For most of the survivors, however, who determined to continue to make Ireland their home, the approach they adopted, as Bishop Thomas Sterling Berry urged in 1923, was to forgive and to forget. In the three-volume history of the Church of Ireland, published in the 1930s and edited by W. Alison Phillips, the author of the chapter on the modern period chose not to recall 'the dark and terrible deeds done in Ireland' at this time.[142] A 1953 history of the Church of Ireland covered these events and losses in one line.[143] Probably, in the circumstances of the times and for the sake of those who remained, this was the best approach. Today, however, in the totally new circumstances of the twenty-first century, we can look at these matters again and investigate them fully. As we do, we can recall once more the words of Archbishop C.F. D'Arcy at the general synod of May 1923, when he praised the 'quiet courage and persistence' of Church members, along with their 'Christian fortitude and true patriotism', which he believed gave hope for the future.[144]

NOTES

Introduction

1   *Report of the Independent Review of Parades and Marches, 1997* (Belfast, 1997), p. 29.
2   Ian McBride, 'Memory and national identity in modern Ireland' in Ian McBride (ed.), *History and National Identity in Ireland* (Cambridge, 2001), p. 2.
3   John Coakley, 'The foundations of statehood' in John Coakley and Michael Gallagher (eds), *Politics in the Republic of Ireland* (Dublin, 1992), p. 8.

Chapter 1: The Past and the Present

1   *Report of the Independent Review of Parades and Marches, 1997* (Belfast, 1997), pp. 5–6.
2   Dermot Bolger, 'Shift your shadow or I'll burst you' in *Sunday Independent*, 16 Aug. 1992.
3   For example, *The Times*, 5 Sep. 1998.
4   *Belfast News Letter* [*BNL*], 10 Feb. 1995.
5   Conor O'Clery, *Ireland in Quotes: A History of the Twentieth Century* (Dublin, 1999), p. 130.
6   *Irish Times* [*IT*], 17 Feb. 1996.
7   *Belfast Telegraph* [*BT*], 13 Oct. 2009.
8   Nicholas Mansergh, *Britain and Ireland* (London, 1942), p. 95.
9   A.D. Smith, *National Identity* (Nevada, 1991, reprinted 1993), p. 14.
10   Eric Hobsbawm, 'Introduction: inventing traditions' in Eric Hobsbawm and T. Ranger (eds), *The Invention of Tradition* (Cambridge, 1983, reprinted 1995), pp. 13–14; John Coakley, 'Mobilising the past: nationalist images of history' in *Nationalism and Ethnic Politics*, vol. 10, no. 4 (2004), pp. 531–60; B.M. Walker, '1641, 1689, 1690 and all that: the unionist sense of history' in *Irish Review*, no. 12 (Summer, 1992), pp. 56–64.
11   John McGarry and Brendan O'Leary, *The Northern Ireland Conflict: Consociational Engagements* (Oxford, 2004), p. 186.

12   Walker Connor, 'A few cautionary notes on the history and future of ethnonational conflicts' in Andreas Wimmer *et al.* (eds), *Facing Ethnic Conflicts: Towards a New Realism* (Lanham, MD, 2004), p. 30.

13   See Ronald McNeill, *Ulster's Stand for Union* (London, 1922), p. 9; Lord Robert Armstrong, 'Ethnicity, the English and Northern Ireland' in Dermot Keogh and M.H. Haltzel (eds), *Northern Ireland and the Politics of Reconciliation* (Cambridge, 1993), p. 203.

14   A.T.Q. Stewart, *The Narrow Ground: Aspects of Ulster, 1609–1969* (London, 1977), p. 16.

15   *Hansard*, lxxxvii, (1985–86), 779, 783, 904 and 907.

16   Martin Mansergh (ed.), *The Spirit of the Nation: The Speeches and Statements of Charles J. Haughey (1957–1986)* (Cork, 1986), p. 738.

17   Richard Davis, *Mirror Hate: The Convergent Ideology of Northern Ireland Paramilitaries, 1966–92* (Aldershot, 1994), p. 3.

18   Shane O'Doherty, *The Volunteer: A Former IRA Man's True Story* (London, 1993), pp. 27–30.

19   Geoffrey Beattie, *Protestant Boy* (London, 2004), p. 126.

20   *IT*, 25 Feb. 1998.

21   Ibid., 3 Mar. 1994.

22   Ibid., 13 Apr. 1994.

23   *Sunday Tribune Magazine*, 31 Mar. 1996.

24   *Report of the International Body on Decommissioning, 22 Jan. 1996* (Belfast and Dublin, 1996), p. 5.

25   Arthur Aughey, 'Learning from the leopard' in Rick Wilford (ed.), *Aspects of the Belfast Agreement* (Oxford, 2000), pp. 184–201.

26   George Mitchell, 'Towards peace in Northern Ireland' in Marianne Elliott (ed.), *The Long Road to Peace in Northern Ireland: Peace Lectures from the Institute of Irish Studies at Liverpool University* (Liverpool, 2002), p. 88.

27   J. Bowyer Bell, *The Irish Troubles: A Generation of Violence, 1967–92* (Dublin, 1993), p. 829.

28   Andy Pollak (ed.), *A Citizen's Inquiry: The Opsahl Report on Northern Ireland* (Dublin, 1993), p. 122.

29   M.E. Smith, *Reckoning with the Past* (Maryland, 2005), pp. 143–79.

30   Jonathan Bardon, *A History of Ulster* (Belfast, 1992).

31   Máiread Nic Craith, *Plural Identities – Singular Narratives: The Case of Northern Ireland* (Oxford, 2002), p. 30.

32   R.D. Edwards, *Patrick Pearse: The Triumph of Failure* (London, 1977); C.C. O'Brien, *States of Ireland* (London, 1972).

33   Ian McBride (ed.), *History and Memory in Modern Ireland* (Cambridge, 2001), p. 38; Ciaran Brady (ed.), *Interpreting Irish History: The Debate on Historical Revisionism* (Dublin, 1994), pp. 13–14; D. George Boyce and Alan O'Day (eds), *The Making of Irish History: Revisionism and the Revisionist Controversy* (London, 1996), pp. 1–14.

34   R.F. Foster, *Modern Ireland* (London, 1988); Marianne Elliott, *Wolfe Tone: Prophet of Irish Independence* (London, 1989).

35   Jane Leonard, *The Culture of Commemoration: The Culture of War Commemoration* (Dublin, 1996), p. 21.

36   *IT*, 12 Nov. 1998.

37   D. George Boyce, "'No lack of ghosts": memory, commemoration and the state in Ireland' in McBride, *History and Memory in Ireland*, p. 270.

38   Mary Daly, 'History à la carte? Historical commemoration and modern Ireland' in Eberhard Bort (ed.), *Commemorating Ireland: History, Politics, Culture* (Dublin, 2004), pp. 34–55; Boyce and O'Day, *Making of Irish History*, p. 4.

39   Peter Collins, *Who Fears to Speak of '98? Commemoration and the Continuing Impact of the United Irishmen* (Belfast, 2004), pp. 168–9.

40   *BT*, 2 Jul. 1992.

41   *IT*, 25 Feb. 1995.

42   Ibid., 17 Dec. 1992.

43   *Irish Independent* [*IND*], 14 Nov. 1992.

44   Ibid., 19 Apr. 1993.

45   *IT*, 8 Nov. 1993.

46   *Sunday Times*, 7 Mar. 1993.

47   *BT*, 28 Oct. 1993.

48   *IT*, 23 Mar. and 19 Apr. 1993.

49   Ibid., 8 Apr. 1993

50   Ibid., 13 Apr. 1994.

51   Elliott (ed.), *Peace in Northern Ireland*, pp. 207–11.

52   *Frameworks for the Future* (Belfast, 1995), pp. iii and 23.

53   *IT*, 2 Oct. 1993.

54   *Irish News* [*IN*], 6 Jan. 1994.

55   *IT*, 26 May 1994.

56   Ibid., 4 Mar. 1996.

57   *BT*, 19 Sep. 1996; *IND*, 30 Jul. 1996.

58   *IT*, 11 Jun. 1996.

59   *Sunday Independent*, 15 Sep. 1996.

60   *BT*, 7 Aug. 1996.

61   Jonathan Powell, *Great Hatred, Little Room: Making Peace in Northern Ireland* (London, 2008), p. 94.

62   *Sunday Times*, 5 Mar. 1995; *BT*, 9 Jun. 1995.

63   *IT*, 1 Aug. 1996.

64   Ibid., 25 Dec. 1995.

65   *IN*, 4 Feb. 1998.

66   *Sunday Times*, 21 Mar. 1999.

67   *Report of the International Body on Decommissioning, 22 Jan., 1996* (Dublin and Belfast, 1996), pp. 5–6.

68   *Report of the Independent Review of Parades and Marches, 1997* (Belfast, 1997), p. 5.

69   B.M. Walker, *Past and Present: History, Identity and Politics in Ireland* (Belfast, 2000), p. 83.

70   *Sunday Times*, 9 Jul. 2000.

71   *IT*, 27 Feb. 1995, 25 Mar. 1996.

72   *BNL*, 10 Feb. 1995.

73   Ibid., 14 Jun. 1996.

74   *The Belfast Agreement, 1998* (Belfast, 1998).

75   Tom Hennessey, *The Northern Ireland Peace Process: Ending the Troubles* (Dublin, 2000), pp. 217–20.

76   *IND*, 8 Apr. 1998.

77 *The Times*, 5 Sep. 1998.
78 Ibid., 13 Dec. 2000; *BT,* 13 Dec. 2000.
79 Ibid., 26 Nov. 1998.
80 From copy of speech in possession of author who attended the lecture.
81 *IN*, 6 Aug. 2005.
82 www.catholicnews.com, Jun. 2006.
83 *IT*, 11 Dec. 1998.
84 *BNL*, 21 Nov. 1998; David Trimble, *To Raise up a New Northern Ireland: Articles and Speeches* (Belfast, 2001), pp. 47–8.
85 *IT*, 2 Mar. 2002.
86 *BNL*, 5 Nov. 2007.
87 *IT*, 9 May 2003.
88 *IT*, 23 Feb. 2007.
89 Bertie Ahern, *Bertie Ahern: The Autobiography* (London, 2009), p. 293.
90 Sir Kenneth Bloomfield, 'The report of the Northern Ireland Victims Commission' in Elliott, *Peace in Northern Ireland*, pp. 235–9.
91 Arthur Aughey, *The Politics of Northern Ireland* (London, 2004), p. 97.
92 Norman Porter, *The Elusive Quest: Reconciliation in Northern Ireland* (Belfast, 2003), p. 145.
93 Dominic Bryan and Gillian McIntosh, 'Sites of creation and contest in Northern Ireland', *SAIS Review of International Affairs*, vol. 25, no. 2 (Summer/Autumn, 2005), pp. 127–37.
94 *BT*, 16 Jul. 2001.
95 *Daily Telegraph*, 12 Jul. 2001.
96 Richard English, *Armed Struggle: A History of the IRA* (London, 2003), p. 316.
97 *IT*, 25 Nov. 2002.
98 Powell, *Peace in Northern Ireland*, pp. 312–13.
99 *IT*, 5 Apr. 2007.
100 Ibid., 11 May 2007.
101 *IN*, 11 Sep. 2007.
102 *BT*, 3 Apr. 2008.
103 Ahern, *Autobiography*, p. 296.
104 *IT*, 1 May 2008.
105 Ibid., pp. 314–15.
106 *The Times*, 17 May 2011.
107 *IT*, 19 May 2011.
108 Ibid., 18 May 2011.
109 Ibid., 19 May 2011.
110 Ibid.
111 Ibid., 14 Jun. 2011.
112 *Sunday Independent*, 19 Jun. 2011.
113 See Fintan O'Toole on Kosovo, *IT*, 30 Apr. 1999; Noel Malcolm, *Bosnia: A Short History* (London, 1994, reprinted 1996) pp. xix–xxiv.
114 Pal Kolsto (ed.), *Myths and Boundaries in South-Eastern Europe* (London, 2005), p. 1.
115 George Mitchell, *Making Peace* (London, 1999), p. 186.
116 Ahern, *Autobiography*, pp. 292–3.
117 *IT*, 27 Nov. 1998.
118 *BNL*, 7 Nov. 2005.
119 *IT*, 5 Nov. 2007.

Chapter 2: St Patrick's Day

1   Kenneth Bloomfield, *Stormont in Crisis: A Memoir* (Belfast, 1994), p. 92.
2   Paul Arthur, *Political Realities, Government and Politics of Northern Ireland* (London, 1980), p. 92.
3   Pauline Mooney, 'A symbol for the nation: the national holiday campaign, 1901–3' MA thesis, Maynooth University College, 1992, p. 76.
4   Ibid.
5   *Irish Independent* [*IND*], 18 Mar. 1926.
6   Ibid., 16 Mar. 1930.
7   Ibid., 18 Mar. 1931.
8   Ibid., 18 Mar. 1932; 19 Mar. 1934.
9   See speech by Éamon de Valera in Maurice Moynihan (ed.), *Speeches and Statements by Éamon de Valera* (Dublin, 1980), pp. 217–19.
10   *IND*, 18 Mar. 1935.
11   *Northern Whig* [*NW*], 18 Mar. 1939.
12   *IND*, 18 Mar. 1939.
13   Ibid.
14   Ibid., 18 Mar. 1953.
15   Ibid., 18 Mar. 1955.
16   *Capuchin Annual* (1962), p. 218.
17   *NW*, 18 Mar. 1930.
18   Rex Cathcart, *The Most Contrary Region: The BBC in Northern Ireland, 1924–84* (Belfast, 1984), p. 32.
19   *Irish News* [*IN*], 18 Mar. 1932; *Belfast News Letter* [*BNL*], 17 Mar. 1932.
20   *NW*, 18 Mar. 1930.
21   *BNL*, 18 Mar. 1946, 18 Mar. 1950, 17 Mar. 1952.
22   Document is quoted in *BNL*, 1 Jan. 1996.
23   *IND*, 18 Mar. 1954; for complaints about schools not closing see *BNL*, 16 Mar. 1961.
24   *IN*, 17 Mar. 1960.
25   *IND*, 17 Mar. 1961.
26   Ibid., 19 Mar. 1956; *BT*, 10 Mar. 1964.
27   *IN*, 17 Mar. 1960.
28   *IND*, 19 Mar. 1962.
29   Ibid., 17 Mar. 1966.
30   Ibid., 18 Mar. 1964, 16 Mar. 1965.
31   *BNL*, 18 Mar. 1960.
32   *IND*, 17 and 18 Mar. 1964.
33   *BNL*, 17 Mar. 1961.
34   *Belfast Telegraph* [*BT*], 17 Mar. 1967.
35   *IND*, 18 Mar. 1971, 18 Mar. 1983, 18 Mar. 1987.
36   *Irish Times* [*IT*], 17 Mar. 1972.
37   Ibid., 19 Jan. 1996.
38   *IND*, 18 Mar. 1985; *BT*, 18 Mar. 1990.
39   See Conor O'Clery, *The Greening of the White House* (Dublin, 1996).
40   *BNL*, 17 Mar. 2008.

41   See B.M. Walker, *Dancing to History's Tune: History, Myth and Politics in Ireland* (Belfast, 1996), pp. 114–16.
42   Ibid., p. 123.
43   *IT*, 4 Jun. 2011.
44   Ibid., 17 Nov. 2004.
45   *BNL*, 5 Apr. 2007.

Chapter 3: Derry and Bodenstown

1   Ian McBride, *The Siege of Derry in Ulster Protestant Mythology* (Dublin, 1997).
2   Marianne Elliott, *Wolfe Tone: Prophet of Irish Independence* (London, 1989).
3   John Hempton (ed.), *Siege and History of Londonderry* (Derry, 1861), pp. 415–17.
4   McBride, *The Siege*, p. 40.
5   Brian Lacy, *Siege City: The Story of Derry and Londonderry* (Belfast, 1990), pp. 154–8.
6   McBride, *The Siege*, pp. 14 and 40–1.
7   *Ordnance Survey of the County of Londonderry, Vol. 1: City and North Western Liberties of Londonderry, Parish of Templemore* (Dublin, 1837), p. 198.
8   *Londonderry Sentinel* [*LS*], 13 Aug. 1889.
9   Ibid., 14 Aug. 1900, 13 Aug. 1912.
10   Ibid., 14 Aug. 1923.
11   *Northern Whig* [*NW*], 13 Aug. 1924.
12   Ibid., 13 Aug. 1924; *LS*, 14 Aug. 1930, 13 Aug. 1936.
13   Ibid., 15 Aug. 1939.
14   Ibid.
15   Ibid., 13 Aug. 1946; *NW*, 13 Aug. 1946.
16   *Belfast News Letter* [*BNL*], 13 Aug. 1947.
17   *LS*, 22 Dec. 1964.
18   Ibid., 16 Aug. 1972; *Belfast Telegraph*, 13 Aug. 1985.
19   Apprentice Boys of Derry member's ticket 1971 (Dungannon, 1971); *LS*, 15 Aug. 1988.
20   Ibid., 16 Aug. 1989.
21   *Official Tercentenary Brochure* (Derry, 1989), p. 3.
22   *LS*, 13 Aug. 2014.
23   Neil Jarman, *Material Conflicts: Parades and Visual Displays in Northern Ireland* (Oxford, 1997).
24   *LS*, 15 Aug. 2012.
25   Ibid., 15 Aug. 2001.
26   *Irish News*, 6 Aug. 2005.
27   *LS*, 7 Aug. 2002.
28   C.J. Woods, 'Tone's grave at Bodenstown: memorials and commemorations, 1798–1913' in Dorothea Siegmund-Schultz (ed.), *Ireland: Gesellschaft and Kultur-vi* (Halle, 1989), pp. 141–5.
29   See Alice Milligan, *Life of Wolfe Tone* (Dublin, 1898), pp. 115–16.
30   C.J. Woods, 'Pilgrimages to Tone's grave at Bodenstown, 1873–1922: time, place, popularity' in *History Ireland*, vol. 23, no. 3 (May–June 2015).
31   Ibid.

32   R. Dudley Edwards, *Patrick Pearse: The Triumph of Failure* (London, 1977), pp. 152–93; *Leinster Leader*, 28 Jun. 1913.

33   D.G. Boyce, *Nationalism in Ireland* (London, 1982; second edition, 1991), p. 308.

34   *Irish Independent [IND]*, 22 Jun. 1925.

35   *Irish Times [IT]*, 23 Jun. 1924.

36   *IND*, 21 Jun. 1926.

37   *IT*, 20 Jun. 1932.

38   Ibid., 19 Jun. 1933.

39   Ibid., 21 Jun. 1948.

40   Ibid., 20 Nov. 1967.

41   Ibid., 26 Apr. 1971.

42   Ibid., 14 Jun. 1974.

43   *Irish Press [IP]*, 24 Jun. 1968.

44   *IT*, 19 Jun. 1972.

45   Ibid.

46   *IP*, 14 Jun. 1976.

47   Richard English, *Armed Struggle: A History of the I.R.A.* (London, 2003), pp. 217–18; Ed Moloney, *A Secret History of the I.R.A.* (London, 2003), p. 151.

48   Martin Mansergh (ed.), *The Spirit of the Nation: The Speeches and Statements of Charles J. Haughey (1957–1986)* (Cork, 1986), p. 673.

49   Moloney, *The I.R.A.*, p. 302.

50   *IT*, 22 Jun. 1992.

51   Tomás MacGiolla, *Bodenstown October 1991: Lessons for Today* (Dublin, 1991), p. 14.

52   *An Phoblacht*, 25 Jun. 1998.

53   *IT*, 19 Oct. 1998.

54   Ibid., 29 Jun. 2013.

55   Ibid., 19 Oct. 2015.

56   McBride, *The Siege*, p. 11.

57   Elliott, *Wolfe Tone*, pp. 1 and 417.

Chapter 4: Commemorating the Two World Wars

1   Programme for official opening of a memorial stone in honour of the Trinity students, staff and alumni who lost their lives in the First World War, 25 Sep. 2015.

2   Ibid.

3   Report of television programme on Magennis, *Sunday Times*, 3 Oct. 2004.

4   *Belfast Telegraph [BT]*, 1 May 2003.

5   *Irish Times [IT]*, 12 Nov. 1919.

6   Jane Leonard, 'The twinge of memory: Armistice Day and Remembrance Sunday in Dublin since 1919' in Richard English and Graham Walker (eds), *Unionism in Modern Ireland* (Dublin, 1996), p. 99.

7   D.G. Boyce, 'Nationalism, unionism in the First World War' in Adrian Gregory and Senia Paseta (eds), *Ireland and the Great War: 'A War to Unite Us All'* (Manchester, 2002), p. 201.

8   Ibid., p. 102.

9   *BT*, 11 Nov. 1924.

10   Donal Hall, *The Unreturned Army: County Louth Dead in the Great War, 1914–1918* (Dundalk, 2005), pp. 24–5.
11   Keith Jeffery, *Ireland and the Great War* (Cambridge, 2000), p. 127.
12   Hall, *The Unreturned Army*, pp. 24–5.
13   *Irish News [IN]*, 12 Nov. 1924.
14   Leonard, 'Twinge of memory', p. 105.
15   See Jeffery, *Ireland and the Great War*, pp. 107–23.
16   Brian Hanley, 'Poppy day in Dublin in the 20s and 30s' in *History Ireland*, vol. 7, no. 1 (Spring 1999), pp. 5–6.
17   Leonard, 'Twinge of memory', p. 106.
18   David Fitzpatrick, 'Commemorating in the Irish Free State: a chronicle of embarrassment' in Ian McBride (ed.), *History and Memory in Modern Ireland* (Cambridge, 2001), p. 194.
19   Ibid.
20   Brian Girvin and Geoffrey Roberts, 'The forgotten volunteers of World War II' in *History Ireland*, vol. 6, no. 1 (Spring 1998), pp. 46–51; Brian Girvin, *The Emergency: Neutral Ireland 1939–45* (London, 2006), pp. 256–81.
21   Ibid.
22   Jane Leonard, '"Facing the finger of scorn": veterans' memories of Ireland after the Great War' in Martin Evans and Kenneth Lunn (eds), *War and Memory in the Twentieth Century* (Oxford, 1997), pp. 59–72.
23   *IN*, 12 Nov. 1919.
24   Jeffery, *Ireland and the Great War*, pp. 107–9.
25   Jane Leonard, *The Culture of Commemoration: The Culture of War* (Dublin, 1996), p. 20.
26   *IN*, 12 Nov. 1924.
27   Keith Jeffery, 'The Great War in modern Irish memory' in T.G. Fraser and Keith Jeffery (eds), *Men, Women and War: Historical Studies*, xiii (Dublin, 1993), p. 151.
28   Jeffery, *Ireland and the Great War*, p. 133.
29   Leonard, *Culture of Commemoration*, p. 20.
30   Jeffery, *Ireland and the Great War*, p. 133.
31   Jeffery, 'The Great War in memory', p. 150.
32   Ibid., pp. 150–1.
33   *BT*, 11 Nov. 1930.
34   *Belfast News Letter [BNL]*, 11 Nov. 1937; *Londonderry Sentinel*, 13 Nov. 1934.
35   Girvin, *The Emergency*, pp. 256–81. Richard Doherty, *Irish Men and Women in the Second World War* (Dublin, 1999), pp. 20–6.
36   *IN*, 5 May 1995.
37   *BNL*, 11 Nov. 1946, 13 Nov. 1950.
38   Leonard, 'Twinge of memory', pp. 102–36.
39   Paul Clark, 'Two traditions and the places between' in John Horne and Edward Madigan (eds), *Towards Commemoration: Ireland in War and Revolution, 1912–1923* (Dublin, 2003), p. 73.
40   *Irish Independent [IND]*, 13 Nov. 1967.
41   *BNL*, 13 Nov. 1961.
42   Ibid., 15 Nov. 1965, 13 Nov. 1967.
43   *IT*, 7–9 Nov. 1978.
44   *BT*, 15 Nov. 1982.
45   *BNL*, 12 Nov. 1984.
46   Leonard, 'Twinge of memory', pp. 107–10.

47   Ibid., p. 103.
48   See Heather Jones, 'Church of Ireland Great War remembrance in the south of Ireland' in Horne and Madigan, *Towards Commemoration*, pp. 74–82.
49   *IT*, 11 Nov. 1998.
50   John Walsh, *Patrick Hillery: The Official Biography* (Dublin, 2008), pp. 466–71.
51   Leonard, 'Twinge of memory', pp. 107–9.
52   Leonard, 'Veterans' memories', p. 9.
53   *BNL*, 13 Nov. 1989, 14 Nov. 1994.
54   Leonard, 'Twinge of memory', p. 111.
55   *IND*, 15 Nov. 1993.
56   Leonard, 'Twinge of memory', p. 111.
57   Ibid.
58   *IT*, 29 Apr. 1995.
59   *BNL*, 14 Nov. 1994.
60   Ibid., 9 Nov. 1992.
61   Ibid., 13 Nov. 1995.
62   *BT*, 10 Nov. 1997; *IN*, 10 Nov. 1997.
63   Keith Jeffery, 'Irish varieties of Great War commemorations' in Horne and Madigan, *Towards Commemoration*, p. 121.
64   Ibid.
65   www.greatwar.co.uk/ypres-salient/memorial-island-of-ireland-peace-park.htm.
66   *BNL*, 12 Nov. 1998.
67   *IN*, 14 Feb. 2002.
68   *IT*, 21 May 2008.
69   Ibid., 21 Feb. 2008.
70   Jeffery, 'Irish varieties of commemorations', pp. 122–3.
71   Article by Neil Richardson, *IT*, 7 Apr. 2016.
72   *Sunday Independent*, 10 Jul. 2016.
73   *IT*, 1 Jul. 2002.
74   Ibid., 1 Mar. 2004, 1 Jul. 2008.
75   *BNL*, 7 Nov. 2005; *IT*, 7 Nov. 2005.
76   *BT*, 3 Jun. 2016.
77   Ibid., 11 Sep. 2007.
78   Ibid., 11 and 15 Nov. 2010; *IN*, 12 Nov. 2010.
79   *BNL*, 13 Nov. 2017; *IT*, 13 Nov. 2017; *IN*, 13 Nov. 2017; *IND*, 13 Nov. 2017.
80   *IT*, 13 Nov. 2017.
81   Ibid., 13 Jan. 2018, article by Diarmuid Ferriter.
82   Fran Brearton, *The Great War in Irish Poetry: W.B. Yeats to Michael Longley* (Oxford, 2000).
83   Jeffery, *Ireland and the Great War*, pp. 144–56.
84   See article by Elaine Byrne about her great-grandfather, Sylvester Cummins who served in the Royal Dublin Fusiliers, *Sunday Business Post*, 17 Apr. 2016.
85   Jeffery, 'Irish varieties of commemorations', p. 121.
86   Tom Burke, 'Rediscovery and rededication: The Royal Dublin Fusiliers Association' in Horne and Madigan, *Towards Commemoration*, pp. 98–104.
87   D.G. Boyce, *The Sure Confusing Drum: Ireland and the First World War: Inaugural Lecture* (Swansea, 1993), p. 24.

Chapter 5: Irish Identity, Past and Present

1   *Northern Whig [NW]*, 1 Oct. 1912.

2   *Hansard*, vol. 37 (1912), 219.

3   Keith Haines, *Neither Rogues Nor Fools: A History of Campbell College and Campbellians* (Belfast, 1993), p. 149.

4   Gearóid Ó Tuathaigh, 'Nationalist Ireland: aspects of continuity and change' in Peter Collins (ed.), *Nationalism and Unionism: Conflict in Ireland, 1885–1921* (Belfast, 1994), p. 49.

5   Charles Townsend, *Ireland: The Twentieth Century* (London, 1999), p. 38.

6   Robert Lynd, *Home Life in Ireland* (London, 1909), pp. 1–2.

7   Quoted in Tony Hepburn, *Conflict of Nationality in Modern Ireland* (London, 1980), pp. 64–5.

8   Marianne Elliott, *The Catholics of Ulster: A History* (London, 2000), pp. 361–9; Valerie Jones, *Rebel Prods* (Dublin, 2016), pp. 23–49.

9   Alvin Jackson, 'Irish unionism, 1905–21' in Collins, *Nationalism and Unionism*, pp. 45–6.

10   A.C. Hepburn (ed.), *The Conflict of Nationality in Modern Ireland* (London, 1980), p. 95.

11   *NW*, 13 Jul. 1923.

12   Patrick Buckland, *Ulster Unionism and the Origins of Northern Ireland* (Dublin, 1973), p. 174.

13   Rogers Brubaker, *Nationalism Reframed: Nationhood and the National Question in the New Europe* (Cambridge, 1996), pp. 1–10.

14   Basil Chubb, *The Government and Politics of Ireland* (London, 1982), pp. 9–10.

15   Tom Garvin, *1922: The Birth of Irish Democracy* (Dublin, 1996; 2005 edition), pp. 147–8.

16   Ewan Morris, *Our Own Devices: National Symbols and Political Conflict in Twentieth-Century Ireland* (Dublin, 2005), pp. 38–69, 168–70, 177.

17   *Dáil Éireann Debates*, vol. 39, 17 Jul. 1931, p. 2348.

18   Brian Girvin, *From Union to Union: Nationalism, Religion and Democracy in Ireland – Act of Union to EU* (Dublin, 2002), p. 98.

19   A.J. Ward, *The Irish Constitutional Tradition: Responsible Government and Modern Ireland, 1782–1922* (Washington, 1994), p. 251.

20   J.J. Lee, *Ireland 1912–1985: Politics and Society* (Cambridge, 1989), p. 300.

21   Brendan Lynn, 'The Irish Anti-Partition League and the political realities of partition' in *Irish Historical Studies*, vol. 24, no. 135 (May 2005), p. 330.

22   Patrick Buckland, *Ulster Unionism and the Origins of Northern Ireland, 1886 to 1922* (Dublin, 1973), p. 174.

23   *Irish News [IN]*, 8 Dec. 1925.

24   *Dáil Éireann Debates*, vol. 22, 22 Mar. 1928, p. 1645.

25   *Irish Independent [IND]*, 14 Dec. 1939.

26   Graham Walker, *A History of the Ulster Unionist Party: Protest, Pragmatism and Pessimism* (Manchester, 2004), p. 103.

27   Ibid., p. 318.

28   Margaret O'Callaghan, 'Language, nationality and cultural identity in the Irish Free State, 1922–7: the *Irish Statesman* and the *Catholic Bulletin* reappraised' in *Irish Historical Studies*, vol. 24, no. 94 (November, 1984), p. 244.

29   Ronan Fanning, *Independent Ireland* (Dublin, 1983), p. 81.

30   Gearóid Ó'Tuathaigh, 'The Irish nation state in the constitution' in Brian Farrell (ed.), *De Valera's Constitution and Ours* (Dublin, 1988), p. 48.

31   Fanning, *Independent Ireland*, p. 140.

32   John Bowman, *De Valera and the Ulster Question, 1917–1973* (Oxford, 1982), p. 107.

33   D.G. Boyce, *Nationalism in Ireland* (London, 1982, second edition, 1991), p. 348.

34   *IND*, 18 Mar. 1935.

35   *Constitution of Ireland (Dublin)*.

36   Elaine Byrne, 'A unique experiment in idealism: the Irish senate, 1922–28' in Mel Farrell, Ciara Meehan and Jason Knirck (eds), *A Formative Decade: Ireland in the 1920s* (Dublin, 2015), p. 64.

37   Ibid., p. 62.

38   Quoted in J.C. Beckett, *The Anglo-Irish Tradition* (London, 1976), pp. 148–9.

39   Quoted by Roy Foster in *Times Literary Supplement*, 1 Oct. 1993.

40   *Irish Times [IT]*, 21 Feb. 1933.

41   Ibid., 10 May 1939.

42   J.L. McCracken, *Representative Government in Ireland: A Study of DAil Eireann, 1919–48* (Chicago, 1976), p. 92.

43   Morris, *National Symbols*, p. 108.

44   *Belfast News Letter [BNL]*, 13 Jul. 1933.

45   *NW*, 13 Jul. 1938.

46   Jonathan Bardon, *A History of Ulster* (Belfast, 1992; updated edition, 2005), p. 581.

47   Thomas Hennessey, *A History of Northern Ireland* (Dublin, 1997), p. 92.

48   J.J. Lee, *Ireland: 1912–1985, Politics and Society* (Cambridge, 1989), p. 300.

49   J.C. Beckett, 'Northern Ireland' in J.C. Beckett *et al.*, *The Ulster Debate* (London, 1972), p. 20.

50   David Fitzpatrick, *The Two Irelands, 1912–1939* (Oxford, 1998), pp. 220–1.

51   Michael McGrath, *The Catholic Church and Catholic Schools in Northern Ireland: The Price of Faith* (Dublin, 2000), pp. 104–5.

52   *Northern Ireland House of Commons Debates*, vol. 2, 15 Jul. 1922.

53   B.M. Walker, *A Political History of the Two Irelands: From Partition to Peace* (Basingstoke, 2012), p. 99.

54   *BNL*, 13 Jul. 1927.

55   David Kennedy, 'Catholics in Northern Ireland, 1926–39' in Francis MacManus (ed.), *The Years of the Great Test, 1926–39* (Cork, 1967), p. 143.

56   *IN*, 13 Jul. 1932. This comment was reported in the *Irish News* but not in the *Northern Whig* or the *Belfast News Letter*.

57   *Northern Ireland House of Commons Debates*, vol. 16, 24 Apr. 1934, 1091.

58   *IN*, 26 Jan. 1928.

59   *Northern Ireland House of Commons Debates*, vol. 16, 24 Apr. 1934, 1095.

60   *IN*, 16 Nov. 1937.

61   Dennis Kennedy, *The Widening Gulf: Northern Attitudes to the Independent Irish State, 1919–49* (Belfast, 1988), pp. 173–4.

62   *IT*, 25 Jan. 1949.

63   Hugh Shearman, *Anglo-Irish Relations* (London, 1948), p. 242.

64   Kennedy, 'Catholics in Northern Ireland', p. 143.

65   *IN*, 6 Jan. 1926.

66   Ibid., 18 Mar. 1926.

67 Cornelius O'Leary, 'Northern Ireland: a failed consociational experiment' in Dennis Kavanagh (ed.), *Electoral Politics* (Oxford, 1992), p. 254.
68 *IN*, 18 Mar. 1929.
69 Eamon Phoenix, *Northern Nationalism: Nationalist Politics, Partition and the Catholic Minority in Northern Ireland, 1890–1940* (Belfast, 1994), p. 377.
70 Quoted in BICO in *Aspects of Irish Nationalism* (Belfast, 1972), p. 7.
71 Mary Daly, 'Irish nationality and citizenship since 1922' in *Irish Historical Studies*, vol. 32, no. 127 (May, 2001), p. 391.
72 J.M. Barkley, *Blackmouth and Dissenter* (Belfast, 1991), p. 51.
73 Quoted in Kennedy, *The Widening Gulf*, p. 230.
74 Paul Bew, Kenneth Darwin and Gordon Gillespie, *Passion and Prejudice: Nationalist–Unionist Conflict in Ulster and the Founding of the Irish Association* (Belfast, 1993), p. 108.
75 *Northern Ireland House of Commons Debates*, vol. 5, 5 Mar. 1929, 434.
76 St John Ervine, *Craigavon: Ulsterman* (London, 1949), p. 561.
77 *NW*, 13 Jul. 1949.
78 Andrew Gailey, *Crying in the Wilderness: Jack Sayers, Liberal Editor* (Belfast, 1995), p. 80.
79 Victor Griffin, *Anglican and Irish Today: Holding the Centre* (Newtownabbey, 2006), p. 44.
80 R.V. Comerford, *Inventing the Nation: Ireland* (London, 2003), p.116.
81 Desmond O'Malley, 'Redefining Ireland' in John Coakley (ed.), *Changing Shades of Orange and Green: Redefining the Union and the Nation in Contemporary Ireland* (Dublin, 2002), p. 64.
82 See Hubert Butler, *Escape from the Anthill* (Mullingar, 1985); Donal Barrington, *Uniting Ireland* (Dublin, 1958).
83 Bowman, *De Valera*, p. 318.
84 *Report of the Committee on the Constitution* (Dublin, 1967), p. 5; Clare O'Halloran, *Partition and the Limits of Irish Nationalism* (Dublin, 1987), p. 188.
85 Bowman, *De Valera*, p. 325.
86 Cabinet documents from 1959 reported in *BNL*, 1 Jan. 1996.
87 Brian Faulkner, quoted in *Aquarius*, 1971, p. 89.
88 *IT*, 30 Oct. 1968, interview with Denis Kennedy.
89 Richard Rose, *Governing without Consensus: An Irish Perspective* (London, 1971), pp. 208–17.
90 Ibid., p. 207.
91 Edward Moxon-Browne, 'National identity in Northern Ireland' in Peter Stringer and Gillian Robinson (eds), *Social Attitudes in Northern Ireland* (Belfast, 1991), pp. 23–30.
92 Ibid., p. 25.
93 Ibid., p. 29.
94 Basil Chubb, *The Constitution and Constitutional Change in Ireland* (Dublin, 1978), p. 97.
95 Ibid.
96 *New Ireland Forum Report*, 2 May 1984 (Dublin), pp. 25–30.
97 D.G. Boyce, *Nationalism in Ireland* (London, 1982; third edition, 1995), pp. 407–8.
98 Eamon Maher, 'The half-life and death of the Irish Catholic novel' in *Irish Times Ticket Magazine*, 23 Dec. 2017.
99 *Belfast Telegraph* [*BT*], 2 Feb. 1994.
100 Marie Jones, *Stones in His Pocket: A Night in November* (London, 2000; reprint, 2012), p. 108.
101 *IT*, 23 Oct. 1995.

102 Ibid., 4 Dec. 1990.

103 *Building Trust in Ireland Studies Commissioned by the Forum for Peace and Reconciliation* (Belfast, 1996), p.v.

104 Typescript of speech in possession of the author.

105 For Belfast Agreement, see Marianne Elliott (ed.), *The Long Road to Peace in Northern Ireland* (Liverpool, 2002), pp. 223–39.

106 Reported in article by Jody Corcoran in *Sunday Independent*, 24 Dec. 2017.

107 'An Irishman's diary', by Aidan Doyle, *IT*, 27 Jun. 2015.

108 Ibid., 27 Nov. 2008.

109 *IND*, 19 Mar. 1962.

110 *IT*, 4 Jun. 2011.

111 Ibid., 21 Jul. 2011.

112 Ibid., 19, 21 and 22 Aug. 2017.

113 Ibid., 22 Aug. 2017.

114 European Sources Online, Speech by Taoiseach Leo Varadker at Queen's University Belfast, 4 Aug. 2017, p. 7.

115 *BT*, 2 Jan. 2018.

116 *BNL*, 8 Apr. 2007.

117 *Northern Ireland Statistics and Research Agency, Census 2011: National Identity in Northern Ireland.*

118 Edward Moxon-Browne, 'National identity in Northern Ireland' in Peter Stringer and Gillian Robinson (eds), *Social Attitudes in Northern Ireland* (Belfast, 1991), p. 28.

119 John Garry and Kevin McNicholl, 'Understanding the "Northern Irish" identity', Knowledge Exchange Seminar Series, www.niassembly.gov.uk, p. 5.

120 *Northern Ireland Statistics and Research Agency, Census 2011; National Identity in Northern Ireland.*

121 Office for National Statistics, *Ethnicity and National Identity in England and Wales*, (London, 2011).

122 Theresa May's speech to Conservative Party Conference 2017, www.conservative.com/sharethefacts/2017/10/theresa-mays-conference-speech.

Chapter 6: 'The Lost Tribes of Ireland'

1   W.E. Vaughan and A.J. Fitzpatrick (eds), *Irish Historical Statistics: Population, 1821–1971* (Dublin, 1978), p. 266.

2   D.H. Akenson, *The Irish Diaspora: A Primer* (Belfast, 1993), pp. 133–40.

3   Original copy of speech in possession of author. See also *Irish Times*, 3 Feb. 1995.

4   See Alan O'Day, 'Revising the diaspora' in D.G. Boyce and Alan O'Day (eds), *The Making of Modern Irish History* (London, 1996), pp. 188–215; Jim McCauley, 'Under an Orange banner: reflections on the northern Protestant experiences of emigration' in Patrick O'Sullivan (ed.), *The Irish Worldwide: Religion and Identity*, vol. 5 (London, 1994), pp. 43–69; Enda Delaney, Kevin Kenny and Donald McRaild, 'The Irish diaspora' in *Irish Economic and Social History*, vol. 33 (2006), pp. 35–48.

5   L.J. McCaffrey, *The Irish Catholic Diaspora in America* (Washington, 1997).

6   See D.H. Akenson, 'The Irish in North America: Catholic or Protestant?' in *Irish Review*, vol. 11 (Winter 1991–92), pp. 17–22.

7   Kerby Miller and Liam Kennedy, 'Irish migration and demography, 1659–1831' in Kerby Miller *et al.* (eds), *Irish Immigrants in the Land of Canaan* (Oxford, 2003), pp. 656–7; Timothy Meagher, 'Diaspora: the Irish in North America' in James Donnelly (ed.), *Encyclopedia of Irish History and Culture*, vol. 1 (Farmington Hills, MI, 2004), pp. 142–4.

8   Akenson, 'The Irish in North America', pp. 19–20.

9   Akenson, *The Irish Diaspora*, pp. 245–50.

10   Joseph Lee, 'Introduction: interpreting Irish America' in Joseph Lee and Marion Casey (eds), *Making the Irish American: History and Heritage of the Irish in the United States* (New York, 2006), p. 4.

11   D.H. Akenson, 'Irish migration to North America, 1800–1920' in Andy Bielenberg (ed.), *The Irish Diaspora* (London, 2000), pp. 115–18.

12   See Kerby Miller, '"Scotch-Irish", "Black Irish" and "Real Irish"' in Bielenberg, *Irish Diaspora*, pp. 139–57; Michael Montgomery, 'Nomenclature for Ulster Emigrants' in *Familia*, vol. 20 (2004), pp. 16–36. See the Montgomery article for good examples of how the term Scotch-Irish was used in the eighteenth century, as well as explanation of the different usage of Ulster Scots, Scotch-Irish and Scots-Irish.

13   See E.R.R. Green, *Essays in Scotch-Irish History* (London, 1969).

14   Samuel Huntington, *Who Are We? America's Great Debate* (London, 2005), pp. 92–8.

15   David Doyle, 'The remaking of Irish America, 1845–1880' in Lee and Casey, *The Irish American*, p. 240.

16   Thomas O'Connor, *The Boston Irish: A Political History* (Boston, MA, 1995).

17   Matthew Mellon (ed.), *Selections from Thomas Mellon and His Times* (Pittsburgh, 1885; abridged edition, Belfast, 1968).

18   Deborah Solomon, *Jackson Pollock: A Biography* (New York, 1987), pp. 15–17.

19   Obituary of Walker in *Evening Telegram* (Portland), 11 May 1917, p. 1.

20   Matthew McKee, '"A peculiar and royal race". Creating a Scotch-Irish identity' in Patrick Fitzgerald and Steve Ickringill (eds), *Atlantic Connections Between Scotland, Ulster and North America* (Newtownards, 2001), pp. 67–83.

21   Wayland Dunaway, *The Scotch-Irish of Colonial Pennsylvania* (Chapel Hill, NC, 1944), p. 3.

22   Akenson, *The Irish Diaspora*, pp. 217–28.

23   Ibid., pp. 243–4, 251.

24   James Webb, *Born Fighting: How the Scots-Irish Shaped America* (New York, 2004).

25   Tom Wolfe article on 'the elite that got away' in review section of *Sunday Times*, 7 Nov. 2004, p. 3.

26   Meagher, 'Diaspora', p. 147.

27   Patrick O'Farrell, 'The Irish in Australia' in Brian Lalor (ed.), *The Encyclopedia of Ireland* (Dublin, 2003), p. 57.

28   Patrick O'Farrell, *The Irish in Australia* (Belfast, 1986); 'The Irish in Australia and New Zealand, 1791–1870' in W.E. Vaughan (ed.), *A New History of Ireland: Ireland Under the Union, 1801–70*, vol. 5 (Oxford, 1989), pp. 661–81; 'The Irish in Australia and New Zealand, 1870–1990' in W.E. Vaughan (ed.), *A New History of Ireland: Ireland Under the Union, 1870–1921*, vol. 6 (Oxford, 1996), pp. 970–91.

29   O'Farrell, 'The Irish in Australia and New Zealand, 1870–1990', p. 703.

30   Ibid., p. 714.

31   Gordon Forth, 'The Anglo-Irish in early Australia: old world origins and colonial experiences' in Philip Bull *et al.* (eds), *Irish Australian Studies:* papers delivered at sixth Irish–Australian conference, July 1990 (Bundoora, 1991), p. 53.

32   David Fitzpatrick, *Oceans of Consolation: Personal Accounts of Irish Migration to Australia* (New York, 1994), p. 14. See also Fitzpatrick, '"That beloved country, that no place else resembles": connotations of Irishness in Irish Australian letters, 1841–1915' in *Irish Historical Studies*, vol. 108, no. xxvi (November 1991), pp. 324–51.

33   Fitzpatrick, *Oceans of Consolation*, p. 14.

34   O'Farrell, *The Irish in Australia*, p. 299.

35   Mike Cronin and Daryl Adair, *The Wearing of the Green: A History of St Patrick's Day* (London, 2002), pp. 204–10.

36   Patrick O'Farrell, 'How Irish was New Zealand?' in *Irish Studies Review*, vol. 9 (Winter 1994–95), pp. 25–30.

37   D.H. Akenson, *Half the World from Home: Perspectives on the Irish in New Zealand* (Wellington, 1990).

38   Brad Patterson (ed.), *Ulster–New Zealand Migration and Cultural Transfers* (Dublin, 2006).

39   Cecil Houston and William Smyth, *Irish Emigration and Canadian Settlement: Patterns, Links and Letters* (Toronto, 1990).

40   See D.H. Akenson, *Being Had: Historians, Evidence and the Irish in North America* (Port Credit, 1985); David Wilson, *The Irish in Canada* (Ottawa, 1989). Also see Robert O'Driscoll and Lorna Reynolds (eds), *The Untold Story: The Irish in Canada* (Toronto, 1988).

41   Akenson, *Being Had*, pp. 82 and 88.

42   J.K. James, 'The Irish in Canada' in Lalor, *Encyclopedia of Ireland*, p. 152.

43   Houston and Smyth, *Irish Emigration*, pp. 3–9.

44   Wilson, *The Irish in Canada*, pp. 20–1.

45   Cecil Houston and William Smyth, *The Sash Canada Wore: A Historical Geography of the Orange Order in Canada* (Toronto, 1980).

46   Wilson, *The Irish in Canada*, p. 21.

47   The above information is from E. Delaney, 'Diaspora: the Irish in Britain', in Donnelly, *Encyclopedia of Irish History*, pp. 141–3.

48   *Census for Scotland, 2001*, Reference volume, p. 276; *Census for England & Wales, 2001*, National report, p. 184.

49   Akenson, *The Irish Diaspora*, p. 210.

50   Roger Swift, 'Historians and the Irish: recent writings on the Irish in nineteenth-century Britain' in Donald McRaild (ed.), *The Great Famine and Beyond: Irish Migrants in Britain in the Nineteenth and Twentieth Centuries* (Dublin, 2000), p. 24.

51   Graham Walker, 'The Protestant Irish in Scotland' in Tom Devine (ed.), *Irish Immigrants in Scottish Society in the Nineteenth and Twentieth Centuries* (Edinburgh, 1991), pp. 44–63; Martin Mitchell, 'Irish in Scotland' in Lalor, *Encyclopedia of Ireland*, p. 970.

52   See, for example, Donald McRaild and D.A.F. Macpherson, 'Sisters of the brotherhood: female Orangeism on Tyneside in the late nineteenth and early twentieth century' in *Irish Historical Studies*, vol. 137, no. xxxv (May, 2006), pp. 40–60.

53   *Focus on Ethnicity and Religion*, 2006 edition of national statistics (London, 2006), p. 48.

54   Ibid., pp. 26–8.

55   Mary Hickman and Bronwen Walter, *Discrimination and the Irish Community in Britain* (London, 1997).

56   *Focus on Ethnicity and Religion*, pp. 26–8.

57   Ibid., p. 11.

58   Grainne O'Keefe, 'The 2001 census: to tick or not to tick? The existence of an Irish ethnic identity in Ireland' in *Études Irlandaises*, vol. 31, no. 1 (Spring 2006), p. 180.

59   Report of Blair speech, *Irish Times*, 27 Nov. 1998, p. 6.

60   John Major, *The Autobiography* (London, 2000), p. 2.

61   Patten interview in *Sunday Times Magazine*, 16 Jul. 2006, p. 68.

62   James Callaghan, *Time and Change* (London, 1987), p. 22.

63   Letter from Denis Healey, 5 May 2000, in *Spark*, vol. 16 (2003), p. 12.

64   O'Keefe, 'The 2001 census', pp. 178–9.

65   B.M. Walker, *Dancing to History's Tune: History Myth and Politics in Ireland* (Belfast, 1996), pp. 123–7.

66   British Council, *Britain and Ireland: Lives Entwined 1* (Dublin, 2005).

67   Marianne Elliott, 'Hyphenated hybrids: Irishness, Englishness and religious identities in Britain and Ireland' in British Council, *Britain and Ireland: Lives Entwined 2* (Dublin, 2006), p. 59.

68   Delaney, 'Diaspora', p. 294.

69   Thomas Hennessey, *Dividing Ireland: World War 1 and Partition* (London, 1998), pp. 2–19.

70   *The Agreement: Agreement Reached in the Multi-Party Negotiations* (Belfast and Dublin, 1998), p. 2.

Chapter 7: The Irish in America

1   From 2013 American Community Survey, as recorded in Tanja Bueltmann and D.M. MacRaild, *The English Diaspora, Ethnicity and Association, 1730s–1950s* (Manchester, 2017), p. 246.

2   National Opinion Research Centre, General Social Survey, 2006.

3   Theodore White, *The Making of the President* (New York, 1961), p. 226.

4   P.J. Blessing, 'Irish' in Stephen Thernstrom (ed.), *Harvard Encyclopedia of American Ethnic Groups* (Cambridge, MA, 1980), pp. 524–45.

5   *New York Times*, 2 May 1981.

6   L.J. McCaffrey, *The Irish Diaspora in America* (Bloomington, IN, 1976).

7   J.G. Leyburn, *The Scotch Irish: A Social History* (Chapel Hill, NC, 1962), p. xii.

8   Ibid., p. 317.

9   M.A. Jones, 'Scotch-Irish' in Thernstrom, *Harvard Encyclopedia*, pp. 896–908.

10   *U.S. Census, 1980; Ancestry of the Population by State: Supplementary Report*. PC-S1 10, p. 2.

11   *Irish Echo*, 15 Feb. 2008, online.

12   D.H. Akenson, *The Irish Diaspora: A Primer* (Belfast, 1993), p. 219.

13   A.M. Greeley, *The Irish Americans: The Rise to Money and Power* (New York, 1981), p. 1.

14   Akenson, *Diaspora*, p. 219.

15   L.J. McCaffrey, *The Irish Catholic Diaspora in America* (Washington, 1997).

16 Bureau of the Census, *Statistical Abstract of the United States, 1975*, p. 3.
17 Collection of Ancestry Data in Census Surveys, draft 12 Aug. 1987. Found on web under Canadian Ancestry Data, p. 2.
18 Reported in *Statistical Abstract, 1975*, p. 34: *Statistical Abstract, 1979*, p. 33.
19 Recorded in *Statistical Abstract, 1982–83*, pp. 4 and 42.
20 Bureau of the Census, *Supplementary Report of Census: Ancestry of the Population by State: 1980*, p. 9.
21 Bureau of the Census, *Detailed Ancestry Groups, 1990*, copy of official census form, E 14.
22 Bureau of the Census, *Supplementary Report of Census: Ancestry of the Population by State: 1980*, p. 5. These figures for single and multiple ancestry are recorded the wrong way round in the table in J.J. Lee and M.R. Casey (eds), *Making the Irish American: History and Heritage of the Irish in the United States* (New York, 2006), p. 691.
23 Social Explorer, database, census 1990 report, statistics on ancestry. Socialexplorer.com.
24 Bureau of the Census, *Census 2000 Special Tabulation, First, Second and Total Responses to the Ancestry Question*.
25 Collection of Ancestry Data in Census Surveys, draft 12 Aug. 1987. Found on web under Canadian Ancestral data, p. 17.
26 Social Explorer, database, census 1990 report, statistics on ancestry. Socialexplorer.com.
27 Bureau of the Census, *Census 2000 Special Tabulation, First, Second and Total Responses to the Ancestry Question*.
28 Bureau of the Census, *Population Division, Ethnic and Hispanic Statistics Branch, Questions*, created 17 March 2003.
29 W.L. Smith, 'Southerner and Irish? Regional and ethnic consciousness in Savannah, Georgia' in *Southern Rural Sociology*, vol. 24, no. 1 (2009), p. 224.
30 Bureau of the Census, *Detailed Ancestry Groups for States, 1990*, p. 6.
31 Akenson, *Diaspora*.
32 Ibid., pp. 244–5.
33 D.N. Doyle, 'Scots Irish or Scotch-Irish' in Lee and Casey, *Making the Irish American*, p. 151.
34 Akenson, *Diaspora*, pp. 245–50; D.N. Doyle, 'The Irish in North America, 1776–1845' in Lee and Casey, *Making the Irish American*, p. 179.
35 Kevin Kenny, *The American Irish: A History* (Harlow, 2000), pp. 72–3.
36 Bureau of the Census, *Detailed Ancestry Groups for States, 1990*, p. 6.
37 See table in Lee and Casey, *Making the Irish American*, p. 689.
38 For information on Irish in the South in the nineteenth century see D.T. Gleeson, *The Irish in the South, 1815–1877* (Chapel Hill, NC, 2001).
39 M.P. Carroll, 'How the Irish became Protestant in America' in *Religion and American Culture: A Journal of Interpretation*, vol. 16, no. 1 (2006), pp. 25–6.
40 James Webb, *Born Fighting: How the Scots-Irish Shaped America* (New York, 2004).
41 John McCain, *Faith of my Fathers* (London, 2008), pp. 22–3.
42 As reported in *Irish Times*, 18 Oct. 2008, from an interview in *Good Housekeeping*.
43 Colm Tóbin, 'Henry James in Ireland: a footnote' in *Henry James Review*, vol. 30, no. 3 (Autumn 2009), p. 212.
44 Ralph McGill, *The South and the Southerner* (Boston, MA, 1962), pp. 38 and 47.
45 See Stephen MacDonagh, *Barack Obama: The Road from Moneygall* (Dingle, Co. Kerry, 2010).
46 See www.ford.ie History of Ford.
47 *Cork Examiner*, 20 Apr. 2017.

48   *Collier's Magazine*, 31 Jan. 1953, pp. 48–50.

49   Article by Gerry Anderson, *Belfast Telegraph*, 15 Oct. 2004.

50   Michael Moore, 'The muckraker: Samuel S. McClure (1857–1949)' in Mark Bailey (ed.), *Nine Irish Lives: The Thinkers, Fighters & Artists Who Helped Shape America* (Chapel Hill, NC, 2018), p. 100.

51   Carroll, 'Irish Protestants', pp. 25–6.

52   Paul Dixon, '"Rosy Catholics" and "dour Prods": President Clinton and the Northern Ireland peace process' in *International Politics,* vol. 47 (2010), pp. 210–28.

53   Pew Forum on Religion and Public Life, report dated 6 Nov. 2009. pewforum.org/rssfeeds/rs.xml. U.S. Religious Landscape Survey.

54   Webb, *Born Fighting*, pp. 15 and 39.

55   See Michael Hout and J.R. Goldstein, 'How 4.5 million Irish immigrants became 40 million Irish Americans: subjective aspects of the ethnic composition of white Americans' in *American Sociological Review*, vol. 59, no. 1 (February 1994), pp. 64–82; Andrew Greeley, 'Achievement of the Irish in America' in Michael Glazier (ed.), *The Encyclopedia of the Irish in America* (Indiana, 1999), pp. 1–4.

56   Obituary in *London Times*, 5 Mar. 2010.

57   Webb, *Born Fighting*, pp. 15 and 133.

58   For extensive family tree see Ancestrymagazine.com and *The Times*, 6 Nov. 2008; for more family information see MacDonagh, *Obama.*

59   Barack Obama, *Dreams from My Father: A Story of Race and Inheritance* (first printed 1995; second edition, New York, 2004).

60   *Irish Times*, 21 Mar. 2009.

61   MacDonagh, *Obama.*

62   A.S. Link (ed.), *The Papers of Woodrow Wilson* (Princeton, 1966), vol. 24, pp. 57–8.

63   W.F. Dunaway, *The Scotch-Irish of Colonial Pennsylvania* (Chapel Hill, NC, 1944), pp. 3–4.

64   See Ralph Hewins, *J. Paul Getty: The Richest American* (London, 1961), p. 23.

65   Akenson, *Diaspora*, pp. 242–4 and 251; D.H. Akenson, 'Irish migration to North America, 1800–1920' in Andy Bielenberg (ed.), *The Irish Diaspora* (London, 2000), p. 132.

66   Greeley, 'Irish in America', p. 2.

67   Carroll, 'Irish Protestants', pp. 25–6.

68   T.J. Meagher, 'Irish' in E.R. Barkan (ed.), *A Nation of Peoples: A Sourcebook on America's Multi-cultural Heritage* (Connecticut, 1999), p. 285.

69   Reginald Byron, *Irish America* (Oxford, 1999).

70   See Feargal Cochrane, *The End of Irish America: Globalisation and the Irish Diaspora* (Dublin, 2010), pp. 193–7; Trina Vargo, 'Congressman Joe Crowley's defeat is further evidence of the non-existent Irish American vote', 28 Jun. 2018, blog, us-ireland alliance.org.

71   From 2013 American Community Survey, as recorded in Bueltmann and MacRaild, *The English Diaspora*, p. 246.

72   Ibid., p. 244.

73   National Opinion Research Centre, General Social Survey, 2006.

74   Kenny, *The American Irish*, p. 3; Greeley, 'Irish in America', p. 3.

75   Akenson, 'Irish migration', pp. 111–15.

76   For example see Patrick Griffin, *The People with No Name: Ireland's Ulster Scots, America's Scots Irish and the Creation of a British Atlantic World, 1689–1764* (Princeton,

2001); K.B. Miller, 'Ulster Presbyterians and the "two traditions" in Ireland and America' in Lee and Casey, *Making the Irish American,* pp. 255–70.

77   Doyle, *Scots Irish*, p. 165. See also his 'The Irish in North America, 1776–1845' in Lee and Casey, *Making the Irish American*, pp. 171–212.

78   Greeley, 'Irish in America', pp. 1–4.

79   Rankin Sherling, 'Irish Protestants in America, 1870–1940' in Elliott Barkan (ed.), *Immigrants in American History: Arrival, Adaptation, and Integration*, vol. 2 (Santa Barbara, 2013), pp. 427–35. Also Sherling, *The Invisible Irish: Finding Protestants in the Nineteenth Century Migration to America* (Kingston, 2017).

80   Leyburn, *Scotch-Irish*, p. 333.

81   See Griffin, *The People with No Name*, p. 175; Miller, 'Ulster Presbyterians', pp. 263–5; Gleeson, *The Irish in the South*, p. 199.

82   Michael Montgomery, 'Nomenclature for Ulster emigrants: Scotch-Irish or Scots-Irish' in *Familia*, vol. 20 (2004), pp. 16–31.

83   Webb, *Born Fighting*, pp. 13–15.

84   For information on this musical tradition see Fiona Ritchie and Doug Orr, *Wayfaring Strangers: The Musical Voyage from Scotland and Ulster to Appalachia* (North Carolina, 2014).

85   Carroll, 'Irish Protestants', pp. 46–7.

86   J.D. Vance, *Hillbilly Elegy: A Memoir of a Family and Culture in Crisis* (London, 2016), p. 3.

87   *Washington Post*, 28 Jul. 2016.

88   Brian Lambkin and Patrick Fitzgerald, *Migration in Irish History* (London, 2008), p. 142.

Chapter 8: General Elections 1885–86

1   For a more detailed study of these elections see B.M. Walker, *Ulster Politics: The Formative Years* (Belfast, 1989); C.C. O'Brien, *Parnell and his Party, 1880–90* (Oxford, 1957); and James Loughlin, *Gladstone, Home Rule and the Ulster Question, 1882–1922* (Dublin, 1986).

2   All information on election results has come from B.M. Walker, *Parliamentary Election Results in Ireland, 1801–1922* (Dublin, 1978).

3   Mary Daly, *Industrial Development and Irish National Identity, 1922–39* (Dublin, 1992), p. 3.

4   B.M. Walker, 'The Irish electorate, 1868-1916' in *Irish Historical Studies*, vol. 7, no. 71 (March 1973), pp. 359–406.

5   *Belfast Morning News*, 10 Nov. 1885.

6   See W.E. Vaughan and A.J. Fitzpatrick (eds), *Irish Historical Statistics, 1821–1971* (Dublin, 1978), pp. 28–37.

7   See B.M. Walker, Mary O'Dowd and Ciaran Brady (eds), *Ulster: An Illustrated History* (London, 1989), p. 164.

8   W.E. Vaughan, *Landlords and Tenants in Ireland, 1848–1904* (Dublin, 1984).

9   Vaughan and Fitzpatrick, *Irish Historical Statistics*, pp. 57–9.

10   See Walker, *Ulster Politics*, pp. 15–38; David Hempton and Myrtle Hill, *Evangelical Protestantism in Ulster Society, 1740–1890* (London, 1992); Emmet Larkin, 'The

devotional revolution in Ireland, 1850–75' in *American Historical Review*, vol. 77, no. 3 (June 1972), pp. 625–52.

11   *Weekly Examiner*, 13 Mar. 1886.

12   Walker, *Ulster Politics*, p. 26; A.C. Hepburn 'Work, class and religion in Belfast, 1871–1911' in *Irish Economic and Social History*, vol. 10 (1983), p. 50.

13   Walker, 'The Irish electorate', pp. 359–406.

14   Walker, *Ulster Politics*, p. 154.

15   O'Brien, *Parnell*, p. 150.

16   Ibid., p. 133.

17   Emmet Larkin, 'Church, state and nation in modern Ireland' in *American Historical Review*, vol. lxxx, no. 4 (October 1975), pp. 1265–7.

18   Walker, *Ulster Politics*, p. 204; Michael Davitt, *The Fall of Feudalism in Ireland* (London, 1904), pp. 466–9.

19   A.C. Murray, 'Nationality and local politics in late nineteenth-century Ireland: the case of County Westmeath' in *Irish Historical Studies*, vol. 25, no. 98 (November 1986), p. 146.

20   Walker, *Ulster Politics*, p. 213.

21   P.J. Buckland, *Irish Unionism, 1885–1923* (Belfast, 1973), pp. 95–9.

22   B.M. Walker, 'Party organisation in Ulster, 1865–92: registration agents and their activities' in Peter Roebuck (ed.), *Plantation to Partition: Essays in Ulster History in Honour of J.L. McCracken* (Belfast, 1981), pp. 201–3.

23   E.g., D.C. Savage, 'The origins of the Ulster unionist party, 1885-6' in *Irish Historical Studies*, vol. 12, no. 47 (March 1961), p. 186.

24   Walker, *Ulster Politics*, pp. 177–92.

25   Ibid., p. 179.

26   Ibid., p. 203.

27   Ibid., pp. 207–8.

28   Ibid., p. 202.

29   T.M. Healy, *Letters and Leaders of my Day*, vol. 1 (2 vols, London, 1928), pp. 231–3.

30   Walker, *Ulster Politics*, pp. 190, 209–11.

31   Ibid., pp. 215–19.

32   P.J.O. McCann, 'The Protestant home rule movement, 1886–95' MA thesis, University College Dublin, 1972; see also James Loughlin, 'The Irish Protestant Home Rule Association' in *Irish Historical Studies*, vol. 24, no. 95 (May 1985), pp. 341–60.

33   James Anderson, 'Ideological variations in Ulster during Ireland's first home rule crisis: an analysis of local newspapers' in C.H. Williams and E. Kofman (eds), *Community Conflict, Partition and Nationalism* (London, 1989), pp. 133–66.

34   For valuable discussions of these movements see D.G. Boyce, *Nationalism in Ireland* (London, 1982; second edition, 1991), and Alvin Jackson, *The Ulster Party: Irish Unionists in the House of Commons, 1884–1911* (Oxford, 1989).

35   Larkin, 'Church, state and nation in modern Ireland', p. 1267.

36   See A.T.Q. Stewart, *The Narrow Ground: Aspects of Ulster 1609–1969* (London, 1977; new edition, 1989), p. 163; John Coakley, 'The foundations of statehood' in John Coakley and Michael Gallagher (eds), *Politics in the Republic of Ireland* (Galway, 1992), p. 8; Tom Garvin, 'Democratic politics in independent Ireland' in ibid., p. 222.

37   See S.M. Lipset and Stein Rokkan, 'Cleavage structures, party systems and vote alignment: an introduction' in S.M. Lipset and Stein Rokkan (eds), *Party Systems and Vote Alignment* (New York, 1967), pp. 50–6; Gordon Smith, *Politics in Western Europe* (London, 1972; fourth edition, London, 1983), pp. 12–14, 44–6; A.R. Ball, *Modern Politics and Government* (London, 1988), pp. 82–4.

38   See Smith, *Politics in Western Europe*, pp. 18–36; Jan Erik Lane and S.O. Erson, *Politics and Society in Western Europe* (London, 1987), pp. 56–64, 97–9; J.H. Whyte, *Catholics in Western Democracies* (Dublin, 1981), pp. 47–75.

39   See Alf Kaartvedt, 'The economic basis of Norwegian nationalism in the nineteenth century' in Rosalind Mitchison (ed.), *The Roots of Nationalism: Studies in Northern Europe* (Edinburgh, 1980), pp. 11–19; Smith, *Politics in Western Europe*, pp. 297–302, 308–10.

Chapter 9: Southern Protestant Voices

1   W.A. Phillips (ed.), *History of the Church of Ireland, From the Earliest Times to the Present Day*, vol. 3 (Oxford, 1933), pp. 412–13.

2   Peter Hart, *The IRA at War, 1916–23* (Oxford, 2003); 'The Protestant experience of revolution in southern Ireland' in Richard English and Graham Walker (eds), *Unionism in Modern Ireland: New Perspectives on Politics and Culture* (Dublin, 1996), pp. 81–98.

3   Barry Keane, *Massacre in West Cork: The Dunmanway and Ballygroman Killings* (Cork, 2013). See review by B.M. Walker in *Irish Independent*, 31 May 2014. Also Stephen Howe, 'Killings in Cork and the historians' in *History Workshop Journal*, no. 77 (Spring 2014), pp. 160–86.

4   Andy Bielenberg, 'Exodus: the emigration of southern Irish Protestants during the Irish War of Independence and the Civil War' in *Past and Present*, no. 218 (February 2013), pp. 199–233; David Fitzpatrick, 'Protestant depopulation and the Irish revolution' in *Irish Historical Studies*, vol. 38, no. 152 (November 2013), pp. 642–70.

5   *Ireland. Census of Population, 1926, Religion and Birthplaces*, vol. 3, p. 1.

6   Easy access to this source is provided by the index to the paper on the *Irish Times* archive website.

7   R.B. McDowell, *The Church of Ireland, 1869–1969* (London, 1965), p. 108.

8   *Irish Times [IT]*, 16 Mar. 1921.

9   *Irish Examiner*, 10 Apr. 1920; *Freeman's Journal*, 7 Jan. 1921.

10   *IT*, 17 May 1919.

11   Ibid., 7 Jun. 1919; for confirmation of these figures see W.E. Vaughan and A.J. Fitzpatrick (eds), *Irish Historical Statistics: Population 1821–1971* (Dublin, 1978), p. 49.

12   *IT*, 1 Aug. 1919.

13   Ibid., 23 Oct. 1919.

14   W.J. Lowe, 'The war against the R.I.C., 1919–21' in *Éire Ireland*, vol. 37 (2002), p. 94.

15   *IT*, 19 May 1920.

16   H.E. Patton, *Fifty Years of Disestablishment: A Sketch* (Dublin, 1922), pp. 303–5.

17   *IT*, 10 Jun. 1920.

18 Ibid., 25 Jun. 1920, 26 Oct. 1920.
19 Ibid., 26 Jun. 1920.
20 Ibid., 31 Jul. 1920.
21 Ibid., 29 Oct. 1920.
22 Ibid., 19 Oct. 1920
23 Ibid., 28 Oct. 1920.
24 Ibid., 29 Dec. 1920.
25 Fifty-first report of the proceedings of the Representative Body of the Church of Ireland, pp. 34–5.
26 *IT*, 11 May, 1921. For another reference to the killing of these farmers see Dennis Kennedy, *The Widening Gulf: Northern Attitudes to the Independent Irish State, 1919–49* (Belfast, 1988), p. 51.
27 *IT*, 2 Jul. 1921.
28 Ibid., 20 Jul. 1921; for information on William Latimer see Brian Hughes, *Defying the IRA? Intimidation, Coercion and Communities During the Irish Revolution* (Liverpool, 2016), pp. 125–6. Eoghan Harris, *Sunday Ind.*, 27 Aug. 2017.
29 *Belfast Telegraph*, 15 Jun. 1921; *IT*, 16 Jun. 1921.
30 Ibid., 23 Jul. 1921.
31 Ibid., 7 and 23 Jul. 1921.
32 Ibid., 23 Jul. 1921.
33 Robin Bury, *Buried Lives: The Protestants of Southern Ireland* (Dublin, 2016), pp. 35–6.
34 For these and other examples of intimidation of Protestants 1920–21, see Kennedy, *The Widening Gulf*, pp. 49–54; Bielenberg, 'Exodus', pp. 206–9; Terence Dooley, *The Plight of Monaghan Protestants, 1912–1926* (Dublin, 2000), pp. 42–5; Bury, *Buried Lives*, chapters 2 and 3.
35 *IT*, 5 Aug. 1921.
36 Ibid., 13 Oct. 1921.
37 Ibid., 26 Oct. 1921.
38 Ibid.
39 Sally Warwick Haller, 'Seeking reconciliation: William O'Brien and the Ulster crisis' in D.G. Boyce and Alan O'Day (eds), *The Ulster Crisis* (London, 2005), pp. 146–64.
40 See J.S. Donnelly, 'Big house burnings in County Cork during the Irish revolution, 1920–21' in *Éire Ireland*, vol. 47, no. 324 (Autumn/Winter 2012), pp. 141–97.
41 Tom Barry, *Guerrilla Days in Ireland* (Cork, 1955 reprint), p. 115.
42 For information on O'Connor, Bradfield and Lindsay see Gerard Murphy, *The Year of Disappearances: Political Killings in Cork* (Dublin, 2010), pp. 73, 89–90 and 64.
43 *IT*, 18 Oct.1921.
44 Ibid., 27 Oct. 1921.
45 Ibid., 26 Oct. 1921.
46 Ibid., 4 Nov. 1921.
47 Ibid., 12 Dec. 1921.
48 Tim Wilson, 'The most terrible assassination that has yet stained the name of Belfast', *Irish Historical Studies*, vol. 37, no. 145 (May 2010), pp. 83–106.
49 *IT*, 5 Apr. 1922.
50 Ibid., 10 Apr. 1922.
51 Keane, *Massacre in West Cork*, and Walker, 'Review'. These murders at Dunmanway were preceded by the murder of three other Protestants at Ballygroman, Co. Cork, and the 'disappearance' of their bodies.

52 In their condemnation of these murders, Michael Collins, Dr Daniel Colohan, Catholic bishop of Cork, and Éamon de Valera all saw them as reprisals for northern murders. *IT*, 13 May 1922; *Cork Examiner*, 1 and 13 May 1922.

53 *Church of Ireland Gazette*, 5 May 1922.

54 See Kennedy, *The Widening*, pp. 114–29; Bielenberg, 'Exodus', pp. 207–13. In the spring of 1922 perhaps as many as 20,000 arrived in Britain as refugees from Ireland, although not all were members of the Church of Ireland, Niamh Brennan, 'A political minefield: southern loyalists, the Irish Grants Committee and the British government, 1922–31' in *Irish Historical Studies*, vol. 30, no. 119 (May 1997), p. 406. See T.A.M. Dooley, 'Protestant migration from the Free State to Northern Ireland, 1920–25: a private census for Co. Fermanagh' in *Clogher Record*, vol. 15 (1996).

55 Bielenberg, 'Exodus', pp. 207–9; S.J. Watson, *A Dinner of Herbs: The History of Old St Mary's Church, Clonmel* (Clonmel, 1988), pp. 190–2.

56 George Seaver, *John Allen Fitzgerald Gregg, Archbishop* (Dublin, 1963), p. 121.

57 *IT*, 10 May 1922.

58 Ibid.

59 Ibid., 13 May 1922.

60 Ibid.

61 Ibid., 30 May 1922.

62 Ibid., 2 Jun. 1922.

63 *Church of Ireland Gazette*, 28 Jul. 1922. See *IT*, 13 Jun. 1922.

64 Ibid., 7 Sep. 1922.

65 Ibid., 7 and 11 Sep. 1922.

66 Ibid., 14 Oct. 1922.

67 Ibid., 2 Oct. 1922.

68 Ibid., 13 Oct. 1922.

69 *Church of Ireland Gazette*, 28 Jul. 1922; *Tuam Herald*, 29 Jul. 1922.

70 Letter from T. Sterling Berry, 10 Jun. 1922 (National Archives of Ireland, Department of Justice papers, JUS/H5/372).

71 Gemma Clark, *Everyday Violence in the Irish Civil War* (Oxford, 2014), p. 90.

72 Correspondence relating to the Biggs family, June 1922 (National Archives of Ireland, Department of Justice papers H.5/386). See also Clark, *Everyday Violence*, pp. 186–7.

73 See condemnation of Moyrus attack by Archbishop Gilmartin of Tuam, *IT*, Dec. 1922.

74 Ibid., 26 Oct. 1922.

75 Ibid., 30 Sep. 1922.

76 Ibid., 17 Oct. 1922.

77 Ibid., 27 Oct. 1922.

78 Ibid., 9 Oct. 1922.

79 Ibid., 6 and 8 Nov. 1922.

80 *Church of Ireland Gazette*, 22 Dec. 1922.

81 W.A. Phillips, *The Revolution in Ireland 1906–1923* (London, 1923), p. 291.

82 Terence Dooley, *The Decline of the Big House in Ireland: A Study of Irish Landed Families, 1860–1960* (Dublin, 2001), pp. 286–7.

83 *IT*, 3 Oct. 1922.

84 Ibid., 3 Oct. 1922.

85   Ibid., 18 May 1923.

86   See Bury, *Buried Lives*, chapters 2 and 3.

87   R.B. McDowell, *Crisis and Decline: The Fate of the Southern Unionists* (Dublin, 1997), p. 129.

88   Clark, *Everyday Violence*, p. 199.

89   *IT*, 17 Feb. 1923.

90   Ibid., 8 May 1923.

91   Fifty-third report of the Representative Body of the Church of Ireland, p. 31.

92   *IT*, 15 May 1923.

93   Ibid., 16 May 1923.

94   Ibid., 29 May 1923.

95   Ibid., 1 Jun. 1923.

96   Ibid., 14 Jun. 1923. See also Murphy, *Year of Disappearances*.

97   Between 1911 and 1926 the total Church of Ireland population fell by 40.0 per cent in Cork County and 52.8 per cent in Cork City. *Census of Population for Ireland, 1926*, p. 10. In 1911 the census recorded 4,390 members of the British army and navy in Cork city and county as Episcopalian (Church of Ireland). We can add another 28 per cent (1,229) to allow for dependants, which gives a total of 5,619. Between 1911 and 1926 the Church of Ireland population fell by 12,675 (43 per cent) from 29,568. After excluding army and navy figures the fall in Church of Ireland population was 7,056, which represents a fall of 29.5 per cent of the original 1911 civilian population. *Census of Ireland. 1911. Province of Munster*, vol. 115, 1912–13, pp. 184–203.

98   *IT*, 14 Jun. 1923.

99   Ibid., 29 Jun. 1923.

100 Ibid., 4 Jul. 1923.

101 Ibid., 6 Jul. 1923.

102 Ibid.

103 Ibid., 1 Aug. 1923.

104 *Freeman's Journal*, 6 Apr. 1924.

105 *IT*, 12 Oct. 1923.

106 *IT*, 3, 13 and 27 Oct. 1923.

107 *IT*, 12 Oct. 1923.

108 *IT*, 29 Oct. 1923.

109 *IT*, 15 Feb. 1929.

110 *Irish Independent*, 15 Feb. 1929.

111 Vaughan and A.J. Fitzpatrick, *Irish Historical Statistics*, p. 49.

112 *Census of Ireland for 1926*, vol. 3, p. 13.

113 Fitzpatrick, 'Protestant depopulation', p. 659; Garrett Fitzgerald, *Reflections on the Irish State* (Dublin, 2003), pp. 147–9. The census records a figure of 30 per cent for Protestant decline, 1861–1911, but Fitzgerald erroneously gives a figure of 45 per cent. *Census of Ireland for 1926*, vol. 3, p. 13.

114 Ibid., pp. 1–2.

115 Kevin Myers, *Ireland's Great War* (Dublin, 2014), p. 5.

116 In 1911 southern Church of Ireland members were 5.5 per cent of the Irish population. This figure is increased to 8.25 per cent to allow for an estimated 50 per cent higher level of southern Protestant enlistments and deaths, acknowledging the claim that the Church had borne 'more than her

proportionate share of the burden' in C.A. Webster, 'The church since disestablishment' in Phillips, *History of the Church of Ireland*, vol. 3, p. 412. This is roughly
the same as the figure of 5,000 Protestant deaths accepted elsewhere, which
is based on a lower figure of total deaths but a higher proportional figure of
Protestant dead. J.J. Sexton and Richard O'Leary, 'Factors affecting population
decline in minority communities in the Republic of Ireland' in *Building Trust
in Ireland: Studies Commissioned by the Forum for Peace and Reconciliation* (Belfast,
1995), p. 314. Also Bielenberg, 'Exodus', p. 223.

117 *Census of Ireland for 1926*, vol. x, p. 46. *Irish Independent*, 15 Feb. 1929, also gives a
figure of 25 per cent, while *IT*, 15 Feb. 1929, gives 20 per cent.

118 *Census of Ireland for 1926*, vol. 10, pp. 46–7. Elsewhere the census put dependants
in Dublin city at 37 per cent, but this is regarded as a special case and outside of
Dublin the figure was a lot lower and has been put in Kildare at fifteen to twenty
per 100. Fitzpatrick, 'Protestant depopulation', p. 648.

119 *Census of Ireland for 1926*, vol. 3, pp. 124–5. In 1926 a total of 11,902 civil servants
included 1,311 members of the Church of Ireland.

120 Bielenberg, 'Exodus', p. 222.

121 Ibid., pp. 230–1.

122 Acknowledgements are due to Don Wood for drawing this to my attention.

123 Garrett Fitzgerald comes up with a figure of 20,000 involuntary Protestant migrants
based on an erroneous figure of 45 per cent decline in Protestant numbers,
1861–1911. Fitzgerald, *Reflections*, p. 148.

124 Sexton and O'Leary, 'Population decline', pp. 263 and 303; Terence Brown,
'Religious minorities in the Irish Free State and the Republic of Ireland, 1922–95',
in *Building Trust in Ireland*, pp. 227–37.

125 *Census of Ireland for 1926*, vol. 3, p. 1.

126 Sexton and O'Leary, 'Population decline', pp. 260–3, 273. See also Bielenberg,
'Exodus', p. 230.

127 *Census of Ireland for 1926*, vol. 3, p. 1.

128 Fitzpatrick, 'Protestant depopulation', pp. 650–2.

129 Registrar-general's review of vital statistics of Northern Ireland and life tables
(1926), (Belfast, 1931), pp. 1–3, 12–13. For example, in Scotland, the number of
legitimate births per 1,000 married women, aged 15–44, fell from 272 in 1901 to
184 in 1926.

130 Sexton and O'Leary, 'Population decline', p. 265.

131 *Census of Ireland for 1926*, vol. 3, p. 1. In contrast Methodists experienced a fall of
8 per cent in this period – their highest in fifty years.

132 David Fitzpatrick, 'The spectre of "ethnic cleansing" in revolutionary Ireland' in
Bulletin of the Methodist Historical Society, vol. 18, no. 34 (2013), pp. 5–69; Fitzpatrick,
'Protestant depopulation', pp. 658–9.

133 *Census of Ireland for 1926*, vol. iii, p. 15. Over the previous three decades before 1911
the Methodist population in the twenty-six counties had gone from an increase
of 4.8 per cent to a decline of 8 per cent, which helps to set the next ten years of
decline in context. Ibid., p. 1. In the past some of the Methodist growth had come at
the expense of Church of Ireland numbers, and perhaps by 1911 this was no longer
the case. In the decade 1901–11 in Co. Cork Methodist numbers fell by 7.8 per cent
compared to a decline of 4.2 per cent for members of the Church of Ireland.

134 For a full discussion of these matters post 1926 see Sexton and O'Leary, 'Population decline'.

135 See also Hart, *The IRA at War*, pp. 223–40.

136 Vaughan and Fitzpatrick, *Irish Historical Statistics*, p. 49.

137 Clark, *Everyday Violence*, p. 152.

138 J.H. Whyte, 'Political life in the south' in Michael Hurley (ed.), *Irish Anglicanism, 1869–1969* (Dublin, 1970), p. 143.

139 *Census of Ireland for 1926*, p. 11.

140 *IT*, 3 Oct. 1922.

141 Out of a total of 153 TDs, Protestants (mostly members of the Church of Ireland) numbered nine in 1922, fourteen in June 1927, twelve in 1932, but seven in 1937 and three in 1948. See B.M. Walker, *A Political History of the Two Irelands: From Partition to Peace* (Basingstoke, 2012), p. 59.

142 Phillips, *History of the Church of Ireland*, vol. 3, pp. 412–13.

143 T.J. Johnston, J.L. Robinson, R.W. Jackson, *A History of the Church of Ireland* (Dublin, 1953), p. 269.

144 *IT*, 16 May 1923.

SELECT BIBLIOGRAPHY

Newspapers

Belfast News Letter, Belfast Telegraph, Church of Ireland Gazette, Irish Independent, Irish News, Irish Press, Irish Times, Londonderry Sentinel, Northern Whig, Sunday Independent, Sunday Times.

Books, Chapters and Articles

Akenson, D.H., *The Irish Diaspora: A Primer* (Belfast, 1993).

Aughey, Arthur, *The Politics of Northern Ireland* (London, 2004).

Bardon, Jonathan, *A History of Ulster* (Belfast, 1992).

Bell, J. Bowyer, *The Irish Troubles: A Generation of Violence, 1967–92* (Dublin, 1995).

Bielenberg, Andy (ed.), *The Irish Diaspora* (London, 2000).

Bielenberg, Andy, 'Exodus: the emigration of southern Protestants during the War of Independence and Civil War' in *Past and Present*, vol. 218 (February 2013), pp. 199–233.

Bowman, Jonathan, *De Valera and the Ulster Question, 1917–1973* (Oxford, 1982).

Boyce, D.G., *Nationalism in Ireland* (London, 1982; second edition, 1991).

Boyce, D.G., *The Sure Confusing Drum: Ireland and the First World War: Inaugural Lecture* (Swansea, 1993).

Boyce, D.G. and Alan O'Day (eds), *The Making of Irish History: Revisionism and the Revisionist Controversy* (London, 1996).

Buckland, P.J., *Irish Unionism, 1885–1923* (Belfast, 1973).

Bury, Robin, *Buried Lives: The Protestants of Southern Ireland* (Dublin, 2016).

Clark, Gemma, *Everyday Violence in the Irish Civil War* (Oxford, 2014).

Collins, Peter, *Nationalism and Unionism: Conflict in Ireland, 1885–1921* (Belfast, 1994).

Comerford, R.V., *Inventing the Nation: Ireland* (London, 2003).

Doyle, David, 'Scots Irish or Scotch-Irish', pp. 151–70; 'The Irish in North America, 1776–1845', pp. 171–212; 'The remaking of Irish America, 1845–1880', pp. 213–54, in J.J. Lee and M.R. Casey (eds), *Making the Irish–American: History and Heritage of the Irish in the United States* (New York, 2007).

Elliott, Marianne, *Wolfe Tone: Prophet of Irish Independence* (London, 1989).

English, Richard, *Armed Struggle: A History of the IRA* (London, 2003).

English, Richard, *Irish Freedom: The History of Nationalism in Ireland* (London, 2006).

English, Richard and Graham Walker (eds), *Unionism in Modern Ireland: New Perspectives on Politics and Culture* (Dublin, 1996).

Fitzpatrick, David, *Oceans of Consolation: Personal Accounts of Irish Migration to Australia* (New York, 1994).

Fitzpatrick, David, *The Two Irelands, 1912–39* (Oxford, 1998).

Fitzpatrick, David, 'Protestant depopulation and the Irish revolution' in *Irish Historical Studies*, vol. xxxviii, no. 152 (November 2013), pp. 642–70.

Glazier, Michael (ed.), *The Encyclopedia of the Irish in America* (Indiana, 1999).

Hart, Peter, *The IRA at War, 1916–23* (Oxford, 2003).

Houston, Cecil and William Smyth, *The Sash Canada Wore: A Historical Geography of the Orange Order in Canada* (Toronto, 1980).

Jeffrey, Keith, *Ireland and the Great War* (Cambridge, 2000).

Kennedy, Dennis, *The Widening Gulf: Northern Attitudes to the Independent Irish State* (Belfast, 1988).

Lambkin, Brian and Patrick Fitzgerald, *Migration in Irish History* (London, 2008).

Lee, J.J. and M.R. Casey (eds), *Making the Irish American: History and Heritage of the Irish in America* (New York, 2006).

Leonard, Jane, *The Culture of Commemoration: The Culture of War Commemoration* (Dublin, 1996).

Leonard, Jane, 'The twinge of memory: Armistice Day and Remembrance Sunday in Dublin since 1919' in Richard English and Graham Walker (eds), *Unionism in Modern Ireland* (Dublin, 1996), pp. 99–114.

McBride, Ian, *The Siege of Derry in Ulster Protestant Mythology* (Dublin, 1997).

McBride, Ian (ed.), *History and Memory in Modern Ireland* (Cambridge, 2001).

McCaffrey, L.J., *The Irish Catholic Diaspora in America* (Washington, 1997).

McDowell, R.B., *Crisis and Decline: The Fate of the Southern Protestants* (Dublin, 1997).

Montgomery, Michael, 'Nomenclature for Ulster emigrants' in *Familia*, vol. 20 (2004), pp. 16–36.

Morris, Ewan, *Our Own Devices: National Symbols and Political Conflict in Twentieth Century Ireland* (Dublin, 2005).

Myles, Kevin, *Ireland's Great War* (Dublin, 2014).

Nic Craith, Máiread, *Plural Identities – Singular Narratives: The Case of Northern Ireland* (Oxford, 2002).

O'Farrell, Patrick, *The Irish in Australia* (Belfast, 1986).

Rose, Richard, *Governing Without Consensus: An Irish Perspective* (London, 1971).

Smith, M.E., *Reckoning with the Past* (Maryland, 2005).

Stewart, A.T.Q., *The Narrow Ground: Aspects of Ulster, 1609–1969* (London, 1977).

Vaughan, W.E. and A.J. Fitzpatrick (eds), *Irish Historical Statistics, Population, 1821–1971* (Dublin, 1978).

Select Bibliography

Walker, B.M., *Ulster Politics: The Formative Years* (Belfast, 1989).

Walker, B.M., '1641, 1689, 1690 and all that: the unionist sense of history' in *Irish Review*, vol. 12 (Summer 1992), pp. 56–64.

Walker, B.M., *Dancing to History's Tune: History, Myth and Politics in Ireland* (Belfast, 1996).

Walker, B.M., *Past and Present: History, Identity and Politics in Ireland* (Belfast, 2000).

Walker, B.M., *A Political History of the Two Irelands: From Partition to Peace* (Basingstoke, 2012).

Wilson, David, *The Irish in Canada* (Ottawa, 1989).

Woods, C.J., 'Tone's grave at Bodenstown: memorials and commemorations, 1798–1913' in Dorothea Siegmund-Schultz (ed.), *Ireland: Gesellschaft and Kultur-vi* (Halle, 1989), pp. 141–5.

INDEX

The History Press Ireland

www.thehistorypress.ie
www.thehistorypress.co.uk